Volcanoes

Volcanoes

Cliff Ollier

Basil Blackwell

Copyright © C. Ollier 1988

First published 1988

Basil Blackwell Ltd
108 Cowley Road, Oxford, OX4 1JF, UK

Basil Blackwell Inc.
432 Park Avenue South, Suite 1503
New York, NY 10016, USA

British Library Cataloguing in Publication Data
Ollier, Cliff
  Volcanoes.
  1. Volcanoes
  I. Title
  551.2'1   QE522
  ISBN 0-631-15664-X
  ISBN 0-631-15977-0 Pbk

Library of Congress Cataloging in Publication Data
Data applied for.

Typset in 10½ on 11½ pt Sabon
by Joshua Associates Limited
Printed in Great Britain by Page Bros (Norwich) Ltd

Contents

Preface

This book gives an account of volcanoes, their activity, their geographical and social importance, and especially their landforms. It is written for secondary school and university students, and general readers interested in volcanoes and scenery.

Many good books on volcanoes already exist, so why write another? My feeling is that most are very strong on eruptive phenomena, petrology and physics, but generally are less informative about landforms, hydrology, and the human response to volcanic phenomena. Once, Cotton's splendid *Volcanoes as Landscape Forms* was the only book devoted to volcanic geomorphology, and many things have been discovered since it was published in 1944. To understand volcanic landforms, however, it is necessary to know how volcanoes work, so the present book inevitably overlaps in content with the mainly volcanological books.

The first version of this book was published by the Australian National University Press and was written primarily for an Australian audience, using Australian examples where possible. In the present edition I have aimed for a world-wide coverage, but an Australian bias will still be evident.

This book is not meant to be exhaustive on terminology. I have tried to use terms and definitions in the way I believe they are commonly applied by geologists and geomorphologists, and for some terms different meanings are discussed. For more advanced work the standard glossaries of geological terms (listed in the bibliography) may be consulted.

The metric system is used throughout the book, necessitating conversion of a wide range of units – fathoms, chains, cubic miles, knots, acres and many others. Many of the figures given will therefore be approximations, but I hope that what is lost in accuracy will be gained in ease of comprehension.

The chapters in this book are all interrelated, but it is not necessary to read them in sequence. Indeed, the chapter on volcanic rocks appears last in the book, almost as an appendix, although it is required reading for all the other chapters. But it is (with apologies to petrologists) the dullest chapter. Catalogues and lists are necessary in any textbook, but they do not make entertaining reading, so these can be read through quickly and used for reference. Most sections end with a few references to enable those interested to follow the topic into modern, specialized literature.

I am grateful to many people who have helped in the production of this book. In the first edition I thanked G. Imbo, P. Gasperini, A. Rapollo, M. Schwarzbach, H. Noll, E. F. Lloyd, M. J. Selby, J. Healy, B. N. Thompson, D. H. Blake, M. J. F. Brown, G. D'Addario, W. Manser, B. P. Ruxton, G. A. M. Taylor, J. F. Harrop, J. N. Jennings and J. Heyward (who drafted the figures in the first edition). Since then many people have helped to teach me about volcanoes and to show me examples in the field; it is impossible to recount them all, but I wish to thank E. B. Joyce, C. F. Pain, N. C. Stevens, P. J. Stephenson, R. W. Johnson, L. A. Lyons, B. Franklin, R. Greely, G. P. L. Walker, J. C. Dohrenwend, W. Halliday, C. Woods and G. Licitra, some of whom have provided illustrations as well as valued comments. Special thanks go to Rudi Boskovic who drafted the new illustrations, and Denise Cumming and Gerda van Houtert who prepared the manuscript.

It is always a bad time to produce a book about volcanoes, because the subject seems constantly to be branching out in new directions, and new frontiers seem just over the hill. In the 1980s there is great interest in physical aspects of volcanic activity and how these can be determined from the rock record; in the effect of volcanoes on climate and earth history; in management of the volcanic hazard; in geothermal energy; in the vital role of volcanoes in aspects of global evolution such as plate tectonics and sea-floor spreading; and in the impact of volcanicity on landscape evolution. This book gives no definitive answers to any of these topics, but I hope it can convey some of the excitement of the study of volcanoes in all their aspects.

Cliff Ollier

1 Volcanoes and People

Active volcanoes are dangerous, and sometimes spectacularly destructive. Whole towns may be destroyed, probably the best-known example being Pompeii, obliterated by the eruption of Vesuvius in AD 79.

Pompeii, 8 km from the eruption centre, was completely buried under the fall-out of ash over a period of two days, and then forgotten until rediscovered in 1595. The eruption seems to have been quiet enough at the start for many people to leave, but those who stayed too long, perhaps to save their possessions, had great trouble because of the darkness and increasing violence of the eruptions. About 16,000 people perished, and many of the bodies later excavated were clutching bags of coins or jewels. Hundreds of casts have been made from the moulds left by the bodies (see plate 1.1).

The 1783 eruption at Skaptar Jokull was a national disaster for Iceland and a fifth of its inhabitants (10,000) died from its effects. Half the cattle, three-quarters of the horses, and four-fifths of the sheep population also perished, and dust even destroyed crops in Scotland, 1000 km away.

The 1815 eruption of Tambora, Indonesia, killed 12,000 people by direct effects and up to 70,000 died from famine following the spoliation of land and crops. The 1902 eruption of Mt Pelée killed 30,000 people in a minute and left only two survivors in the town of St Pierre. In the same year the eruption of La Soufrière (St Vincent) took 2000 lives and caused the extinction of the Caribs, the original inhabitants of the island when Columbus discovered it. In 1909 Kelut (Indonesia) killed 5000 people.

A long-continued seismic and volcanic crisis in the Phlegrean Fields, Italy, persists in the 1980s. About 400,000 people are at risk including 72,000 in Pozzuoli (*Bulletin Volcanogique*, 47, 1984).

Volcanoes continue to be a menace up to the present time. The eruption of Mt Lamington, New Guinea, in 1951 killed 6000 people; Mt Agung, in Bali, Indonesia, killed 1500 people in 1963; Mt Villarica, Chile, caused 30,000 people to evacuate their homes in 1963 and 1964; Mt Taal, Philippines, took another 500 lives in 1965.

The menace of volcanoes is greater than would be supposed from disasters that have happened so far. Some ignimbrite deposits are on a tremendous scale, but by good fortune most of the large historical

1

Plate 1.1   Cast of victim of eruption of Vesuvius, AD 79, at Pompeii. The attitude of many victims with hands close to mouth indicates death by suffocation (Ente Provinciale per il Turismo, Naples)

eruptions – such as the 1912 eruption at the Valley of Ten Thousand Smokes and the 1956 eruption of Bezymianny, Kamchatka, have taken place in uninhabited areas. If such an eruption should occur – as it has before – in Japan, New Zealand, California, or other densely populated area, there will be a catastrophe of unheard-of proportions.

For this reason the main bread-and-butter work of volcanologists is to predict eruptions, and all the ancillary research is justified if it helps towards this aim.

Prediction of Eruptions

Observations of many volcanoes have led to the discovery of various phenomena that may be taken as warning signs of impending eruption. These are seldom certain, and frequently there is very little time between warning and eruption – the 1872 eruption of Vesuvius gave no warning up to the previous night, even to trained observers – but at least people may be given such warning as is possible.

Warning signs include the melting of snow caps, the disappearance of crater lakes, the drying-up of wells and springs, death of surrounding vegetation, and movement of animals and birds. It seems that many

2

animals left Mt Pelée before its eruption in 1902. The sort of observation described above depends on special circumstances, and for most volcano prediction more routine methods must be used, as will be described below.

Seismic Methods

The measurement of earth tremors is now the commonest method of eruption prediction. The ascent of magma causes tremors, and before an eruption there is usually a marked increase in the number and violence of local tremors with a focus at shallow depth. A number of synchronized seismographs can give an accurate location of the eruption point, and seismic shocks may give several days' warning. The method cannot be certain, however. Some eruptions, such as that of Coseguina (1815), apparently take place without preliminary tremors. On the other hand, Vesuvius has given strong warning tremors on several occasions in the past few years, without producing an eruption.

When an elaborate seismic net is utilized, quite remarkable feats of forecasting can be achieved. In the eruption of Kilauea in December 1959, seismographs provided six months' notice of eruption by recording tremors from the remarkable depth of 50 km. As time went by the focal depth of tremors became less and less, and by measuring the speed of the rise the date of eruption could be forecast. Extra field seismographs were used to locate the epicentres accurately, and the exact point of eruption (Kilauea Iki) and time of eruption were predicted with unprecedented accuracy. Furthermore, when the eruption stopped, the time and place of recurrence were forecast, and the village of Kapoho, 42 km from Kilauea Iki, was evacuated with sufficient warning to allow removal of portable belongings before the area was buried by lava.

The eruption of Talbachik, Kamchatka, in 1975, was forecast by P. I. Tokarev entirely from the seismograph recordings of five stations. Eruptions of Bezymyanny in October 1959, April 1960, and March 1961, and Sheveluch in 1964 were also predicted. Tokarev predicted an eruption of Klyuchevskoy would take place between 4 March and 9 March 1983. It occurred on 8 March, 2 km from the place predicted.

The possibility of using long-range forecasting of volcanic activity (several months, to possibly several years) was presented by Blot (1964) and is based on the apparent relationship between some deep (550–65 km) and intermediate (150–250 km) seismic effects and certain eruptions in the New Hebrides group. In the first three years of observations after publishing the hypothesis, the volcanoes Gaua, Ambrym, and Lopevi erupted on dates forecast months in advance. The relationship between volcanic eruption and deep effects cannot be direct since magma does not originate at these great depths, but some sort of activity is traced in depth and direction, and appears to take 12 ± 2 months to travel from 650 to 200 km depth, and 6 ± 2 months between 200 km and eruption at the surface.

3

Tilt Measurements

Before an eruption a volcano is liable to swell because of lava pushing up inside it. This swelling or tumescence can be measured by tiltmeters. After eruption the volcano sinks back, often below its original position. Changes observed in Hawaii amount to increases of between 2ft (0.6 m) and 3.5 ft (1 m). Such changes could be determined by occasional surveys, but a quicker method is needed for volcanic prediction, preferably a single measurement. Tiltmeters measure very accurately any tilt of the ground and any change in tilt may be regarded as a warning. By careful placement of tiltmeters some information may be gained about the possible location of an eruption. On Hawaii they are placed so that tumescence of Kilauea gives a northward tilt, while swelling of Mauna Loa gives an eastward tilt. Tiltmeter readings on Manam Island volcano, New Guinea, showed a slow tilt of 30 seconds during the five months preceding the climactic explosions of 1958. A tilt of 8 seconds preceded the eruption of March 1960, and then during the initial lava outpourings there was a reversal of 11 seconds.

The eruption of Kilauea in 1959 was predicted by seismic and tiltmeter records (Eaton and Murata, 1960).

Uplift and outward tilting of caldera edges prior to eruption causes horizontal expansion, which can be measured by tellurometers. Distance measurements across Kilauea caldera, Hawaii, showed a line of 3098 m lengthened by 12 cm prior to eruption and then rapidly shortened by 28 cm during and after eruption. The method is said to be accurate to four parts per million (Decker et al., 1966).

Swelling and sinking of the land is most easily observed at the coast, for a change in relative sea level has very marked effects. The sea is said to have retreated some distance the day before the eruption of Monte Nuovo near Naples in 1538; in all probability it was the land swelling. The Temple of Serapis at Naples records many changes of sea level by the level at which marine borers have lived on its pillars during their numerous submergences. Much of the movement in this area is probably related to volcanic activity.

Temperature Measurement

The temperature of crater lakes, hot springs, and fumaroles often shows a sharp increase before eruption. By constant or regular readings it may be possible to give some warning.

However, in both Indonesia and in New Guinea it has been found that there is no good correlation of temperature increase (measured in summit craters) and eruption, so the general reliability of the method is in considerable doubt (Neumann van Padang, 1963).

Gas Composition

The composition of gases erupted from craters or fumaroles may vary before eruption. There is likely to be an increase in the amount of hydrochloric acid (HCl). The composition of gases emitted from volcanoes depends on the temperature. Iwasaki et al. (1966) say that high temperature emanations include water (H_2O), HCl, hydrogen fluoride (HF), sulphur dioxide (SO_2), carbon dioxide (CO_2), hydrogen (H_2), hydrogen sulphide (H_2S), nitrogen (N_2) and others, but low temperature emissions have only CO_2 and H_2S as main components.

A great deal of water is produced by volcanoes, though it is not easy to determine whether this is original water or if some has been recycled from sedimentary rocks. In the eruption of Bezymianny, Kamchatka, 1956, for instance, it was estimated that 2.5 per cent by weight of the eruption products consisted of water, and that 2.7 per cent of the original magma was water (Markhinin, 1962).

A very good correlation between eruptive activity and the composition and amounts of gas, was demonstrated at Mt Mihara, Japan, by Noguchi and Kamiya (1963). From April to early July 1957, amounts of fluorine (F), chlorine (Cl), and sulphur (S) were low. They increased markedly from 27 to 30 July, and the eruption took place on 5 and 6 August. The increase in the amounts of these gases was repeated in early October, and eruption occurred on 13 October.

Tazieff and Tonani (1963) used rapid methods of gas analysis and could trace changes in content of H_2O and CO_2 over a three-hour period inside the crater of Stromboli. The range and rapidity of changes were amazing: CO_2 increased from 0 to 25 per cent in less than 3 minutes, H_2O from 0 to 45 per cent in a similar period. This appears to diminish the value of the almost isolated analyses obtained previously by conventional methods.

Gravity and Magnetism

Movements of lava at depth cause slight changes in local gravity and magnetic fields, and so measurement of these effects may give some way of predicting possible eruption. At present such measurements are not very much used, perhaps because they are not sufficiently sensitive indicators. The potential value of magnetometric work is discussed by Bernstein (1960).

Regular Behaviour of Volcanoes

If some pattern could be found in the times of eruption of a volcano, if some rhythm or cyclical behaviour could be demonstrated, then prediction would be very much easier. There have been many attempts at finding

5

periodicity, varying from wild numerology to serious scientific attempts, and also efforts to link volcanic activity with other events such as sunspots or phases of the moon.

Jaggar (1931) believed that Hawaiian eruptions exhibited 11- and 132-year cycles, corresponding with sunspot cycles. However, Stearns and Macdonald (1946) found no support for this claim, and maintain that 150 years of observations are not enough for such speculation.

Mt Etna has a fairly regular pattern within individual eruptions. Each starts with a fracture on the flank. Lava flows out at the bottom and a scoria cone is built up at the top. Succeeding eruptions occur at higher and higher spots along the rift until the fracture is sealed. Imbo (1928) has suggested that the periodicity involves cycles with eruptions at fairly regular intervals:

1755–1809; a 54-year cycle with 9-year intervals
1809–1865; a 56-year cycle with 6-year intervals
1865–1908; a 43-year cycle with 7-year intervals.

We are now supposed to be in a cycle with 7-year intervals. Each new cycle starts on a new fissure.

Vesuvius has the best long-term records of any volcano. Even from early days the dates of eruption are known because of the strange fact that the relics of St Januarius were paraded at eruption time to quell the activity. No kind of mathematical periodicity fits all the events, but a rough general sequence of events can be made out as follows:

Period of repose	average 7 years
Explosions build cinder cones on the crater floor / Crater fills with lava and may overflow	average 30 years
Earthquakes, explosions, cone splits and great floods of lava erupt	average a few weeks
Gas 'blow off' – a continuous emission of high-pressure gas	average a few hours

The last great eruption of Vesuvius was in 1944 when the towns of Massa and San Sebastian were destroyed. Since then the volcano has been quiet, and eruption appears long overdue. Whatever one may think of the scientific value or otherwise of the search for periodicity it is hard not to be somewhat alarmed, and fear that the next eruption will be particularly violent.

Modern summaries of volcano forecasting are provided by Tazieff and Sabroux (1983) and Decker (1986). One of the successes Decker reports comes from the Indonesian island volcano of Colo. In 1983 following earthquakes and a small eruption, and knowing the history of the volcano, 7000 inhabitants were evacuated by boat. On 23 July an eruption destroyed all the houses, stock and coconut plantations. It will take many years for the island to recover, but at least the people were saved.

What to do when a Volcano Erupts

Volcanologists spend a lot of time trying to predict eruptions. When an eruption seems imminent, evacuation will usually be advised. Little can be done to save property, but many lives may be saved. Thus in the 1914 eruption of Sakurajima, Japan, seven out of eighteen villages were destroyed on the island, property damage was estimated at $19,000,000 and nearly 25 km$_2$ were covered by new lava, but no lives were lost and an estimated 15,000 people were evacuated from within the death radius of the volcano (Wilcoxson, 1967). When eruption actually occurs instrumental observations become secondary to direct observations, and the volcanologists' work changes from prediction to actively warning people of possible dangers from flow, explosions, and ashfall (taking into account the effect of wind), and drainage diversion and flooding. Let us consider these aspects a little further.

Flows

Flows usually move sufficiently slowly for people to get out of their way. It may be possible to move to higher ground, making sure not to be surrounded by lava and possibly engulfed. It is normally better to get right away. Although people generally escape from flows, their homes and farms cannot be moved and will generally be destroyed. However, if natural and political circumstances permit, it may be be possible to prevent such destruction.

The 1669 flow of Mt Etna threatened the town of Catania. A man called Pappalardo, deservedly a hero of volcanology, took fifty men to divert the flow. Covered with wet skins to protect them from the heat and armed with iron bars they breached the crust and diverted part of the lava at least, so that the main flow slowed down. Unfortunately the diverted lava headed for the town of Paterno, and five hundred Paterno citizens drove off the Catanians. The flow then destroyed a large part of Catania.

In Hawaii Jaggar organized the bombing of flows during eruptions in 1935 and 1942. By making extra breaches the lava spread out laterally and eventually stopped. In this sort of experiment it can always be argued that the flow would have stopped anyway, but at least the bombings may have helped. In 1955 Macdonald had low walls built that proved sufficient to divert flows, and thus saved large areas of plantations. Bombing and diversion are only useful if there is sufficient waste land to receive the lava. If a flow is advancing across valuable land this policy is of no use, and then dams may be built to prevent its spread, as reported by Macdonald (1962) from Hawaii. In January 1960 eruption of the eastern rift zone, 40 km east of Kilauea caldera, produced 113 m^3 of lava covering 5–6 km^2. A number of walls were built, several hundred metres long, 5 m high and 20 m wide. These were not diversions but simply dams impounding the lava. In fact lava overflowed the dams, but it is thought that it was sufficiently slowed down to justify the dam construction. It was found that such walls need to be heavy and broad-based to withstand the thrust of lava flows, and that overflow causes erosion of the walls.

On strato-volcanoes, flows run down radial valleys, and may possibly be diverted into neighbouring valleys of less value. The 1929 Vesuvius flow could have been diverted into earlier lava fields where no harm would be done, but military authorities refused to allow it. Villages in the main Vallone Valley were therefore evacuated and were extensively damaged.

Explosions, Pyroclastics, and Gas

Pyroclastic eruptions are very hard to deal with, and early evacuation is the best policy, especially if there is any danger of pyroclastic flows. Once a nuée ardente erupts there is nothing, absolutely nothing, that can be done except to look for possible survivors around the edge of the flow.

In the town of St Pierre, prior to the eruption of Mt Pelée, many people were quite anxious to evacuate, for there were plenty of warning signs. Horses were dropping dead in the street, dead birds fell from the sky, a fine ash covered the city, and there were muted sounds, the air was sulphurous, and an incandescent mass could be seen rising in the volcano. However, the Governor was anxious that people stay for the elections to be held on 10 May.

On 6 May troops were stationed to prevent people leaving town.

On 7 May, Professor Landes of the Lycée opined in the local newspaper that 'the Montagne Pelée presents no more danger to the inhabitants of Saint-Pierre than does Vesuvius to those of Naples'.

On 8 May at 7.30 a.m. four great explosions came from Pelée, one of which shot laterally to St Pierre. The town clock stopped at 7.32 a.m., when the town's 30,000 people were killed.

In quiet ash falls evacuation is still the best policy. If this is impossible light protection should be sought – during the eruption of 4 April 1906, Neopolitans went about with umbrellas to keep off the rain of volcanic sand. It may even be possible to spend some time shovelling ash from the roofs of houses. It is probably not a good idea to go to church for shelter or prayer. During the 1906 eruption of Vesuvius villagers of San Giuseppe assembled in church for refuge, but the weight of ash on the roof caused the building to collapse, and 105 people were killed.

It must not be forgotten that even quiet eruptions can do a lot of damage.

The volcano Irazu is only 30 km from San Jose, capital of Costa Rica, with a quarter of a million inhabitants. Eruptions of ash and gas between 1963 and 1965 were not fatal, but were nevertheless a great nuisance to everyday life and many crops and much good land was ruined. Losses were estimated at $150,000,000.

Santiago, Nicaragua, was a quiet volcano in the solfataric stage, but the fumes did a great deal of damage, estimated at $10,000,000, between 1946 and 1951. Many solutions were considered for stopping or ameliorating the nuisance, but in 1953 the emissions fortunately stopped of their own accord.

Pyroclastic eruption can produce total darkness, and artificial light is of little help. If people were aware of this possibility it might at least prevent some panic, which is an incidental danger in all eruptions. In the 1835 eruption of Coseguina, Nicaragua, the tremendous noise and ashfall was taken to indicate the coming of Judgment Day, and 'the terror of the inhabitants of Aloncho was so great, that three hundred of those who lived in a state of concubinage married at once' (Galindo, 1835, quoted in Wilcoxson (1967), p. 320).

Floods and Lahars

Drainage diversions can be a great danger. The commonest kind is the sudden displacement of a crater lake, producing a lahar, either hot or cold, which flows in very mobile fashion though carrying large boulders. Lahars are fairly common on strato-volcanoes. Attempts may be made to divert them by walls, but little success has been achieved by such structures. Furthermore, there is not sufficient warning for most lahars. A known lahar path ought not to be inhabited, though in many instances it is.

In Kelut, Indonesia, which has a long history of lahar eruptions, massive walls were built, 3 m high, but proved useless against lahars. Later the crater lake was drained by tunnels and the next eruption caused significantly less damage than usual. However, this eruption destroyed the tunnels. A new set of 'seepage pipes' was constructed which, while not actually reaching the crater, would drain it if the rock were permeable. However, Zen (1965) reported that the pipes had failed to drain the lake, so lahars are again a potential danger.

In Iceland the Jokulhlaup, produced when sub-ice volcanoes melt the great quantities of water, causes total devastation, but fortunately of uninhabited areas.

Secondary effects of an eruption may present serious problems to inhabitants, and to some extent modify landforms. The increased runoff caused by the destruction of vegetation can cause flooding, rapid erosion, and silting up of stream beds.

Taylor (1958) has described how such flooding after the disastrous 1951 eruption of Mt Lamington, New Guinea, caused some loss of equipment

9

and necessitated removal of one of the evacuation camps. Mudflows frequently descended the mountain as roaring torrents, disrupting communications, and at river crossings a permanent labour force was needed to remove the debris left by daily flash floods.

Climatic Effects of Volcanoes

Major eruptions produce sufficient high-level ash to reduce incoming sunlight, and cause a notable cooling of the earth. The Dust Veil Effect is described by Lamb (1971) and a fairly good correlation between volcanicity and climate is evident. Hirschboeck (1980) noted that there were three great eruptions in both 1883 and 1963; the 1880s had 15 great eruptions and the 1960s had 21 great eruptions. More emphasis should therefore be placed on episodes of increased volcanicity than on large individual eruptions. Episodes of frequent and intense ash production are associated with cooler temperatures; volcanically quiet episodes with warm climates.

Carbon dioxide is also produce by volcanoes, and is well known for its potential greenhouse effects and warming of the earth's atmosphere. Leavitt (1982) has calculated the annual volcanic CO_2 emission for the world as about 1.5×10^{11} moles CO_2 per year, which is about three orders of magnitude less than man's current CO_2 production.

A review of the many effects of volcanoes on climate is provided by Newell and Walker (1981).

Volcanic Hazard Management

In recent years natural hazards have become an area of systematic study, as many hazards – whether they be floods, locust plagues, cyclones and so on – have many features in common, such as prediction, warning, monitoring, evacuation, health risks and public relations. Clearly, volcanoes are one of the classic natural hazards, though until recently hazard research has been relatively trivial and uncoordinated. A modern text on volcanic hazards (Blong 1984) describes the hazards, the effects on humans, the social responses, the economic effects, and hazard perception. A special issue of *Volcano News* (85 (22)) was devoted to volcanic hazard management, especially the practical side, and another (No. 25, Dec. 86) to social aspects of volcanic activity, including epidemiology, mental health, and the role of the media.

Modern knowledge of volcanic hazards is heavily weighted to activity associated with the eruption of Mt St Helens, including a whole book on warning and response (Saarinen and Sell, 1985). Most other areas are much worse off, especially the Third World, but there are exceptions such as the study of surveillance and contingency planning for the Rabaul caldera, Papua New Guinea (McKee et al., 1985).

The Benefits of Volcanoes

In case this parade of disasters should be too depressing, we might briefly try to see volcanic damage in perspective. In the past 500 years volcanoes have probably killed, directly or indirectly, over 200,000 people, of whom about half died in the eruptions of Tamboro, Krakatoa and Mt Pelée. This toll is in fact very low when compared with those of earthquakes, floods, wars, or road accidents.

On the credit side, volcanoes produce fertile land, energy and materials for industry, and a livelihood for many people in the tourist trade. There is an increasing trend towards viewing the totality of volcanic phenomena as part of human ecology (Sheets and Grayson, 1979).

Blong (1982) has collated numerous instances in which tephra fall was beneficial. Varenius wrote in 1683 of an eruption of Vesuvius 'but then the Conflagration ceasing, and the showers watering the Sulphureous *Embers* and *Ashes*, in the Superficies of the Mountain here and there was great fertility of *Wine*'.

After the 1918 eruption of Katla, Iceland, there was improved grass growth on low-lying lands, and in areas where Paricutin, Mexico, deposited 3 cm of tephra, crops of wheat and barley were excellent. Three years after the 1912 eruption of Katmai-Novarupta everyone agreed that the ash fall was 'the best thing that ever happened to Kodiak'. 'Never was such grass before, so high or as early. No one ever believed that the country could grow so many berries, nor so large, before the ash' (Griggs, 1918).

On Tristan da Cunha, the volcano that supports the remotest permanent human settlement on earth, agriculture is carried on in a small area of young pyroclastic deposits about 5 km from the settlement, the only fertile land on the island.

Even when other land is fertile, the benefits of an ash cover are clearly visible (see plate 1.2).

Volcanic rocks can be used as building materials (plate 1.3). Basalt provides massive masonry although comparatively difficult to work. Boulders or rock fragments may be used. In Tristan da Cunha old walls of rounded boulders needed careful fitting, but the eruption of 1961 provided jagged and spiny blocks that stick together with ease. Ignimbrites often combine strength with lightness, and so yield prized building material. Pozzolana is a pyroclastic deposit which, when mixed with lime, produces a valuable cement that will set under water.

Volcanoes are associated with certain economic mineral deposits. Obsidian was a tool of early man and a rival to flint for providing a good cutting edge. Diamonds occur in kimberlite pipes, but not all kimberlites contain diamonds. Volcanogenic ores are those mineral deposits, usually restricted to particular strata, that are formed by volcanic activity under water. Most are sulphide deposits, including the Kuroko (Kuromono)

11

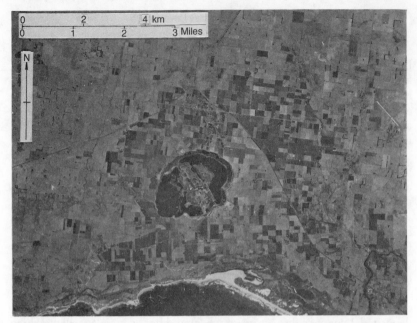

Plate 1.2 Tower Hill, Victoria, Australia. Vertical photograph showing the asymmetrical distribution of ash reflected in the intensity of cultivation (Crown copyright. Courtesy of the Director of National Mapping, Department of National Development, Canberra)

deposits of Japan. The black ores are mixtures of sphalerite, galena and other sulphide minerals, either bedded or irregular and are usually unmetamorphosed (Watanabe, 1970).

Much modern research is concerned with minerals associated with 'black smokers' on modern submarine eruptions, where metallic sulphides are produced, as they provide insight for the formation of ancient volcanogenic sulphide deposits. Volcanic sulphide deposits are reviewed by Franklin et al. (1981).

In several of the world's volcanic areas there are resources of hot groundwater that can be used for the production of energy, known as geothermal energy.

Minor use has been made of such heat for a long time for such purposes as cooking. laundering, and bathing. Nowadays shallow bores provide domestic hot water to many homes in Rotorua, and the hot water needs of Reykjavik's 80,000 population are practically all met by the municipal water works from geothermal heat.

For the modern production of commercial energy, however, high-pressure steam is required, which is only produced under special circumstances.

The use of geothermal energy has increased very much in the last few decades; about one third of Italy's energy output is now geothermal, and

Plate 1.3 Volcanic rocks as building materials, Cappodocia, Turkey. This area was covered by a volcanic ash flow, which was eroded naturally into many conical hills. These have been excavated to make houses (Ministry of Culture and Tourism, Republic of Turkey)

about 11 per cent of New Zealand's energy requirements are met by geothermal sources (see plate 1.4 on p. 14). At the Geysers in California, electrical energy is generated by geothermal heat at a cost of 23 per cent cheaper than that from nearby conventional sources. Many other countries are now investigating the use of geothermal energy, including Japan, Chile, and the Soviet Union. Geothermal energy is becoming an almost independent branch of technology, with its own journals. Texts are provided by Rinehart (1980), Heiken (1982) and Kruger and Otte (1973).

Even when activity has long ceased, most volcanic regions retain a great natural beauty, and frequently display most spectacular scenery. Such areas are often tourist attractions, and a large number of national parks are located on volcanic centres. On balance volcanoes do more good than harm.

Plate 1.4 Wairakei Geothermal Power Station, New Zealand. The clouds of waste steam mark bores. Superheated water is passed along the pipes to the power station at the top of the picture, conveniently situated next to a river for cooling and waste discharge. The U-bends in the pipes are to allow for expansion (C. D. Ollier)

2 Volcanic Eruptions

Volcanic eruptions may be classified in many ways, based on their activity, their relationships through time, their spatial relationships, or their violence.

Active, Extinct, and Dormant Volcanoes

The categories of active, extinct and dormant divide volcanoes into one of the most familiar classifications, and one that is of importance to people living in the vicinity of a volcano. Active volcanoes can be recognized easily, but distinction between dormant and extinct is difficult and sometimes dangerous. Vesuvius had long been thought extinct, until the great eruption of AD 79 proved it had only been dormant. Many volcanoes of the world are presumed to be extinct, with varying degrees of risk. The younger the volcano, the more risky it is to pronounce it extinct.

Booth and Fitch (1979) suggest 'live' to denote a volcano that may erupt, and 'dead' to replace 'extinct', leaving 'active' to denote actually in eruption. They retain the dangerous term 'dormant'.

Continuity of Eruption

Tsuya and Morimoto (1963) have classified the active volcanoes of Japan into two main groups:

(a) those that erupt every few years, usually from a persistently open crater;
(b) dormant volcanoes that erupt once in several scores of years or less frequently. These tend to have closed craters and to erupt from new craters that are more or less unrelated to earlier craters.

Such a classification could be extended to other areas.

Volcanoes in almost permanent eruption include Stromboli, first recorded 2400 years ago; Masaya and Amatitlon in Nicaragua; Sangay in Eduador; and Kilauea in Hawaii. Izalco in El Salvador was almost continuously active after it first appeared in 1770, and was long known as 'The Lighthouse of the Pacific', but eruption ceased in 1957.

Central Eruption, Fissure Eruption, and Areal Eruption

Volcanic eruptions may be divided into those that issue from a central pipe or vent, known as central eruptions; those that issue from cracks or fissures, called fissure eruptions; and eruptions scattered over wide areas, areal eruptions. This classification can be difficult to apply at times, for an eruption may start along a fissure but later erupt from a number of separate centres. A lot of centres all in line are clearly associated with a fissure at deeper levels. On the other hand, a large central-type volcano may erupt at numerous parasitic centres along a fissure on its flank, as commonly happens on Mt Etna, Italy. Another good example comes from Chile. Two days after the great earthquake of May 1960, a lateral fissure eruption occurred on the north-west flank of Puyehue volcano. After initial pumice ejection, dacitic lava poured from 28 craters aligned along a new fissure 14 km long. There was no activity in the central crater.

Thus the distinction between central and fissure eruption depends partly on the scale and stage which interest the observer, but nevertheless the distinction has some merit. Some very high volcanoes such as Cotopaxi in Ecuador (about 3000 m above its base) and Muhavura, Uganda (2500 m above its base) appear to have erupted entirely from one central crater, while many Icelandic volcanoes obviously erupted from fissures. The Laki (Iceland) eruption of 1783 came from a fissure about 32 km long; Hekla, the best-known Iceland volcano, is clearly built over a fissure for it is a ridge rather than a cone, and has a series of craters along its crest. Fissure eruptions are most often associated with basalt.

Areal volcanism (also known as polyorifice volcanism) is characterized by the absence of any tendency for eruption centres to be localized at definite points for any length of time (Karapetian, 1964). The individual volcanic structures tend to be of small size, seldom attaining a height of over 450 m. Scoria and lava cones, domes and maars are the dominant volcanic type, and strato-volcanoes are absent or very rare. The volcanic regions of Auvergne, Armenia, Mexico and Victoria (Australia) are examples of areal volcanic fields. Individual volcanoes are short lived, ranging from the 45 days from initiation to extinction of Muhobili, Congo, to perhaps twelve years. The spatial distribution of the volcanoes is irregular in general, but there may be some clustering and occasional linear groups. The petrographic composition within an areal field remains fairly constant.

Karapetian (1964) believes that areal fields gravitate towards tectonic trenches or to zones of deep faults, which allow lava to penetrate into intermediate chambers. This is in contrast to polygenic central or fissure volcanoes, which stand directly on deep faults.

Classification by the Type of Product

A classification of volcanic activity based on the type of product has been offered by Gèze (1964). The basic subdivision is based on the proportions of the gas, liquid, and solid components, which can be represented on a triangular diagram as shown in figure 2.1. The four basic triangles represent the domains of four basic kinds of volcanic activity, and each triangle is subdivided into smaller triangles by Gèze. The course of volcanic activity that changes through time can be plotted on this type of triangular diagram.

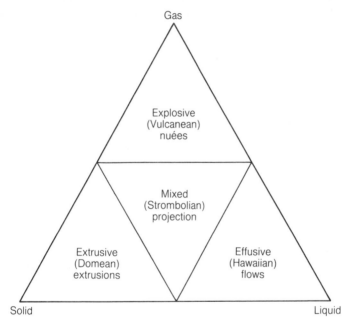

Figure 2.1 Classification of eruptions by Gèze. The proportions of gas, liquid and solids correlates with the type of eruption

Violence of Volcanic Eruptions

Volcanic activity is commonly classified by its violence, which in turn is usually closely related to rock type, the course of eruptive activity and the resulting landforms. In general we may distinguish between lava eruptions, generally associated with basic and intermediate magmas, and pumice eruptions, usually associated with acid magmas.

The percentage of the fragmentary material in the total volcanic material

17

produced can be used as a measure of explosiveness, and if calculated for a volcanic area can be used as an explosion index (E), useful for comparing one volcanic region with others. Some examples are shown in table 2.1; data are from Rittmann (1962) except the Victorian figure from Ollier and Joyce (1964).

Walker (1973a) classified eruptions on two parameters: area of dispersal and degree of fragmentation. Arbitrary measures are needed to determine these (see figure 2.2), and it is difficult to apply in practice because the method requires a lot of sieving, and the determination of thickness of deposits.

Newhall and Self (1982) proposed a volcanic explosivity index (VEI) which helps to summarize many aspects of eruptions, and is best shown in a table (table 2.2). Despite these quantitative suggestions, degrees of eruptive violence are commonly named after type volcanoes or regions that exemplify particular kinds of activity. Some of these types are listed below, and are shown diagramatically in figure 2.3.

Table 2.1 Explosion index for selected volcanic regions

Area	Approximate E (%)
Indonesian island area	99
Solomon Islands–New Hebrides	95
New Guinea–New Britain	90
Southern Italy	41
Iceland	39
Central Pacific Ocean	3
Volcanic plains of Victoria	1

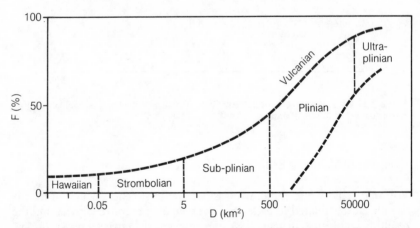

Figure 2.2 Walker's classification of pyroclastic fall deposits. F% is percentage weight of deposit finer than 1 mm along dispersal axis where it is crossed by isopach line that is 10% of maximum thickness. D is the area enclosed by the isopach line 0.01 of the maximum thickness

18

Table 2.2 Volcanic explosivity index (VEI)

VEI	0	1	2	3	4	5	6	7	8
Description	Non-explosive	Small	Moderate	Mod.-large	Large	Very large			
Volume of ejecta (M³)[a]	$<10^4$	10^4–10^6	10^6–10^7	10^7–10^8	10^8–10^9	10^9–10^{10}	10^{10}–10^{11}	10^{11}–10^{12}	$>10^{12}$
Column height (km)[a]	<0.1	0.1–1	1–5	3–15	10–25	>25			
Classification	——— Hawaiian ———		——— Strombolian ———	——— Vulcanian ———	——— Plinian ———	——— Ultra-Plinian ———			
Duration (hours of continuous blast)		<1	——— 1–6 ———		6–12	——— >12 ———			
Tropospheric injection	Negligible	Minor	Moderate	Substantial	Definite	Significant			
Stratospheric injection	None	None	None	Possible	Definite	Significant			
Eruptions (total in file)[b]	443	361	3108	720	131	35	16	1	0

[a] For VEI's 0–2, given as km above crater; for VEI's 3–8, given as km above sea level.
[b] Catalogue of active volcanoes (Simkin et al., 1981).
Source: after Newhall and Self (1982).

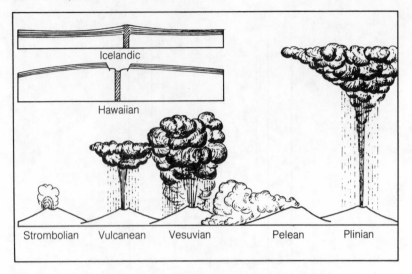

Figure 2.3 Types of volcanic eruption based on geographical examples

Lava Eruptions

Icelandic

In Icelandic activity, fissure eruption is dominant and persistent. Vast floods of basaltic lava are quietly erupted, the lava flowing almost as easily as water and building wide horizontal lava plains. At the end of eruption a string of small cones may be built along the fissure.

Repeated Icelandic eruptions on a grand scale give rise to the great basalt plateaus and provinces such as the Columbia Plateau, the Snake River basalts, and the Deccan. The only really vast outpouring in historic times is that of Laki, Iceland, which in 1783 erupted 12 km^3 of lava and covered an area of 600 km^2 (Thorarinsson, 1969).

Hawaiian

In Hawaiian eruptions basaltic magma is erupted as in the Icelandic type of eruption, but central activity is more pronounced. Fire fountains of lava spray at times and build small scoria mounds, but pyroclastics are very much subordinate to lava flows (see plate 2.1).

Eruption often starts along fissures, making a curtain of fire of frothing lava that may be several kilometres long, but in a matter of hours or days most of the fissure seals up and eruption continues through separate points. Small cones built in this way are of minor importance, and it is the piling up of many lava flows that builds up most of the Hawaiian type of volcanic landform.

Plate 2.1 Eruption in Halemaumau, Hawaii, 1967: a lava lake. There were 12 fountains that sent lava spurting to heights of 80 m (Hawaii Visitors Bureau)

Viscous Lava Flows

Eruptions of rhyolitic to andesitic composition are often too viscous to flow very far, and build up small flows and domes. These are commonly destroyed by explosions, like that of the Mt St Helens' eruption of June, 1980, but some survive, like the dome of Lassen Peak, California.

Pyroclastic Eruptions

Strombolian (from Stromboli, Italy)

The Strombolian is a more explosive type of eruption than the Hawaiian (see plate 2.2) and a higher proportion of fragmental or pyroclastic rocks are produced, though the magma is still basaltic. Activity may be rhythmic or continuous, and fragments of incandescent lava that cool into scoria are thrown out of the crater. The type volcano, Stromboli, has a nearly continuous succession of minor eruptions a few minutes or a few hours apart. Occasionally lava may be poured from the crater, so volcanic deposits consist of alternating lava and pyroclastics. Strombolian eruption is commonly marked by a white cloud of steam emitted from the crater.

Plate 2.2 Strombolian eruption, Ngauruhoe, New Zealand, 1954 (D. R. Gregg)

Vulcanian (from Vulcano, Italy)

Vulcanian eruption occurs where there are relatively viscous lavas which solidify rapidly. Explosions are violent and wreck earlier volcanic structures. Discrete eruptions take place at intervals of minutes to hours. A lot of volcanic ash is produced, and Vulcanian eruption is characterized by dark cauliflower clouds. Many volcanic eruptions start in this way when a blocked vent has to be cleared. If no lava is discharged during an eruption and the fragmental ejecta are made up entirely of old rock fragments, the activity is said to be of Ultra-Vulcanian type. Activity of similar appearance at the end of a complex eruption may be termed Pseudo-Volcanian.

Vesuvian (from Vesuvius, Italy)

The Vesuvian is a more violent type of Vulcanian or Strombolian eruption, in which a cloud of ash is thrown to a great height and scatters ash over a wide area (see plate 2.3). The great cloud is incandescent and luminous at night.

Plinian

Even more extreme in violence than the Vesuvian eruption is the Plinian, which produces a cloud several kilometres high. It is named after the scholar Pliny who died while investigating the Plinian eruption of Vesuvius in AD 79. The amount of ash produced is not great by mountain-building standards, but sufficient to bury a town such as Pompeii. Plinian eruption is characterized by a high column, wide dispersal, and continues for hours to 4 days.

An eruptive column has two main parts: the lower gas thrust part, and the upper convectional thrust part. When the density of the gas thrust is less than that of the atmosphere, convectional rise takes over. The smaller the fragments the greater the heat exchange and the higher the column. The convectional part commonly makes up 90 per cent of the height.

Pliny described two characteristic features of the eruptive type named after him, namely the flashes of fire as vivid as lightning, and darkness more profound than night. He also described 'a thick dark vapour just behind us (which) rolled along the ground like a torrent and followed us'. This rather suggests the base surge described later in this chapter.

The pino (pine tree) is the name sometimes given to the black mushroom cloud produced by Plinian eruption.

Peléan (from Mont Pelée, Martinique)

Peléan is a general name for very violent eruptions and explosion of a very viscous magma. Large quantities of pumice are erupted very rapidly. The magma is usually intermediate to acidic, but basaltic examples have been reported from Manam Island, New Guinea (Palfreyman and Cooke, 1976). Nuées ardentes (glowing clouds of ash, see chapter 7) are characteristic (see plate 2.3). Peléan eruptions may be subdivided into a number of types, including the following:

(a) Peléan (*sensu stricto*), where ash clouds erupt laterally;
(b) St Vincent (or La Soufrière), where ash clouds are vertically directed rather than laterally;
(c) Merapi, where ash clouds are blown laterally from the flanks of a cumulo-dome;

Plate 2.3 Vesuvian eruption of Mt Mayon, Luzon, Philippines, in 1968. Mayon, one of the world's most perfect cones, rises to a height of 2421 m above a nearly level plain, but is dwarfed by the huge eruption cloud. Note also the nuées on the left flank. (Courtesy of the US Air Force and the Smithsonian Institution for Short-Lived Phenomena)

(d) Katmai, with eruption of pumice from fissures. (Actually it is not certain that the Katmai eruption, or any other, emitted pumice from fissures.)

To express the dimensions of the Katmai eruption of 1912, Griggs (1921) worked out what the effects would have been if it had taken place in New York instead of remotest Alaska. New York itself would have been totally devastated, Philadelphia would have received one foot of ash, and ash would have reached Washington and Buffalo. The explosion would have been heard in St Louis and Atlanta, and fumes would have reached Denver and Jamaica. Approximating these dimensions to Australia, an eruption in Canberra would have deposited ash in Melbourne and Sydney, and the sound and fumes may have reached New Zealand.

Krakataun (from Krakatau, Indonesia)

The most violent volcanic eruption in recent times was that of Krakatau in 1883 (Simkin and Fiske, 1983).

Krakatau was an island off Java. On 20 May 1883, noises of explosions were produced that could be heard 150 km away. On 26 August a Vesuvian stage set in, and eruption climaxed with four colossal Krakatau explosions on 27 August, which were heard over about 57 per cent of the earth's surface, and at Rodriguez Island, 4750 km distant, the sound was reported as resembling the distant roar of heavy guns. A wave 17 m high on the open sea was set up, and 36,000 people were killed. The island was destroyed.

The eruption of Santorini near Crete in about 1400 BC appears to have been of the same type as Krakatau and even more violent. It seems to have been responsible for the disappearance of the Minoan civilization, and it is possible that the disappearance of the island gave rise to the legend of Atlantis (Ninkovich and Heezen, 1965; Luce, 1969).

Island-building Eruptions

In 1953 the *Catalogue of Active Volcanoes of the World* added a new category to its eruptive types, the Island-building Eruption. In 1981, 96 new islands were recorded from 45 locations, indicating that some of the islands were short-lived and rebuilt. Santorini had eight island-forming eruptions between 197 BC and AD 1866; Kavechi, Solomon Islands, has grown about sea level eight times since 1950.

Typical eruptions produce spectacular steam clouds, fountains, and dark clouds of tephra. Eventually lava flows may consolidate the ejecta and protect it from erosion. Surtsey, Iceland, provides a spectacular modern example and some use the term 'Surtseyan' as the name for this volcano type. In 1963 it rose from an ocean depth of 160 m to a height of 163 m making a 2.6 km^2 island in 18 months.

Special Features of Eruption

Phreatic and Gas-blast Explosions

The adjective 'phreatic' refers to groundwater of surface origin in the zone of saturation. Phreatic explosion usually refers to violent explosion caused when ascending magma meets groundwater and rapidly produces great quantities of steam. The idea is frequently invoked to account for maars (see chapter 4) which in many areas are found in those places with abundant groundwater (near sea level, on river gravels, etc.) and thus favourable for phreatic eruption, while on nearby sites with little or no groundwater, eruptions are quietly effusive or make simple scoria cones. Stearns and Macdonald (1946) restrict phreatic eruption to those instances in which the ejecta contain no igneous rock, and use phreato-magmatic for those eruptions with igneous rock included in the ejecta.

Unfortunately the term phreatic eruption has been used for eruptions other than those caused by the meeting of magma and groundwater.

The 1962 eruption of Mt Yake, Japan, formed a fissure 700 m long from which issued milkly muddy hot water. Morimoto and Ossaka (1964) called this a low-temperature phreatic eruption.

Rittman (1962) explains the Bandai-San eruption of 1888 as being caused by the superheating of groundwater by juvenile gases ascending from depth, and he calls this phreatic eruption.

He also uses the term for another mechanism that produced some diatremes in Egypt. In Oligocene to Miocene times sills were intruded which heated up groundwater in porous sandstone beds beneath a caprock of impervious clay. High-pressure steam was produced, which bored its way to the surface where it formed explosion craters. The craters contained no igneous material as the sill was largely solidified and only supplied heat. These and other eruptions which produced no new lava whatsoever may be described as gas-blast explosions.

The following terms seem to be generally agreed:

Hydroclastic eruptions – eruptions caused by explosions due to steam from any kind of water.

Phreatic eruptions – eruptions driven by conversion of groundwater to steam.

Phreatomagmatic eruptions – eruptions partly driven by conversion of groundwater to steam but including new lava and its contained volatiles.

Flank Collapse

Landslides are part of the normal erosion process, and happen on many scales during the dissection of volcanoes. There are some failures, however, which are on such a scale that they produce huge effects outside the range of normal landslides, and they are triggered by direct volcanic action, as in the case of Mt St Helens. Indeed this mechanism is very probably the cause of many flank collapses, though with the more ancient ones it may not be easy to prove.

On La Grande Decouverte volcano, Guadeloupe, there were two catastrophic flank collapses, 8000 years apart, both accompanied by explosive eruptions. The great scar on Mt Etna known as the Valle del Bove is thought to have formed by massive slope failure about 5000 BC. The eruption of Bezymianny was accompanied by a directed blast very similar to that of Mt St Helens. Popocatpetl has an earlier volcano partly destroyed by a major blast, on which the younger volcano is built. A volume of about 30 km^3 was moved forming an elliptic amphitheatre 6.5 $\times$ 11 km, and the debris flow covered about 300 km^2. Much of this information comes from the Abstracts of the 1986 International Volocanological Congress and will eventually be published. It is interesting how detailed observations of Mt St Helens have led to re-interpretation of many other volcanoes, and emphasized what might prove to be a common volcanic mechanism.

Sequences in Volcanic Eruption

Many volcanoes have patterns in their eruption depending on their regularity, periodicity, and sequence.

The simplest type is continued eruption. Stromboli is the finest example, as it has been erupting more or less continuously since ancient times and has exhibited several thousand years of virtually uninterrupted but seldom violent eruption. Izalco in El Salvador was similar to Stromboli for over a hundred years, but in 1957 eruption ceased.

Many scoria cones are built as late-stage eruptions on lava plains, but in the Paricutin type, also exemplified by Jorullo (both of these are in Mexico), there is first a building up of a large scoria cone, followed by the emission of large quantities of basalt from the base of the cone. It seems that the lava is too heavy to reach the summit, and finds an easier route near the base of the volcano.

Etna and Vesuvius appear to show typical patterns, described in chapter 1, with cycles of activity and a typical sequence of events within any given cycle. In Hawaii no cyclic behaviour has yet been proved, but there does appear to be a fairly unpredictable sequence within any one eruption.

Hekla, Iceland, is another volcano that seems to have a repeated pattern in its eruptions. There have been fifteen eruptions since the settlement of Iceland, the first in 1104 and the latest in 1981. Tephrochronological studies (Thorarinsson, 1967) show that each eruption starts with a Plinian eruption of silica-rich ash, which lasts for only a few hours, and is followed by production of large amounts of basic lava and ash. The silica content of the initial ash is related to the length of the interval between eruptions, during which differentiation occurs.

Volcanoes classified as pumice-producing commonly alternate explosive activity with the production of domes and other bodies of viscous lava, which are often destroyed during the following explosive phases.

In the central volcanic region of the North Island of New Zealand there is possibly a protracted sequence of eruption with pumice first, followed by the extrusion of rhyolite domes. In the Taupo area there are no domes, so it may be that the eruptive cycle is not complete. Possibly an even later event is caldera collapse and extrusion of basalt around the rim.

In contrast to those volcanoes that have a fairly constant, though rhythmically variable, type of eruption, there are some volcanoes that merely show a succession of widely different types of volcanic action.

Usu volcano, Japan, may be taken as an example (Oba, 1966). Usu formed in early Holocene times on the wall of an older caldera. A strato-volcano was built of basalt, mafic andesite and scoria. Violent explosion then destroyed the cone, pyroclastic flows occurred, and a crater 15 km in diameter was produced. After quiescence for 1500–2000 years, eruption started again, but this time completely different in petrology and style. Dacite plug domes were extruded in almost solid form, with striae along their sides, accompanied by explosive eruptions of pumice and ash. Oba believes all the lavas could be derived from a tholeiitic parent magma by fractional crystallization, without any assimilation of wall rock.

A common sequence of eruption in the Auckland district (New Zealand) and Western Victoria (Australia) is first, a maar explosion, then lava flows, and finally a scoria cone eruption. The products of the later stages may obliterate earlier products to varying degrees.

Various types of eruption may even occur simultaneously as at the new volcano Surtsey, off southern Iceland, which resulted from repeated sub-marine and subaerial fissure eruption of basaltic ash and spatter beginning on 14 November 1963. At one stage there were phreatic and Strombolian eruptions from vents within 15 m of each other in the same crater.

Late Stage Volcanic Activity

In the dying stages of vulcanicity no lava is produced, but eruption continues with the production of water, gases, and sublimates.

Hot springs usually occur in downfaulted areas, where there are suitable geological conditions for the circulation of groundwater and where heat can be provided by hot volcanic rocks. The water emitted by hot springs is usually of meteoric origin, that it derived from rain, and only a very minor part is likely to be derived from magma. Evidence for this comes from the fact that in many volcanic areas, including New Zealand, the hot springs and geysers are much more active some time after heavy rain (when the groundwater has been recharged) than after a prolonged dry spell.

Geysers are jets of hot water that are periodically spurted into the air (see plate 2.4). The name comes from the Great Geyser in the Geysir region of Iceland, which has been inactive, except when artificially stimulated, since 1918. The highest geyser recorded was Waimangu in the Tarawera region of New Zealand in 1901, when the spray reached heights of 500 m. Old Faithful, a geyser in Yellowstone Park, USA, commonly reaches 60 m. Geyser water usually contains much dissolved silica which is deposited in a mound around the orifice of the geyser as sinter or geyserite. These mounds and terraces can attain the size of distinct landforms.

Not all hot springs produce geysers, and there are many areas where hot water appears in quiet pools. The thermal springs of the world have been catalogued by Waring et al. (1965).

Plate 2.4 Waikiti Geyser, Whakarewarewa near Rotorua, New Zealand, with water erupting approximately 10 m high. Sinter deposits in foreground (E. F. Lloyd)

29

Mud volcanoes are simply dirty hot springs. The mud is sometimes brightly coloured, giving rise to interesting displays like the 'Paint Pots' of the USA.

Fumaroles are vents that emit steam or gas, as are solfatara, named after Solfatara near Naples, Italy. There is a tendency to use the term fumarole for high temperature emissions (200–1000°C) and solfatara for low temperature emissions (below 200°C).

Mofettes are openings that exhale carbon dioxide and water only. The heavy carbon dioxide tends to collect in hollows or in low ground, where it can be dangerous. Hence the sinister names of two examples, Death Gulch in Arizona, USA, and Death Valley in Java.

Isotopic analysis of carbon dioxide from some Victorian volcanoes are consistent with values for deep-seated juvenile carbon, rather than derivation from re-cycled atmospheric or sedimentary sources (Chivas et al., 1987).

Complex Eruptions – Mt St Helens

Eruptions can be very complex, as illustrated by the best studies of all volcanoes, Mt St Helens (Peterson, 1986). After over a century of quiet, earthquake activity began on 20 March 1980. An arcuate east–west graben formed across the northern summit area at the head of a 1 × 2 km 'bulge' on the volcano flank that was moving laterally as much as 2 m per day. Intermittent phreatic activity continued through succeeding weeks, as did deformation and seismicity.

On 18 May an earthquake (magnitude 5.1) triggered a catastrophic chain of events. Several immense landslides (flank collapses) sliced off the summit area. The resulting debris avalanche sped north to Spirit Lake and west down North Fork Toutle River. The abrupt loss of pressure on the magma-hydrothermal system led to a minutes-long lateral blast that devastated about 600 km^2 in a 180° sector north of the mountain.

Then came vertically directed explosions, producing a tephra column over 24 km high. Ashfall blanketed thousands of square kilometres to the east. From about noon the vertical column was accompanied by pyroclastic flows that raced north and covered the debris avalanche deposits. Snow and ice melted by the blast-generated lahars. The largest lahar resulted from dewatering of the debris avalanche, and swept down Toutle and Cowlitz Rivers.

The new mountain summit was 400 m lower than the old, and a 600 m crater exposed the core of the cone (see figure 2.4). About 2.5 km^3 of the old mountain had slid away, and about 0.5 km^3 of new magma and old rock had been erupted. Five smaller eruptions occurred in the next five months. A lava dome has grown in the crater, and by 1985 its volume was about 60×10^6 m^3.

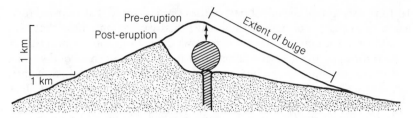

Figure 2.4 Diagrammatic N–S section of Mt St Helens, showing pre- and post-eruption (May 1980) shapes of Mt St Helens, and presumed position of the new magma chamber (shaded)

The Birth of New Volcanoes

Most volcanic activity takes place on well-established volcanoes, but the actual first eruptions of completely new volcanoes have occasionally been observed.

Monte Nuovo erupted about 10 km from Naples in 1538. After preliminary tremors a depression appeared from which water issued. Later the ground swelled and a fissure opened, through which incandescent material could be seen. Then rocks, pumice, and mud were thrown in the air. The most violent activity occurred on the first two days and in eight days the eruption was over. Monte Nuovo is an entirely pyroclastic cone, about 150 m high and rather less than 1 km in diameter.

A new volcano started in Chinyoro, Tenerife, on 18 November 1909. Observers were only 100 m away when the first eruption threw bushes, rock, and soil 80 m into the air. The eruption went on to erupt more lava than ash, and lasted 10 days.

The most thoroughly observed, documented, and well known of all new volcanoes is Paricutin in Mexico, 320 km west of Mexico City. In a cornfield there was a small hole that had existed for many years, and an old inhabitant recalled that even fifty years earlier the hole emitted noises and a pleasant warmth. On 5 February 1943 a series of tremors commenced which increased in number and intensity until on 19 February there were about three hundred. At about 4.00 p.m. on the 20th, witnesses noticed a fissure extending through it, at first only half a metre deep. The fissure then started to erupt smoke or fine grey dust, accompanied by a continuous hissing noise and sparks. Nearby trees began to burn. By 5.00 p.m. a thin column of smoke rose from the hole, and a little later a hole at the end of the fissure, only half a metre across at first, emitted red hot stones and smoke. By 8.00 a.m. the next morning a cone about 10 m high had formed, and by midday was 30–50 m high. The first lava issued on the second day. At the end of the first week the cone was 140 m high, eruption was increasingly violent, and the noise could be heard 350 km away.

In mid-April lava issued from the south-western base of the cone, and on

10 June a section of the upper part of the cone collapsed. Lava flowed for a while from the lower part of the break; this was the only time that lava flowed from the crater. All other lava flows came from sources or *bocas* at or near the base. In October a parasitic vent opened at the base of the cone, and a new cone grew over a hundred metres within weeks. A lava flow then issued from its base, and carried a wide section of the cone with it. This breached cone was eventually buried by a succession of lava flows.

At the end of the first year Paricutin reached 325 m, and growth then became slower. When eruption ceased in 1952 the cone was 410 m above the original cornfield.

3   Types of Volcano

In popular imagination volcanoes are always symmetrical cones like Fujiyama, but in reality volcanoes vary widely in shape, size, and composition.

As a first classification we shall consider the common forms of volcano associated with basic lava, acid lava, scoria eruption, mixed eruption, and finally some types of volcano recognized by features other than the type of material erupted. It must be remembered that different volcanologists may use different terms for the same features.

Basic Lava Volcanoes

Basic lavas are characteristically very fluid, so spread easily and give rise typically to volcanoes of low gradient (see figure 3.1).

Lava Shields

A succession of wide sheets of volcanic rock, built by repeated outpourings of basaltic lava, can pile up to produce huge 'shields' with gentle slopes (of less than 7°) and convex outlines. The Hawaiian islands are the classic example. Mauna Loa, the largest shield, rises 10,000 m above its sea-floor base, which is 100 km wide, and projects over 4000 m above the sea. Several shields may group together like Kilauea and Haulalai on Mauna Loa. Volcanic masses such as the island of Hawaii, formed by the overlapping of a group of shield volcanoes, may be termed volcanic shield-clusters. It is important to realize that the great shields of Hawaii are very much bigger than the largest terrestial volcanoes such as Rainier, Etna or Vesuvius (see figure 3.2).

Parasitic cones, flank eruptions, and fissure eruptions are commonly associated with shield volcanoes. 'Shield volcano' is a less exact term that usually refers to a lava shield, but may be used for a large strato-volcano or volcanic complex, such as the Tweed shield volcano of New South Wales, Australia.

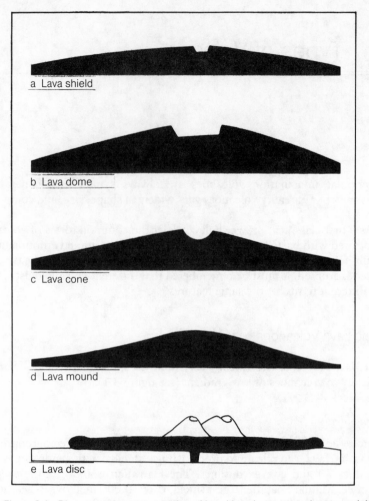

a Lava shield

b Lava dome

c Lava cone

d Lava mound

e Lava disc

Figure 3.1 Diagrammatic representation of basaltic volcano types (not to scale)

Lava Dome

A smaller-scale volcano that erupts liquid lava may produce a convex dome rather than a shield. Any of the individual peaks on Hawaii, such as Mauna Kea, may be regarded as lava domes. The distinction on size used here is not standard practice and many authors use shield and dome inter-changeably.

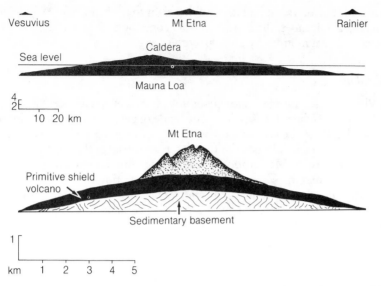

Figure 3.2 (top) Relative size of Mauno Loa shield volcano and some large terrestrial volcanoes (bottom) Enlargement of Mt Etna (simplified from Romano, 1982) showing the doming of the sub-volcanic rocks which is characteristic of many large central volcanoes (Wellman, 1986)

Lava Cones

Central eruption on a still smaller scale may give rise to simple straight-sided cones built of successive lava flows. These usually have flanks of low angle (7° or less), but some examples are much steeper.

Beerenberg on the Arctic island of Jan Mayen, for example, consists of a broad basalt lava dome some 15–24 km in diameter at sea level, on the crest of which is a lava cone with steep 45° slopes, some 5 km in diameter and 750 m high (Fitch, 1964).

The Kolotta Dyngja, a typical Icelandic cone, rises to a height of 460 m with an average slope of 7°, approaching 8° towards the summit. The volcano has a diameter of 5 km and the crater a diameter of 550 m. A ring of scoria about 15 m high surrounds the crater, and has slopes of up to 30°.

In the Victorian volcanic province (Australia) a final stage of scoria eruption often obliterates lava cones formed earlier.

Lava Mounds

Some basaltic volcanoes have no sign of a crater, but are gently sloping mounds, such as Mt Cotterill, Victoria. These extinct volcanoes may owe their shape partly to erosion, although they probably never had very

35

pronounced craters but had lava welling right to the brim before solidification. Such volcanoes, distinguished from cones by their lack of crater, may be termed lava mounds by analogy with scoria mounds.

Lava Discs

In Victoria there are a few anomalous volcanoes which have been described as lava discs (Ollier, 1967a). They are made of basalt, and display jointing perpendicular to the lava skin on both the upper surface and the sides. The smallest one, Lawaluk, has the form of a steep-edged, flat-topped disc of basalt. The disc of Mt Porndon is a similar feature though larger (3 km in diameter). These hills appear to be made by eruption of a single mass of lava that develops a tough skin and then spreads out from the centre without breaking the skin, like of a water-filled balloon collapsing into a disc.

Acid Lava Volcanoes

Acid igneous rocks are generally very viscous, and if they do not explode their limited flow gives rise to a number of distinctive landforms (see figure 3.3).

Cumulo-domes

When viscous lava is extruded, it sags and spreads into convex dome-like bodies without craters called cumulo-domes (see plate 3.1). These may be almost independent, or may be associated with and partly intrusive into previously deposited pyroclastics.

The main part of Lassen Peak, California, is a large-scale example, rising 800 m above pyroclastics and having a diameter of 2.5 km.

In the central volcanic region of the North Island of New Zealand, there are many rhyolite domes, akin to cumulo-domes, but with more mobile flows or *coulées* on their flanks (see figure 3.4). These appear to erupt in the late stage of a volcanic cycle after vast ignimbrite flows and caldera formation.

Sometimes several cumulo-domes may coalesce. Tauhara volcano, New Zealand is a multiple volcano of late Pleistocene age consisting of five coalescing dacite cumulo-domes. Internal flow structures suggest that each dome was formed from lava continuously extruded, but each had a separate vent (Lewis, 1968).

The Tarawera Rift explosion of 1886 exposed excellent sections through a number of domes, enabling a better interpretation of internal structure than is usually possible. There is well-developed circular jointing at the centre of domes, becoming vertical towards the edge and in the coulées.

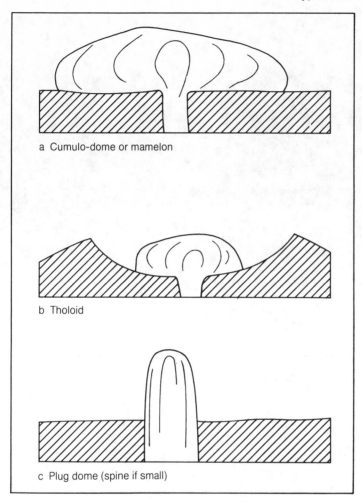

a Cumulo-dome or mamelon

b Tholoid

c Plug dome (spine if small)

Figure 3.3 Diagrammatic representation of acid lava landforms (not to scale)

The tops of both domes and coulées are very irregular due to fissuring (see figure 3.4).

The puys or volcanic hills of the Puy-de-Dôme landscape of Auvergne are typically scoria cones with craters, but some, such as the craterless Grand Sarcoui, are trachytic cumulo-domes and the term puy is occasionally and unfortunately used to mean cumulo-dome.

Plate 3.1 Whakapapaterenga rhyolite cumulo-dome (foreground) and Tutukau rhyolite cumulo-dome beyond, New Zealand (E. F. Lloyd)

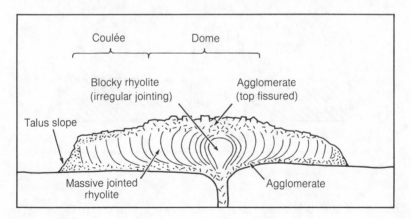

Figure 3.4 Cross-section of cumulo-dome at Tarawera, New Zealand

Mamelons

The term mamelon is often used as synonymous with cumulo-dome, but Cotton (1944) suggests that the term be reserved for those domes built up by the eruption of successive flows of trachytic material, in contrast to the true cumulo-dome, which expands from within. Mamelons, like cumulo-domes, have no crater.

Tholoids

The term tholoid refers to cumulo-domes or mamelons when they occur in the crater of a larger volcano. They may be hundreds of metres high and in diameter. They are often covered with rubble and may be mistaken for nested cones, but they have no crater. The formation of a tholoid in a crater does not necessarily mark the end of activity, for they may be repeatedly built and shattered during the growth of large volcanoes. But apparently not all siliceous domes are explosive. Eichelberger et al. (1986) describe the quiet eruption of Obsidian Dome in California. There is a well-marked tholoid in the crater of Mt Egmont, New Zealand (see plate 3.2). Novarupta, Alaska, has a dome 400 m in diameter and 70 m high lying in a 2.6 km-diameter tephra basin.

Plug Domes

In its most viscous form, the magma extruded from a vent may be so rigid that it moves up like a piston, producing a roughly cylindrical body known as a plug dome. The landform is also known as a piton. In American usage plug domes may refer to what are called cumulo-domes in this book. In New Zealand, Mt Edgecombe is an andesite volcano that was apparently

Plate 3.2 A large strato-volcano, Mt Egmont, New Zealand, with a parasitic cone (Fantham's Peak) on the left (National Publicity, New Zealand)

extruded through a jagged orifice, for it has huge grooves on the side and top that are not due to erosion, but are giant scratches.

The Pitons of Carbet, Martinique, are thought to be plug domes, and Merapi, Indonesia, is an active volcano which builds successive plug domes that are explosively destroyed.

Plug domes can emerge rapidly, but they are repeatedly shattered by explosions and broken by uneven growth, and the accumulation of broken spines and extrusion ridges causes many plug domes to be covered by a jumble of debris, which make a scree-like deposit around the flanks with rocks piled up at their angle of rest.

Spines

Whereas plug domes are large bodies of nearly mountain size, smaller-scale extrusion of very rigid lava, through chinks in the cracked skin of plug domes or cumulo-domes, gives rise to ridges and spines. The spine of Mont Pelée, Martinique, was produced after the catastrophic eruption of 1902. With a basal diameter of 100 m it reached a height of over 300 m, but was rapidly eroded. At one stage it grew 13 m in a day. Spines are frequently irregular in shape, and are not extruded uniformly as in cylindrical pillars. The two views of the Mont Pelée spine (see figure 3.5) show this. A spine on Santa Maria, Guatemala, that grew between 1922 and 1925, reached a maximum size of 200 m high and 1300 m across the base.

Figure 3.5 Two views of the spine of Mont Pelée (left) from the east, after a photograph by Lacroix (right) from the south, after a drawing by Cotton (1944). The eastern side is convex, grooved, and slickensided, while the western side is broken and ragged

Pyroclastic Volcanoes

When explosively produced fragments of lava fall around a volcanic vent they build up a heap of debris, the slope of which depends on the angle of rest of the fragments concerned (see figure 3.6). Fine particles have lower slopes than coarse ones, and as the coarser fragments tend to accumulate near the vent, beautiful concave slopes are formed, like those of Fujiyama (Japan) and Mt Egmont (New Zealand).

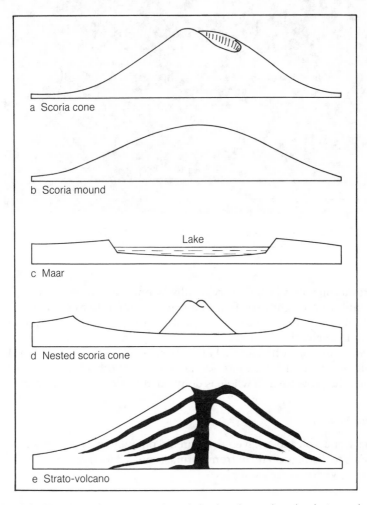

Figure 3.6 Diagrammatic representation of dominantly scoria volcanic types (not to scale)

Scoria Cone

The ideal scoria cone is single, steep, with straight or gently concave sides, and with a crater at the top (see figure 3.6). Mt Elephant, Victoria, 240 m high, is a good example (see plate 3.3). The even height of the crater rim often causes scoria cones to appear flat-topped when viewed from a distance.

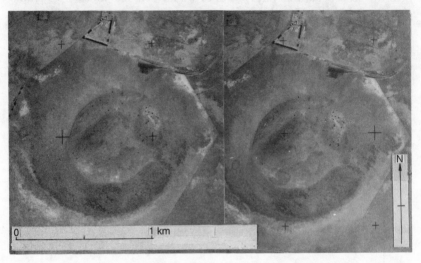

Plate 3.3 Mt Elephant, Victoria; stero-pair of a scoria cone (Crown Copyright, courtesy of Director of National Mapping, Canberra)

Scoria cones may be built very rapidly. Monte Nuovo near Naples, Italy, was built to a height of 130 m in a single eruption lasting a few days in 1538. Barcena, on the island of San Benedicto, Mexico, built a cone of 300 m in twelve days in 1952.

Scoria cones are often formed in the last stages of basaltic eruption. Thus in Victoria there are far more scoria cones than other types of volcano, though the province as a whole is dominated by flows of basaltic lava.

Scoria Mound

Some scoria volcanoes have no apparent crater and may be termed scoria mounds to distinguish them from normal scoria cones (see Figure 3.6). The Anakies, Victoria, are examples.

Nested Scoria Cones

Scoria cones are frequently produced as the last phase of an eruption on the site of larger volcanoes of other types. When they are in the centre of a large crater or caldera they are called nested cones (see figure 3.6). The V-sectioned trough between the inner cone and the crater wall is called a fosse.

Littoral Cones

When lava reaches the sea it explodes and the ejecta pile up to form a cone up to 100 m high and 1 km in diameter. Twin cones are common, one on each side of the lava stream (Wentworth and Macdonald, 1953). Littoral cones are often crescent shaped ridges breached by the feeding lava flow. More rarely they occur as complete cones with craters above lava tubes. They are up to 100 m high, and typically consist of poorly sorted, weakly defined beds. Their formation probably requires rapid delivery of large volumes of lava to the ocean.

There are about 50 prehistoric littoral cones along the shores of Mauna Loa and Kilauea. Twenty-one lava flows have reached the sea along the shores of Hawaii since about 1800, of which only four developed littoral cones.

Maars (Tuff Rings)

Maars are landforms caused by volcanic explosion and consist of a crater which extends below general ground level and is considerably wider than deep, and a surrounding rim constructed of material ejected from the crater. The rim consists of pyroclastic material, either igneous or comminuted bedrock, and is often markedly asymmetrical in plan, with greater deposition on the downwind side of the crater. The rim deposit is also asymmetrical in cross-section, with a steep side towards the crater, and a gentle slope (commonly 4° or less) away from the crater, parallel to the bedding of the pyroclastics (see figure 3.6). The craters have a diameter often about 1 km and a depth of 10–500 m. The rim is commonly less than 50 m high, although it may reach 100 m (see plate 3.4).

Some authors regard tuff rings as the same as maars; others think they have craters above general ground level. Maars are usually associated with basaltic igneous activity, but andesitic maars are known in Chile, and those of Basotu, Tanzania, are produced by carbonatite eruptions (Downie and Wilkinson, 1962). Maars are discussed in detail in chapter 4. Fisher and Schmincke (1984) list ten maar-forming eruptions of the twentieth century.

Plate 3.4 A maar. Pulvermaar, Eifel, Germany (C. D. Ollier)

Mixed Eruption Volcanoes

In many volcanoes there is a mixture of lava and fragmental deposits.

Strato-volcanoes

Many of the world's great volcanoes, such as Vesuvius, Fujiyama, Egmont and many others, are strato-volcanoes, built up of both lava flows and pyroclastic deposits. Many of these have erupted over a long period, and indeed the strato-volcano is the commonest form developed by long-lived central volcanoes. The cones become gullied by erosion and lava flows commonly follow such gullies (see plate 3.5). New gullies then form on the edges of flows, and so on (see figure 3.6). Scoria cones are built around the top of the volcano and pyroclastic flow and fall deposits may have a wide distribution on the flanks. Ngauruhoe, New Zealand, is a typical strato-volcano, almost perfectly conical and about 1000 m high. The slopes are about 30° steep and the crater is about 400 m across. The highest point on the rim is to the east, possibly because of the prevailing westerly wind. Young lava flows have reached the base on all sides except the east.

Some strato-volcanoes are isolated, but many occur in groups. In McMurdo Sound, Antarctica, for instance, the large young strato-volcanoes, Mts Erebus (altitude 3700 m), Bird, Terra Nova, and Terror coalesce to form Ross Island.

Plate 3.5 Ngauruhoe, New Zealand. Flank of a strato-volcano showing lava flows (C. D. Ollier)

Hekla, Iceland, is intermediate in many respects between a typical Icelandic shield volcano and a strato-volcano such as Vesuvius. It has been built by repeated eruptions from a fissure, often with several craters active at the same time.

Intra-glacial Volcanoes

Intra-glacial volcanoes are those that formed from eruptions beneath a thick ice sheet. Such volcanoes have several phases of growth (see figure 3.7).

(1) Volcanic heat causes a melt-water vault to form within the ice, within which pillow lavas and hydroclastics pile up around the vent. Eventually the roof of ice collapses and activity takes place in an intra-glacial lake.

(2) As the pile of lava reaches the water surface, explosive activity increases, and tuff deposits mantle the pillow lavas.

(3) When the volcano builds above water level, lava flows are produced. These flow into the surrounding lake, where they are brecciated, and a flow-foot breccia is deposited. This is made up of breccia, pillows,

45

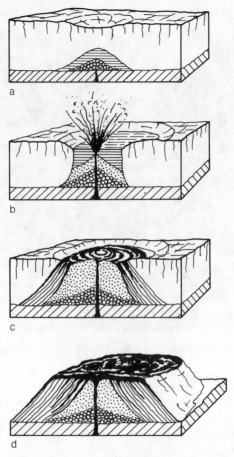

Figure 3.7 The formation of intraglacial volcanoes (a) eruption melts ice and forms pillow lava (b) pyroclastic eruptions when enough ice melts (c) when sediment accumulates above water level, lava flows erupt, with hydroclastics at the edge (d) when ice melts, a table mountain with a lava cap over clastics remains

and ash (mixed hydroclastics), deposited as cross-bedded sediments with a dip of about 3°.

(4) If the volcanic mass grows large enough, there will be a mass of pillow lava, flow-foot breccia, and pyroclastics overlain by 'normal lava'. Since the lava is fluid it builds a low-angle sheet or shield which is virtually a caprock over the underlying hydroclastics. These processes produce two main kinds of volcano.

Tablemountains (Tuyas) Tablemountain is the name given to a particular kind of volcanic mountain in Iceland; examples include Hrutfell,

Kjalfell, and Skridufell (Kjartansson, 1966). Tablemountains are isolated plateaus roughly circular in plan, with gently convex tops and abrupt sides. They are built in the manner described above of a mixture of pillow lava and hydroloclastics (locally known as moberg in Iceland) but capped by basalt lava flows. During the whole volcanic process the material has been moulded within the walls of ice, more or less into the present shape.

Occasionally the process was only partially operative, as at Leggjabrjotur. This is a shield volcano except on its southern side, where it has an abrupt scarp of 300 m formed where lava was ponded against a thick ice margin.

The 'tuyas' of British Columbia, Canada, appear to be similar to the Icelandic tablemountains (Mathews, 1947).

Ridges   Another kind of Icelandic volcano, formed in association with tablemountains, is known as a ridge (Kjartansson, 1966). Ridges are ridge-shaped, serrated mountains, built up by fissure eruption of moberg under a thick cover of ice. The volcanic products have not been sufficient to reach the surface of the ice at the time of eruption.

Miscellaneous Volcanoes

Composite Volcanoes

The term composite volcano in a strict sense refers to those volcanoes which have a mixture of lava and scoria forms, but not in a simple layered sequence. Mt Rouse, Victoria, is an example, with an elongate crater in a scoria hill and with a smaller and more distinct crater with a basalt rim on the south. The composite Mt Porndon, Victoria, has a large basalt disc with a diameter of about 3 km, in the centre of which are a number of scoria cones and mounds. Staughtons Hill, Victoria, consists of a maar, a scoria cone, and a basalt-rimmed separate crater. Most composite volcanoes appear to consist of individual hills which are genetically related, but it is possible that some are due to accidental superimposition of unrelated eruption points of different ages.

Parasitic Cones (also called Adventive Cones and Secondary Cones)

When a volcano becomes very high, very great pressure is required for the rising lava to reach the summit crater. The lava may then find an easier route to the surface at a lower level, and will erupt on the flanks of the main volcano. After such an eruption the conduit is blocked, and in the next eruption another opening must be made. In this manner a large volcano comes to have many small parasitic cones on its flanks. Mt Etna, Sicily, with over 200 parasitic cones and over 800 small mounds of lava known as

47

boccas, is the finest example. Here each new series of eruptions occurs along a rift, and succeeding new cones appear higher and higher up the fissure until it is sealed. Another fine example of a major volcano and parasitic cones is Tristan da Cunha (see figure 3.8).

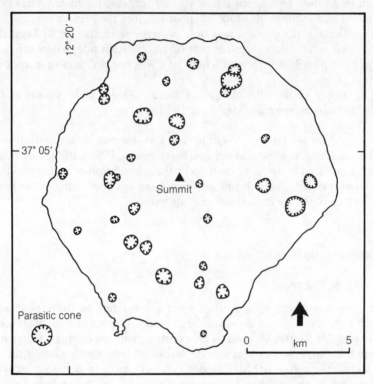

Figure 3.8 Tristan da Cunha, showing many parasitic cones (after Baker et al., 1964)

Alternatively, a volcano may have a single parasitic cone, such as Fantham's Peak on Mt Egmont, New Zealand (see plate 3.2).

It must be noted that volcanoes do not inevitably produce parasitic cones when their column of lava becomes very high. Cotopaxi (Ecuador) for instance, attains a height of 5897 m and 3000 m above its base, yet its volcanic activity is confined to the summit crater where lava flows and pyroclastics are produced. Flank eruptions are unknown on Cotopaxi.

Multiple Cones

In regions of areal eruption, such as on the volcanic plains of Victoria, a number of scoria cones are built very close together. The general mechanism appears to be the same as for parasitic cones, that is the first cone blocks the vent, and the second one occurs on a new vent close by. The difference here is that no cones grow very big, and all the separate cones tend to be of about the same size; that is, there is no main volcano with parasites, but a series of equal volcanoes. These may be called multiple cones.

Seamounts and Guyots

Thousands of submarine mountains or seamounts are known from all oceans, but especially from the Pacific (Menard, 1964). These are of volcanic origin and many, distinguished by a flat and horizontal top, are known as guyots.

They are large mountains, rising over 1000 m above their bases, and their flat tops commonly lie at a depth of between 1000 m and 2000 m. A guyot south of Eniwetok atoll in the Marshall Islands is 55 km across the base and 14 km across the plateau; one to the north of Eniwetok is 55 km across the top and 95 km wide at its base. There is no regularity in the levels of guyot tops. Oceanic volcanoes build up rather like sub-glacial volcanoes, with pillow lavas first, then various hydroclastic deposits, and sub-aerial flows when the volcano rises above sea level (see figure 3.9).

Guyots frequently occur in groups, especially on swells on the ocean floor, though they are also common on deep ocean floors. One guyot is known from the Aleutian trench in the Gulf of Alaska, at a depth of 2500 m. Many guyots have now been dredged and photographed. There is no doubt that they are basaltic and they often have thin veneers of Cretaceous or Tertiary fossiliferous sediment on the tops and slopes.

Guyots represent a late stage in the development of oceanic volcanoes, which erupt, are planated at sea level, and then sink beneath the sea too fast for coral growth to keep pace.

The speed with which erosion can reduce a volcano to a flat-topped shoal is demonstrated by many examples given in chapter 11.

When a volcano erupts, the weight of the volcanic pile adds a load concentrated on a small area of the earth's crust already weakened by withdrawal of magma from beneath it. The mechanism for subsidence of guyots is probably the overloading of the ocean floor caused by the weight of the volcanoes themselves. Some guyots even have an annular depression around their base, supporting the sinking hypothesis.

Crypto-volcanoes

Crypto-volcanoes are roughly circular holes or rims, sometimes with disturbed strata, where a volcanic origin is postulated, but where no igneous rock can be found. Such structures may be due to eruption of gas only, or may be surface expressions of volcanic pipes that have not quite

49

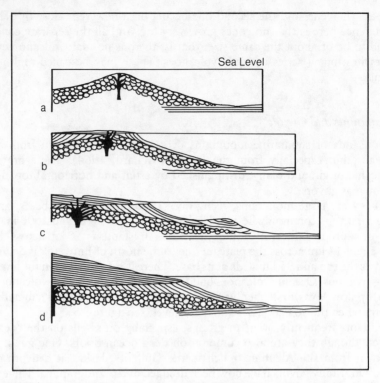

Figure 3.9 Formation of oceanic volcanoes Ovals: pillow lavas; steep lines: hydroclastic flows and breccias; gently sloping lines: sub-aerial lava flows

reached the surface. Mt Abbott is an example in Western Australia (Prider, 1960); Bucher (1933) has described examples from the USA.

Meteorite craters have a superficial similarity to volcanoes. The best known of all, Meteor Crater, Arizona, is a rimmed basin 170 m deep and 1200 m wide. At Henbury in central Australia there are thirteen craters with inconspicuous rims, the largest of which is 200 × 110 m, and the circular Wolf Creek crater of Western Australia is 840 m across and 50 m deep.

When a meteor strikes the earth it explodes, and it is the explosion rather than the impact that forms the crater. Meteoritic iron is seldom found inside the crater, but is scattered outside the rim by the explosion. Other indications of meteoritic origin are the presence of fused bedrock fragments, the development of outward dipping rocks in the rim, and imbricate structures in the bedrock due to impact.

Morphology

The classification of volcanoes used so far is not systematic, but based on shape, petrology, volcano mechanism, and other factors. Geomorphologists are particularly concerned with shape or morphology, and have produced some classifications in which this aspect dominates. Some, such as the classification of scoria cones into five types by Breed (1964) are largely subjective (see figure 3.10). Moriya (1978) studied 142 Japanese

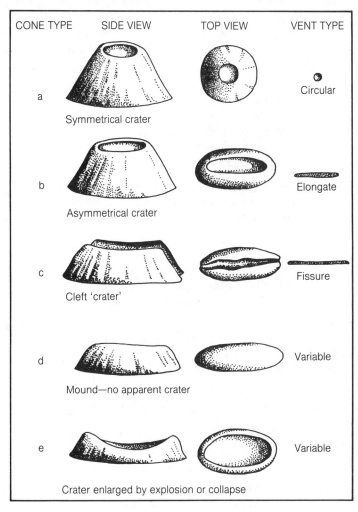

Figure 3.10   Classification of scoria cones by crate shape (after Breed, 1964)

lava domes and classified them into plug domes, typical domes, domes with flow, flat lava domes, and crypto domes. He was then able to correlate his morphological types with chemical composition and dominant mineralogy.

Some classifications are based on mathematical analysis of morphological data. Pike (1978), for instance, analysed the data for 655 volcanoes including height, flank width, crater diameter and depth, and circularity. Multivariate analysis brought out eight groups – lava shields, strato-volcanoes (with crater or caldera), cauldron-centred ash-flow plains, small tephra cones, maars, table mountains (tuyas), and silicic lava domes. These groups suggest that particular combinations of volcano-forming processes commonly work together.

Suzuki (1977) analysed the morphology of 699 volcanoes and found they grouped into six 'volcano series'. The series, with the global population percentages, are:

Strato-volcano	62
Strato-volcano with caldera	10
Shield volcano	11
Shield volcano with caldera	3
Caldera volcano	7
Monogenetic volcano	6

Happily, almost three-quarters of the volcanoes conform to the popular image of a volcano – a conical strato-volcano.

Suzuki further divided the world's volcanoes into five regional groups:

I	Island arc volcanoes
A	Alpine zone volcanoes
C	Continental volcanoes
O	Oceanic volcanoes
R	Rift and ridge volcanoes

It then becomes possible to rank the regional groups according to the percentage of volcano types that they contain. Perhaps the most remarkable finding is that the strato-volcano series decreases in almost the same order as the shield series:

Strato-volcano series	I	A	C	R	O
Shield series	I	A	C	O	R

Suzuki also related the volcanic groups to his own Morphological Explosion Index (MEI):

Volcano type	MEI %
Island arcs	97
Alpine	77–88
Rift and ridge	38–41

As Simpkin et al. (1981) point out, different volcanologists have used different terms for the same features and there is still no standardized usage. Their own catalogue uses about 20 morphological volcano types. This is an area where geomorphologists could make a contribution, for there is little doubt that form reflects more important volcanological truths.

4   Craters and Calderas

Depressions on volcanoes are usually known as craters or calderas. These are formed in a number of ways and have many variations of form, some of which have been given specific names.

Craters in Scoria Volcanoes and Strato-volcanoes

The simplest craters are the depressions usually found at the top of scoria cones (see plate 3.3) and strato-volcanoes (see plate 4.1). These are generally 1 km or less in diameter, and seldom exceed 2 km. They are thus

Plate 4.1   Crater of Ngauruhoe showing subsidiary cone built during 1954 eruption with formation of fosse (E. F. Lloyd)

different in scale from calderas, described later, which are often over 5 km in diameter.

Summit craters mark the vent from which pyroclastics were ejected, and around which scoria was heaped to build the cone. Craters vary in depth, and in general the wider the crater the deeper it will be. The particle size of the pyroclastics largely controls the angle of the inner slope, and the crater may not exhibit its greatest depth because of later fill by lava, eroded debris, or by pyroclastics which have been emitted with insufficient energy to leave the crater, or in such a way that they have fallen directly back into the crater. When the crater rim is of even height the volcano often has the appearance of a truncated, flat-topped cone when seen from the side.

Many craters are breached. That is they have a low gap on part of their rim, which may be caused in a number of ways. The eruption may be directed laterally by an inclined or partly blocked vent. If a strong wind blows during eruption it may cause preferential accumulation on the down-wind side and an apparent breach on the upwind side. A lava flow may be erupted from the crater and erode a channel through pyroclastics, as for example, Cerro El Ciguatepe, Nicaragua (McBirney and Williams, 1965). Alternatively a Paricutin-type flow may erupt from the base of the scoria cone, causing collapse of the overlying pyroclastics and thus a breach of the crater rim. The breach of Mt Elephant (see plate 3.3) may be of this type. Breaching may be caused by land-sliding during eruption, as was actually observed at Paricutin on 10 June 1943.

The shape of the crater may be used to classify scoria cones into the various kinds shown in Figure 3.10.

Craters are normally a few times wider than the pipes beneath them. Exceptionally violent explosions may produce much wider craters, such as maars. The diameter of craters may also increase by the caving-in of the walls. In this way the crater of Irazu, Costa Rica, widened from 200 m to 525 m during the eruption of 1963–5.

The relative depth of the crater to the surrounding cone can also be of significance (see figure 4.1). In the majority of scoria cones, the crater is a comparatively small feature on the large cone. In what has been termed the 'Noorat' type (Ollier, 1967b) the crater is as deep as the volcano is high; in other words the volcano consists almost entirely of a ring of scoria around a vent and there has been very little accumulation over the vent itself. If the crater is actually below the general ground level then the volcano is usually of the maar type.

Open Volcanic Vents

At Mt Eccles, Victoria, Australia, there are examples of vertical and inclined volcanic vents in cones interpreted as hornitos. The main one, 'The Shaft', is a vertical hole with a total depth of about 30 m. It is about 4 m wide at the narrowest part, becoming wider to the surface crater, and also

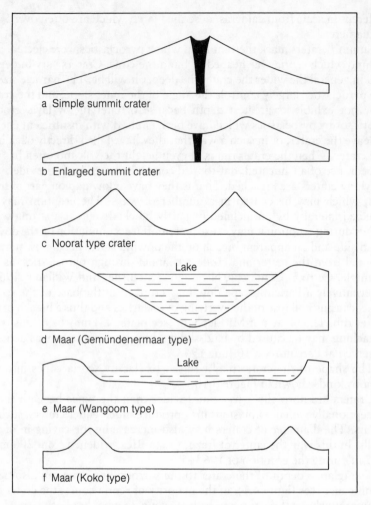

a Simple summit crater

b Enlarged summit crater

c Noorat type crater

Lake

d Maar (Gemündenermaar type)

Lake

e Maar (Wangoom type)

f Maar (Koko type)

Figure 4.1 Diagrammatic representation of kinds of crater

opening out at depth like an inverted wine glass. The walls are completely lined with lava stalactites, the floor is covered with blocks of very vesicular scoria (Ollier, 1964b).

A somewhat similar open vent is present in 'The Hill With A Hole In It' on the Atlantic island of Tristan da Cunha, but this vent is in the main volcanic cone, not a hornito. No geologists have descended this vent, but from the account of the single islander who has been down it appears to be very similar to Mt Eccles, but with horizontal continuation, probably in the direction of an associated lava flow.

At Red Crater, Tongariro, New Zealand, a thick dyke intruded the crater wall, chilled at the edges and then was partially drained to form a lava cave within the dyke.

Cave vents can sometimes be entered in still active volcanoes. A small vent goes down at a shallow slope from the floor of the crater of Matupi near Rabaul, New Guinea. Steam and fumes still issue from the vent, which is lined not with lava stalactites but with a beautiful array of crystals, mainly of unstable sulphates.

Maars

Maars are landforms caused by volcanic explosion and consist of a crater which extends below general ground level and is considerably wider than deep, and a surrounding rim constructed of material ejected from the crater. The word comes from the German *Maar*, a name given to numerous lakes in craters of this type in the Eifel district of Germany. The rims of maars are characteristically low, the slopes are generally low, about 4° being characteristic, and the diameter of maars is usually between 500 m and 1 km. There is a distinct difference between the size of the largest maars and that of calderas which are normally 5 km or more in diameter.

A very frequent suggestion in connection with maars is that they are formed by phreatic explosion due to the violent reaction of ascending magma and groundwater (Lorenz, 1973). In most areas with maars this is very feasible. In Hawaii (Stearns, 1935) and on Ambrym, New Hebrides (Stephenson et al., 1967) there are pyroclastic cones of apparently phreatic origin near sea level with coral limestone fragments in the ejecta, suggesting possible reaction of ascending magma with water in a coral reef. Volcanoes on higher ground in both areas have normal scoria cones, and presumably did not erupt phreatically. Similarly, in the Auckland area of New Zealand, the volcanoes near sea level have a form that suggests phreatic eruption, while those on higher ground are normal scoria cones (Searle, 1964). In the Mud Lake area of Idaho there are five possible maars on the gravel fan of the Snake River which is saturated with groundwater; elsewhere in the region, where groundwater is negligible, quiet fissure eruptions occurred (Stearns, 1926). The maars of Victoria usually occur over porous limestone which would have provided ideal conditions for phreatic explosions.

Maars with nested scoria cones (the Zuni type) may be explained satisfactorily on the phreatic hypothesis by supposing that the first ascending magma hits groundwater and explodes violently, using up the groundwater and drying the ground. If emission of lava continues, it cannot explode violently as there is no longer any groundwater, and so erupts as a lava flow or more commonly as a scoria cone.

However, there are some areas of maars, including the type area of the Eifel district, where conditions seem unfavourable for phreatic eruption. In these (and perhaps other) maars, explosive eruption may result from high carbon dioxide content in the initial magma which expands violently near the surface (Chivas et al., 1987).

Holmes (1965, p. 313) divides ring craters (here called maars) into explosion vents and fluidization craters. The former are said to give rise to small funnel-shaped craters and coarse angular debris, and the latter have wide shallow craters with nearly flat floors and low rims of distinctive material due to fluidization. In fact this regular association of form and type of ejection is not generally found.

Maars may be classified by means of their approximation to type examples (Ollier, 1967b) including the following:

(1) Pulvermaar (see figure 4.2; plate 3.4) – a simple, circular maar. This is the commonest type, and includes both flat-floored maars and funnel-shaped maars.
(2) Zuni – maar with a scoria cone or cones inside on the same centre of eruption. The nested cone may be very small or large enough almost to bury the maar, as at Mt Wellington, Auckland.
(3) Koko – maar with steep walls both inside and outside the crater, and thus a sharp crest.

Some authors (for example, Macdonald, 1972; Fisher and Schmincke, 1984) distinguish between tuff rings and maars, on size, or on whether the

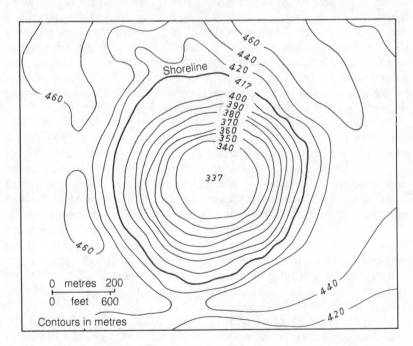

Figure 4.2 Plan of Pulvermaar

crater is above or below general ground level. Others (for example, Wohletz and Sheridan, 1983) see a hydrostatic continuum from cinder cones to pillow lavas related to environment and mechanical energy. Clasts in maar sediments show no thermal metamorphism, and so indicate low temperatures. Ballistic calculations on large ejected blocks show eruptive velocities reaching 500 m/s, and unaltered mantle xenoliths also suggest rapid ascent approaching the speed of sound.

Maars are often located on the top of diatremes. Cloos (1941) studied such pipes in Germany. They are funnel-shaped (see figure 4.3) and it was found that the larger blocks within the pipes had subsided rather than being thrown out, and were separated by 'tuffisite', or intrusive tuff. The eruption evidently took place by streaming of material around the large blocks. There may nevertheless be phreatic explosion nearer the surface.

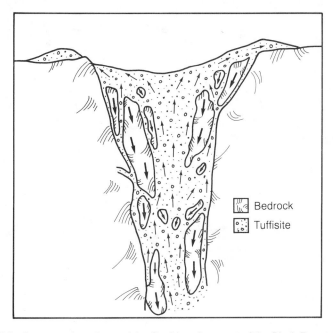

Figure 4.3 Cross-section of one of the Swabian pipes east of the Black Forest. While a highly mobile mixture of gas and particles is intruded, the large blocks of bedrock subside (after Cloos, 1941)

Craters in Lava Volcanoes

In lava volcanoes no mound is built up around the vent as in scoria cones, but the lava volcano builds up by periodical overflows of the lava in the vent, which is then sometimes called a crater. This may be enlarged by the collapse of the crater walls. An even larger area around the vent may also sink to form a caldera. Both the caldera and crater formed in this way have sometimes been called lava sinks, and this term is better than crater for the actual top of the vent, though the larger depression is more simply called a caldera. The Hawaiian volcano Kilauea has a summit caldera, in the base of which is Halemaumau, the lava sink (see figure 4.4). This was formerly continuously active, and was known by yet another term, a fire-pit. Nyiragongo in Zaire is another volcano, in this case a strato-volcano, exhibiting both a caldera and a lava sink, in which a lava lake is still active (see figure 4.5).

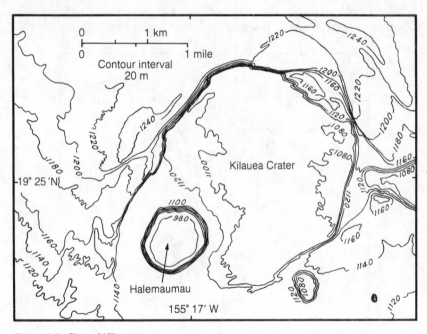

Figure 4.4 Plan of Kilauea

Long records have been kept of the lava levels in the lava sinks of Hawaii. Lava is occasionally withdrawn to great depths; in 1924 Halemaumau sank 400 m and then exploded.

Pit Craters

Pit craters reported from Hawaii (Wentworth and Macdonald, 1953) are circular or elliptical features sunk below a lava surface. They never have been full to the brim and there is no accumulated material surrounding them. They are collapse features on lava shields or domes, and in their

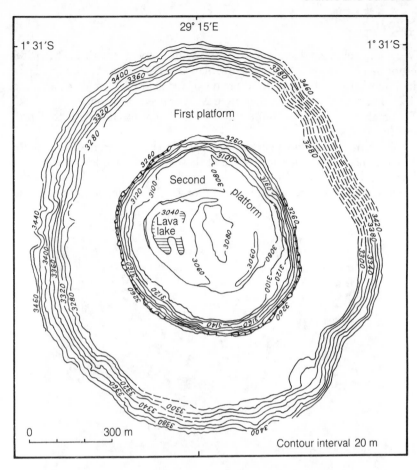

Figure 4.5 Plan of Nyiragongo. The laval lake disappeared in 1977 and reappeared in 1982

nearly vertical walls the edges of horizontal lava flows are exposed. In some groups there is a tendency to alignment, suggesting a distribution following a fissure or a rift zone. At the largest size, pit craters merge topographically into lava sinks such as Halemaumau, but besides a size difference it seems that pit craters form rather rapidly and then become inactive, whereas lava sinks may remain active for very long periods.

Similar pit craters have been described from lava volcanoes of the Chyulu Range, Kenya, including one 500 m across and 30 m deep (Saggerson, 1963).

Rifts

Very long elongated craters are commonly known as rifts. The 1886 eruption of Tarawera, New Zealand, blew out a rift or line of elongated pits in a trench 15 km long, 100–400 m deep, and about 200 m wide (see plate 4.2). The rift passes across the top of Mt Tarawera and continues to Lake Rotomahana, which is rimmed by a thick deposit of fragmented pre-existing rocks.

The term rift (Icelandic *gja*) is also applied to large open fissures that are found in Hawaii and Iceland. Some of these have emitted lava and scoria, but others appear to be simply tension cracks. The largest in Hawaii is the Great Crack, Kilauea, which is 13 km long, 12 m wide, and has a visible

Plate 4.2   Tarawera Rift, New Zealand (C. D. Ollier)

depth of 15 m (Wentworth and Macdonald, 1953). The Eldgja in Iceland is an exceptional rift that has been enlarged by explosion and is over 30 km long (Cotton, 1944). Most rifts are very much smaller.

Crater groups

In Iceland there are 'crater groups' consisting of hundreds or even thousands of craters in an area of about 50 km². The craters are 1–2 m high, and 2–3 m in diameter, ranging to over 30 m high and 300–400 m in diameter. The best-known crater group is the Skutustadir group south of Myvatn. The craters in these groups are all pseudo-craters, formed by lava overflowing ground soaked in water. The water turned to steam and was explosively erupted through the lava. Crater groups appear to be especially common in Iceland because of the combination of thin basalt flows, flat topography, and plentiful water.

Impact Craters

Eruption on Arenal Volcano, Costa Rica, in 1968 threw out numerous incandescent blocks. Most of these disintegrated when they hit the ground, but they left numerous large craters ranging up to 30 m in diameter, and craters up to 2 m in diameter were found as far away as 10 km from the volcano.

Calderas

Very large volcanic depressions, commonly over 5 km in diameter, are called calderas. The world's largest caldera is that of Aso, Japan, which measures 23 × 16 km. Ngorongoro, Tanzania, is 19 × 17 km and the caldera floor is 650 m below the rim.

At one time calderas were classified into explosive calderas, collapse calderas, and erosion calderas. The term erosion caldera refers to a depression formed by completely different processes from the others and leads to confusion, but no alternative has been generally accepted. It now seems doubtful if any true calderas are due to explosion, so the old classification is of little use and the word caldera will nowadays almost always refer to a volcanic depression caused largely by subsidence.

Topographically many calderas are marked by distinct fault lines bounding subsided blocks, and the tops of fault blocks sometimes make topographic benches within the caldera rim.

One kind of caldera is the large, fault-bounded depression found on top of lava shields. The largest caldera in Hawaii is on the summit of Mauna Loa and is called Mokuaweoweo, and is approximately 6 km long, 3 km wide, and 200 m deep. Kilauea (see figure 4.4; plate 4.3) ranks next in size,

Plate 4.3   Kilauea and Halemaumau from the air (J. Dohrenwend)

but since it is much better known, having the volcano observatory and tourist hotel on its rim, its name is used for this kind of caldera.

It was noticed at many volcanoes that after great eruptions, large parts of the original mountains were missing and great calderas had appeared. In 1772 Papandayand (Indonesia) was reduced in height by 1300 m by a great Plinian eruption. In 1815 Tambora (Indonesia) lost 1400 m of height and the eruption produced a caldera 12 km in diameter. It seemed fairly obvious that calderas were formed as huge explosion craters when the volcano 'blew its top'.

As an example, the eruption of Vesuvius near Naples, Italy, in AD 79 was often cited. The top of the old volcano was completely missing after the eruption, and in its place was a huge depression 2.5 km across, within which a new volcano, Vesuvius, had grown. The wreck of the old volcano was a ragged ring, the larger part of which is now Monte Somma. Somma has become a general term given to such relics of volcanoes, and somma caldera may be used as a term for the depression formed by this kind of eruption.

It seemed natural to suppose that the old mountain had been shattered into countless fragments during the eruption and scattered around the countryside. However, when the deposits of the eruption were examined it was found that they consisted almost entirely of new pyroclastic rock, and that fragments of the old volcano were present only in small quantities in the first deposits laid down. It therefore seemed that the volcano had not blown its top but had emitted vast quantities of lava until it emptied itself out, and the summit of the old volcano had then collapsed into the empty magma chamber.

The summit caldera of Ruapehu, New Zealand, about 3 km × 1.5 km, has likewise produced little lithic ejecta, and is thought to be due to subsidence like the somma caldera at Vesuvius (O'Shea, 1954). Eruption and caldera collapse may be repeated many times on one volcanic site, as in the case of Somma–Vesuvius complex (see figure 4.6).

A similar story of collapse was found in many other calderas, such as Krakatau (Indonesia), Coseguina (Nicaragua), Santorini (Crete) and Crater Lake (Oregon), on the site of the original Mt Mazama, where Williams (1941) has calculated that the volume lost is almost 70 km³, but ejecta from the volcano amount to only one-third of this.

Figure 4.7 shows the stages in the development of this kind of caldera as envisaged by Williams (1941). The early stages of eruption discharge enormous quantities of pumice, much of which is expelled as pyroclastic flow deposits. Eruption continues to a stage where the upper part of the magma chamber is emptied and so there is no longer any support for the top of the cone, which therefore collapses. The collapsed material is presumed to be broken up considerably, but most of the material engulfed disappears completely or is hidden under a cover of later volcanics. Such calderas may be referred to as of Krakataun type.

The collapse hypothesis had been described in detail by Verbeek in 1885, but was apparently lost to the English-speaking world until rediscovered by Simkin and Fiske (1983). These calderas are similar in general mechanism of formation to those of the somma type, but differ in degree. Krakataun calderas are generally larger than somma calderas, they are associated with more violent eruptions, generally including pyroclastic flows, and the remnants of the old volcanoes are smaller than those found around somma volcanoes.

Another mechanism for caldera making is shown in figure 4.8, in which a cylinder of material falls as a single unit, and is surrounded by a ring dyke of igneous rock. This mechanism is called cauldron subsidence, and gives rise to calderas known as the Glencoe type, after an example in Scotland.

Branch (1966) described cauldron subsidence areas of enormous size from North Queensland, including one of 120 × 55 km, and he suggests a distinction between *cauldrons*, formed by collapse resulting from the subterranean withdrawal of magma from a deep magma chamber, and *calderas*, caused by collapse as a result of colossal eruptions of pumice derived from a high-level magma chamber.

A modern example of a Glencoe-type caldera may be the Askja cauldron in Iceland which has a rim of volcanoes pouring lava into the great subsidence hollow. Another example is Niuafo'ou near Tonga, where a complex of fissures forms a ring 5 km in diameter around a central caldera. The caldera of Ambrym, New Hebrides, appears to have subsided quietly and there is no evidence for any dramatic cataclysmic eruption accompanying

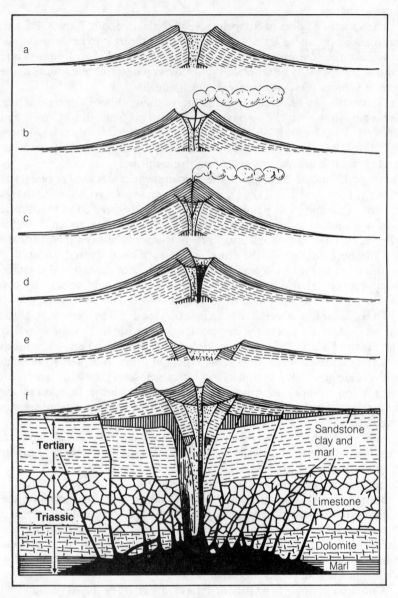

Figure 4.6 Evolution of Vesuvius (according to Rittmann, 1933) (a) the Old Somma volcano (This covers the Primitive Somma volcano, not shown in this figure) (b) a new volcano (Young Somma) begins to grow in the caldera. (c) Young Somma has reached its maximum height, completely covering the Old Somma. (d) on the top of Young Somma is a partially filled caldera (around 800 BC, described by Strabo). (e) large caldera formed at the great Plinian eruption of AD 79. (f) Vesuvius has grown in the caldera, largely filling it

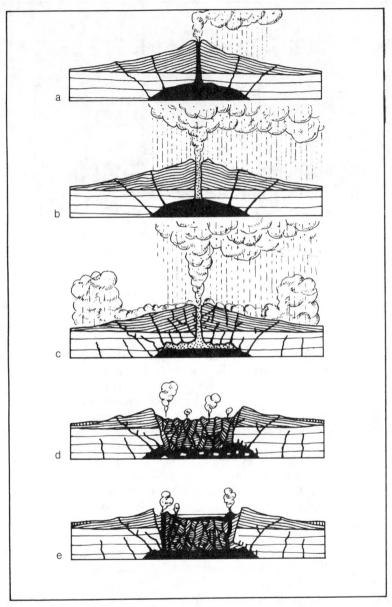

Figure 4.7 Stages in the formation of a caldera (after Williams, 1941) (a) mild explosions. Magma stands high in the conduit (b) increase in violence of activity. Magma sinks to the top of the magma chamber (c) activity climaxes in Plinian or Pelean eruptions. Magma sinks below the roof of the magma chamber, removing support (d) collapse of the cone into the magma chamber (e) Renewed eruptions on the caldera floor, especially near the rim

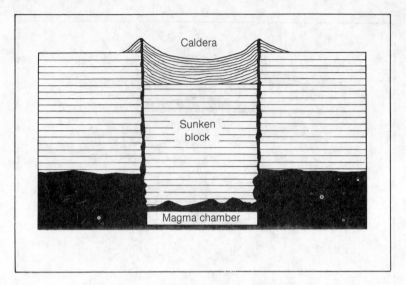

Figure 4.8 Cauldron subsidence, Glencoe type. A cylindrical mass of crust sinks into the magma chamber, forming a caldera at the surface. Ascending magma forms a ring dyke around the sunken block and erupts at the surface around the edge of the caldera, which becomes partially filled with lava

caldera formation (Stephenson et al., 1967). Silai caldera, in the Rift Valley of Kenya, is a Glencoe-type structure, 8 × 5 km, the floor of which has subsided 300 m without any violent eruptions, and there is negligible mantling of pumice associated with the caldera formation.

It thus appears that violent volcanic eruption is not normally associated with Glencoe-type subsidence, and the main distinction between Krakataun and Glencoe types of calderas is that the former emits enormous quantities of pyroclastics, and the latter tends to be quietly effusive. The Glencoe type of caldera appears to be more often associated with basaltic provinces and the Krakataun with orogenic, acidic provinces. Nevertheless, the two processes may be in some ways related. McCall (1963) has suggested that the Glencoe mechanism is the primary mechanism involved in the majority of subsidence calderas, and that the Krakataun mechanism is in the nature of a special case, a complication of the Glencoe mechanism operating where volatiles are particularly abundant within the magma chamber at the time of subsidence. He believes that a complete gradation is possible between calderas showing only the effects associated with ring-fracture and the truly catastrophic Krakataun calderas.

This proposed interrelationship of calderas is supported by the fact that different kinds of caldera may occasionally occur in close proximity or even on one site. For example, McCall and Bristow (1965) interpret Suswa volcano, Kenya, as having an earlier caldera of 100 km² of Glencoe type with Krakataun elements, and an inner caldera of 18 km^2 of Glencoe type, on the edge of which is a small Kilauean caldera.

Several calderas appear to have been formed by lateral withdrawal of support. The Katmai eruption of 1912 occurred on the southern coast of the Alaskan peninsula. Mt Katmai lost 240 m from its top, and produced a caldera 5 km in diameter, and at first it was thought that this was the main source of the eruption. Later investigation showed that the main eruption produced an altogether new mountain, Novarupta. In 60 hours Novarupta and associated fissures ejected 30 km^3 of rock; 150 km^2 of valley floor was covered by up to 200 m of ash flow deposits. It is remarkable that although the main eruption took place from Novarupta, it was Katmai, 8 km distant, that collapsed. The new vent tapped magma located under the old mountain. In a way Novarupta can be regarded as a distant parasitic cone, 8 km distant and 1500 m lower than Katmai, and probably connected by fissures. Groundwater buried by the pyroclastic flow deposits produced thousands of fumaroles that played for many years; this was the Valley of Ten Thousand Smokes.

Another example is the Atitlan basin in Guatemala, a cauldron subsidence caused principally by collapse resulting from subterranean withdrawal of magma (Williams, 1960).

Resurgent Calderas (Valles-type Calderas)

Studies of the Valles Caldera in New Mexico led to the concept of resurgent calderas (Smith and Bailey, 1968). In this type of caldera, renewed volcanic activity is accompanied by up-arching of the caldera by as much as a kilometre. Resurgent calderas are commonly much larger than the other types, and have central mountains as a result of uplift of the caldera floor. Valles Caldera itself is 20 × 24 km, with walls rising 600 m above the present floor. Near the centre is a structural dome forming a mountain mass 15 km across.

Volcanism began about 11 million years ago, but eruption of 200 km^3 of thyolitic ash flows (Lower Bandelier Tuff) about 1 million years ago led to the first caldera collapse (Toledo Caldera). After 300,000 years the same volume of Upper Bandelier Tuffs were erupted, completely burying the Toledo Caldera. Collapse followed along arcuate fractures.

Volcano-Tectonic Depressions

Volcano-tectonic depressions as defined by Van Bemmelen (1930) are depressions due to collapse of the roofs of magma chambers brought about by rapid eruptive evacuation of the magma. The type area for such depressions was the basin of Lake Toba, Indonesia, and the explanation was also applied to the Rotorua-Taupo depression in New Zealand. In the Lake

Toba area, however, it has been shown that the depression already existed as a fault trough before the paroxysmal outburst that produced enormous quantities of ignimbrite. In New Zealand, too, the deformation of the Rotorua-Taupo area is largely tectonic and occurred before the eruptions of ignimbrite, though some major faults are younger than the earlier ignimbrite eruptions. The subsidence has taken place intermittently over a long period, and the evidence is inconsistent with a hypothesis of volcano-tectonic depression in the sense of development in a single major paroxysm by collapse of an arched roof (Cotton, 1962).

5   Lava Flows

Liquid lava flows away from its point of eruption under the influence of gravity, partly impelled by further lava arriving behind it. Some lava is very fluid, some very viscous. Acid, rhyolitic lavas are the most viscous, and never flow freely: at most they give rise to bulbous, thick short flows or tongues, often known as coulées. Basic, basaltic lava can flow much more readily, though it may sometimes flow quite slowly. Intermediate lavas have intermediate properties.

The fastest lava flows can attain speeds of 15 m/s, though 3 m/s is more common for a fast flow, and many flows move along at barely perceptible rates.

The nature of lava flow profoundly affects the resultant landforms, and the landforms provide a lot of evidence constraining ideas about the nature of lava flow.

Dimensions of Lava Flows

Basalt flows of tens of kilometres are not uncommon. Eight unusually long flows in Queensland travelled over 90 km from their source, and the longest, the Undara flow, reached a length of 160 km (see figure 5.1). The longest flow in Victoria is the Tyrendarra flow from Mt Eccles, 48 km long and in parts only 100 m wide. Basalt flows are usually several metres thick, rarely over 10 m, and Icelandic lava flows are commonly less than 1 m in thickness.

The greatest lava flow of historic times was the Laki flow of 1783 in Iceland; it erupted from the Lakagigar crater row which is 25 km long and has about 100 craters. The eruption lasted for seven months. Lava streams were up to 64 km long on the western side and 50 km long on the eastern side. The flow covered an area of 565 km^2 and had a volume estimated at 12–15 km^3.

On level topography lava may spread widely to form extensive veneers of basalt on a pre-existing plain. The volcanic plains of western Victoria are a fine example of this kind of lava plain, covering an area of about 15,000 km^2. Some lava plains may be produced by extensive fissure

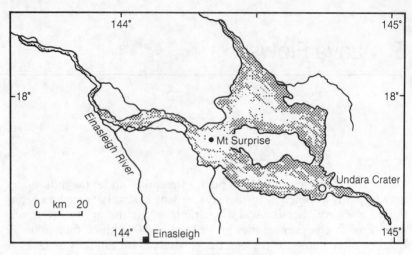

Figure 5.1 The Undara lava flow, Queensland, Australia

eruptions, but the Victorian one was made by lava from many distinct points. Islands of old land that project through a 'sea' of surrounding lava flows are called 'steptoes'. Kipuka is the equivalent Hawaiian term.

On irregular topography basalt tends to flow down valleys, sometimes filling them and spilling over interfluves. Such flows disrupt the pre-existing drainage, displace rivers to new courses, and sometimes completely alter drainage patterns, as will be described in detail in chapter 9. On the cones of strato-volcanoes flows also tend to follow gullies (see plate 3.5).

The outpouring of lava in a region may sometimes be on so vast a scale that even the valleys of originally mountainous areas may be completely filled, and a lava plateau produced (see figure 5.2). The Columbia River Plateau is one of the best-known examples. These lavas are mainly of Miocene age. The original topography had a relief of over 1500 m which was eventually all buried, and new valleys have been incised in the plateau of up to 1500 m deep, deeper than the Grand Canyon of Colorado, USA. This great thickness of lava was attained by the piling up of hundreds of individual flows, averaging only 10 m with the largest only 120 m thick. The Columbia Plateau basalts average 1000 m thick and in places are over 1500 m thick. Besides this great thickness the plateau basalts covered a vast area, about 130,000 km². The Snake River basalts in southern Idaho, USA, are Quaternary volcanics covering an area of 50,000 km². The Snake River and Columbia Plateau basalts are often described together as if they were parts of one province, but they are in fact quite different in location, age, and physiography.

Other major basalt plateaus are those of the Deccan of India, Eocene in age, with a present area of 500,000 km², but originally of a considerable

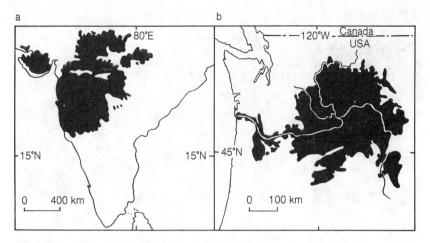

Figure 5.2 Lava plateaus: (a) Deccan Plateau (b) Columbia River Plateau

greater area. The Deccan traps attain thicknesses up to 2000 m, and are made up of many flows varying in thickness from less than 1 m to about 60 m. The Paraña plateau basalts of Brazil cover an area of 750,000 km²; the Karroo basalts of South Africa cover over 50,000 km² and were once probably as large as those of Brazil. Both are of Jurassic age. The flood basalt province of Ethiopia covers an area of 600,000 km² and was originally 750,000 km², with an estimated volume of 350,000 km³. It was emplaced between the Oligocene and the present, with the most voluminous eruptions in the periods 30–15 and 4.5–0 millions of years ago, which may match two stages in the opening of the Red Sea (Mohr, 1983).

The Tertiary volcanic province of Northern Ireland and Scotland is an example of the many smaller regions of flood basalts, some of which are small remnants of once much more extensive areas.

Kinds of Lava Surface

The basalt flows of Hawaii have been divided into two types depending on the nature of the flow.

Pahoehoe

Pahoehoe flows are the most liquid type of lava with little froth (see plates 5.1; 5.2). Cooling forms a very thin skin that may be dragged into folds by movement of the still mobile lava underneath. This produces varieties known as sharkskin, filamented, corded, ropy, entrail, festooned, elephant hide lava, and numerous other kinds.

Plate 5.1 Pahoehoe. Ropy lava, Iceland (D. H. Blake)

Plate 5.2 Pahoehoe. Slab lava, east rift, Kilauea, Hawaii (Hawaii Visitors Bureau)

Aa (pronounced 'ah ah')

Aa lava is blocky, spiny, and slow moving. The lava has a thick skin, broken into blocks that ride on the massive, pasty lava underneath. Such flows have the appearance of slowly advancing heaps of boulders (see plate 5.3), and their movement is accompanied by loud grinding noises. Aa and blocky lava are often used synonymously, but Finch (1933) and Macdonald (1953) distinguish between aa, which is spinose and clinkery, and block lava which has the form of fairly smooth angular blocks.

Plate 5.3   Advancing aa lava flow, Nguaruhoe, New Zealand (E. F. Lloyd)

The terms pahoehoe and aa have been adopted all over the world, but a few other terms have been used at times. Rittman (1962) used 'slab lava' for that in which a skin several centimetres thick solidifies and then is broken by further movement so that the slabs are jumbled together. Another kind of slab lava has been described from Acicastello, Mt Etna (Italy) by Re (1963). These slabs are tens of metres thick, and made of pillow lava and hyaloclastics.

Internal Features of Lava Flows

Pillow Lava

If lava flows into water or is erupted under water a special structure known as pillow lava is commonly formed (see figure 5.3). The lava chills rapidly to form a glassy but plastic skin around still liquid lava, and rolls along in the manner of plastic bags full of liquid. The round or sausage shaped bags are known as 'pillows', and are usually heaped one on another. They have rounded tops, but their base fits into the shape of the underlying surface. This feature, together with the glassy, tachylitic skin and radial cracks makes pillows easy to distinguish from rounded basalt boulders produced by spheroidal weathering. Most pillow lava is formed in the sea, but some is formed in fresh water. Pillow lava is often associated with hyaloclastic deposits.

Figure 5.3 Pillow lava in cross section. Upper pillows sag into hollows between lower pillows. Each pillow has a glassy skin and radial cracks. Unbroken pillows may have a breadcrust surface. Sketch by C. D. Ollier

The formation of pillow lava has been observed by divers, and by observers in submarines in the deep sea, and described in considerable detail. Moore (1975) wrote:

... pillowed lava flows ... are composed of elongate, interconnected flow lobes that are elliptical or circular in cross section. The flow lobes are fed from upslope by larger, connected lava tubes that maintain lava pressure within the growing lobes. Isolated pillow sacks are rare but may form when a flow tube pinches off on a steep slope and tumbles a metre or so downhill.

Jointing

Cooling of a lava flow causes shrinkage, and this results in the formation of joints. These may be irregular in originally pasty masses, but attain geometric regularity in originally widespread, very fluid basalts. If centres of contraction develop in the cooling lava, and lines joining these centres are directions of greatest tensile stress, then cracks eventually appear perpendicular to such lines. When contraction centres are evenly spaced the cracks will join to form hexagons (see figure 5.4a). The pattern of vertical joints divides the lava into columns, which ideally are vertical, hexagonal in cross-section, and broken into blocks by cross-fractures that are often concave-up, resembling ball-and-socket joints. The vertical joint faces may have distinctive scratches known as 'chisel-marks'. Joints in some flows form in a definite sequence with master joints first, mega-columns next, then normal columns and finally cross-fractures. Detailed examinations led Spry (1962) to propose that columnar basalt results from regular crack propagation (see figure 5.4b).

Columns may be tens of metres thick, depending on the thickness of the original flow and its cooling history, and a few decimetres across. They are

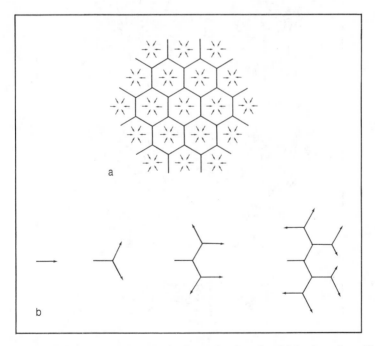

Figure 5.4 The formation of hexagonal columns in a lava flow (a) the formation of ideal hexagonal pattern of joints by uniform contraction towards evenly spaced centres. (b) the formation of hexagonal pattern by continual fracture propagation (after Spry, 1962)

77

seldom perfectly hexagonal, but polygonal, and the columns are not always vertical but take on a wide range of patterns (see figure 5.5). Columnar direction is controlled by the orientation of planes of equal tensile stress, which are normally parallel to the isotherms, which are in turn normally parallel to the flow surface. However, this parallelism is not always maintained, and complicated curved forms of columns can be produced. Curved columns make various patterns such as fans, chevrons, and basins, which

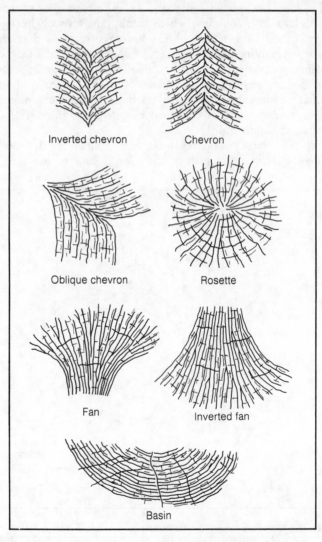

Figure 5.5 Patterns formed by columnar basalt (after Spry, 1962)

are often given local names such as 'harps' or 'fans', while the vertical columns are most commonly known as 'organ pipes'.

In some flows a threefold division is recognized with a 'lower colonnade' with good vertical columns, a central 'entablature' which often contains various patterns of curved columns, and an upper layer that may be columnar, crudely columnar, devoid of columns or scoriaceous (see plate 5.4).

Plate 5.4 Lava flow at Narre Warren, Victoria, Australia, showing lower colonnade with vertical columns, a central entablature with curved columns, and an upper scoriaceous zone without columns (A. A. Baker)

Presumably the upper and lower parts of a flow with this threefold division became immobile before shrinkage caused joint formation, but the central part took longer to cool, developed an irregular isotherm pattern, and so formed curved columns.

A horizontal surface eroded across columnar lava has the appearance of being paved with polygonal flagstones, and is known as a tesselated pavement. The Giant's Causeway in Ireland (see plate 5.5) is perhaps the most famous example of columnar lava.

Some lava flows develop a platy jointing in a roughly horizontal direction. In Australia this is confined to the older lava, over about 2 million years old, and may result from the weathering out of an obscure flow

Plate 5.5 The Giant's Causeway, Northern Ireland. Perfect hexagonal columns and a tessellated pavement in the foreground (Northern Ireland Tourist Board)

structure. Rittmann (1962) suggests that rapid cooling may produce some platy jointing.

Jointing in pyroclastic flow deposits is not nearly so regular as that of lava flows, and is sometimes said to have a rectangular rather than a hexagonal pattern. Sills frequently have very well developed hexagonal joints, very similar to those of lava flows.

Vesicles and Amygdales

Vesicles are small cavities in lava, frozen bubbles of gas. Amygdales are vesicles filled with secondary minerals such as zeolite, calcite or agate. Diameters of about 1 cm are common, but some tens of centimetres are known. Pipe amygdales are cylindrical and perpendicular to the direction of lava flow, and due to movement over wet ground. Some long cylinders of tiny vesicles in Victorian basalts are termed 'corks', and possibly have the same origin. Marathe et al. (1980) report that the lava flows making up the Deccan Traps consist of two main types, *compact*, which are thick flows with well-developed jointing, but no amygdales, and *amygdaloidal*, which are free from joints (massive), comparatively thin, and with abundant amygdales.

Layered Lava and Flow Units

A cross-section of a lava flow may reveal lava in distinct layers, often associated with tubes or lava caves (see plate 5.6). The 'layers' are usually a few decimetres to a metre thick, varying rapidly in thickness and not traceable for long distances. Layers have been interpreted as successive flows (for example, Skeats and James 1937), flow units (for example, Nichols, 1936; Wood, 1971), shearing planes formed during flow just before solidification (Ollier and Brown, 1965a), and as lava levee overspills (for example, Peterson and Swanson, 1974).

Plate 5.6 Bear Trap Lava Tube, Idaho, USA, showing layered lava partly covered by a lava tube lining (from Greeley, 1971)

Flow units are 'lenses and sheets of basalt, one piled on the other, each of which resembles a separate and distinct flow. However, these lenses and sheets have no great continuity and merge into the main body of the flow. . . . There is no evidence of weathering or erosion between flow units.' (Nichols, 1936).

The formation of flow units, as envisaged by Nicholls, is shown in figure 5.6a, and it is seen that a succession of thin flow units may be extruded from the front of an advancing lava flow. But how does such a flow continue to advance? Each successive front has a few layers at the base, but as these are overtopped the flowing lava becomes confined to a higher level – a continuous course is developed, which becomes a line of continued heat

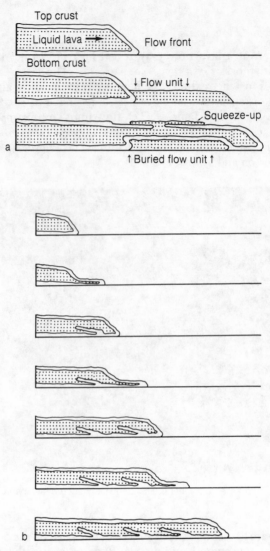

Figure 5.6 (a) the formation of flow-units (after Nichols, 1936) (b) the continued formation and overtopping of flow units, to show how a major conduit is required to transmit lava from a source to the front of the flow

supply, and where a lava cave might form (see figure 5.6b). It is important to realize that a heap of flow units cannot simply be piled one upon another like a stack of pancakes. For the lava flow to continue its advance there has to be at least one conduit going through or over the flow-units, all the way from the volcanic source to the furthest front of the flow. When distances of several kilometres are involved it is unlikely that through-flow takes place in narrow flow-units; more probably the lava travels through a major tube cut though earlier structures, that is, through the layered lava. The formation of flow units and levee overspills has been directly observed and described by Peterson and Swanson (1974).

Sometimes trains of vesicles define layers that are not distinctly separated by partings and sometimes partings fail to cross a unit of lava completely, a feature which would not occur in a series of separate flows. In areas of flow units, many flow units have a parting in the middle, and other partings may occur where layers of vesicles coalesce, so the number of 'layers' exceeds the number of flow units. Since the layers do not correspond exactly with flow units and are more numerous, the term layered lava is useful as a less specific term.

Lava Tubes

Lava tubes, also known as caves, tunnels, and caverns, are hollow tubes inside lava flows, formed not by erosion but as primary features of the flow (see plate 5.6). They are elongated in the direction of lava flow, and may be several kilometres long.

The longest single passages are Leviathan Cave, Kenya (11,122 m); Kazumura in the USA (9,994 m) and Man Jang Kul in Korea (8,994 m). The longest continuous network of completely underground tunnel in Australia is that of Mt Hamilton, Victoria, with a total surveyed length of 950 m (see figure 5.7). Many individual caves are clearly linked as remnants of former continuous caves that were broken by subsequent collapse.

To express the matter simply, lava tubes are formed by the withdrawal of still liquid lava from beneath a solid lava crust. Actually the mechanism is very much more complicated. There is considerable controversy on the origin of lava tubes, and there have been four international symposia on the topic. Three mechanisms appear to be dominant.

Lava Caves Associated with Lava Channels Lava channels are elongated depressions bounded by levees. Greeley and Hyde (1971) found that some tubes in the Mt St Helens area, Washington, were formed by accretion of spatter, leading to arched levees and eventually a complete roof. The same process was described from Hawaii by Greeley (1971). Also from Hawaii, Wentworth and Macdonald (1953) describe how near the vent a flow may be confined to a narrow channel, spattering and overflow build up levees, and a roof may be formed by the jamming of crustal slabs across the lava river. Waters (1960) also mentions how 'some lava tubes are underground continuations of lava rivers that emerge from vents, pour down steep slopes, and gradually crust over and disappear into the flows they feed'.

A similar process is recorded for lava tubes near the source vents by Peterson and Swanson (1974), who add the important process of the

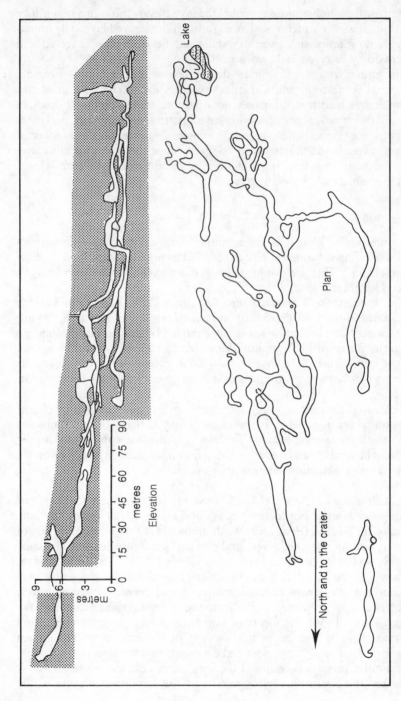

Figure 5.7 Mt Hamilton lava cave, Victoria, in plan and elevation

growth of stationary crust directly on the flowing stream, both downstream from the point of emergence of the stream, and outward from the banks.

In Iceland Kjartansson (1940) observed a flow confined to a narrow channel, and noted how it crusted over partially, and as bits of crust were added to levees they grew together until they completely covered the channel.

Subcrustal Lava Caves   This name is here given to a common type of lava cave found beneath a fairly level groundsurface and with no associated lava channel. Subcrustal lava caves have the following features:

(1) The lava tubes are often partly of circular cross-section; the original tubes were circular in cross-section and the ultimate shape of the tunnel depends on how much lava is drained out.
(2) Many tube caves are found within a flat-topped valley flow.
(3) The tube is within layered lava, parallel to the flow surface, approximately horizontal and not concentric around the lava tube.
(4) The diameter of the tubes is many times greater than the thickness of the layers, so the cave cuts through the layers.

Perhaps the best general statement about this kind of tube is that of Hatheway and Herring (1970) 'The lava tubes . . . appears to have been formed by the development of mobile cylinders of lava in a cooler, more viscous host rock. These cylinders transported fluid lavas to the toe of the flow as long as the source provided a continuous supply. When this ceased, the tube probably drained rapidly.'

Tubes may occur at several levels, and may branch and anastomose in a braided pattern, like Mt Hamilton Cave (see figure 5.7), which also appears to be part of a radial drainage pattern on a lava cone.

Drained Pahoehoe Toes or Flow Units   Pahoehoe flows advance by outbreak of toes or flow units at the front, which flow for a while, develop skins, burst, and so on – the lava moves by advancing one toe after another. Cliff and roadside exposure in Hawaii often reveal superimposed pahoehoe toes, some of which may be over 1 m thick and contain small, drained tubes which are irregular in shape, and do not cross the toe boundaries. Examples of drained tubes are illustrated in Green and Short (1971), figures 5-xxx, 5-xxA and B, and a Hawaiian example, figure 5-xxB.

In his explanation of the lava caves of Raufarholshellir, Wood (1971) proposes a theory of draining both toes and flow units followed by coalescence of the resultant minor caves to make a much larger one with an irregular cross-section.

The three main types of lava tube have a consistent spatial relationship. Nearest the volcanic vent the lava runs between levees, and here the roofed-over lava channel type of cave is formed. Beyond this the lava flow tends to be flat-topped, but under the level crust the flowing lava is simplified into a few major conduits, which, if drained, become subcrustal lava tubes. At the front of the flow, most distant from the vent, single small caves may form in drained pahoehoe lobes.

Small-Scale Features of Lava Flows

The number of small features associated with lava flows must be almost infinite, but some of the commoner ones have been given names, and can be classified and explained (see figure 5.8).

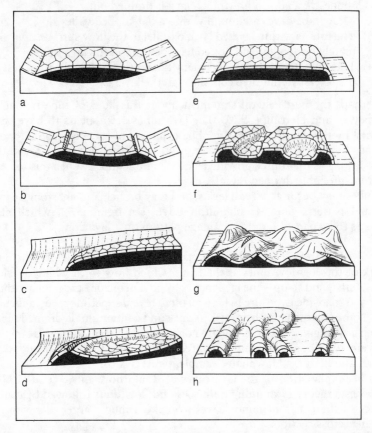

Figure 5.8 Some features of lava flows (a) simple convex surface of valley flow (b) lateral ridges formed by sagging of a simple convex flow (c) toe, at front of a lava flow (d) toe ridge, formed by sagging behind toe (e) broad, flat-topped lava flow (f) stony rises formed by collapse of broad lava flow, parts of which remain at accordant heights (g) stony rises formed by irregular collapse (h) stony rises formed of divided, narrow lobes

Features Associated with Pressure Changes

Toes   The mechanism of lava flow by the successive formation and breaching of toes has been described already. The toes are convex lobes, often about 3 m high and tens of metres long.

Convex Lava Surface   In cross-section many flows have a convex surface, and the more viscous the lava the greater the convexity. Even the most fluid lavas cool fastest on the edges, where the solid sides present some obstacle to spreading and a convexity develops at the edge of the flow. This is important in locating lateral streams.

Lateral Ridges (sometimes inaccurately called pressure ridges)   Suppose a flow has a convex top, and then the liquid in the centre is drained away. The crest will then sag, but the edges, solidifying faster because thinner, will be stronger than the centre and the collapse therefore stops some distance in from the edge. This collapse leaves two ridges, one on each side of the flow. The ridges are usually cracked at the top, and the broken edges reveal cross-sections of the original crust of the flow.

Toe Ridges   Sagging of the main part of a flow may push lava into a stationary toe, so that it swells, the crust is pushed up and sometimes broken at the top in the same way as a lateral ridge.

Pressure Ridges   Pressure ridges, also known as barriers, are elongate ridges of basalt pushed up by movement of the underlying lava. They are often in pairs, with a trough in between. They curve convex downstream, and are found most often some distance above bottle-necks where there is sufficient width for a pressure ridge to form, and sufficient differential flow between the centre and the edge of the flow to cause dragging.

Tumuli (the singular is tumulus, the name coming from the Latin term for ancient burial mounds)   Tumuli are humps on the surface of a generally flat lava flow (see plate 5.7). They are often about 3 m high and usually unbreached, that is, the lava crust runs continuously from flat areas right over the hump. However, if the curvature becomes too extreme the crest of the tumulus cracks. Tumuli are caused when pressure changes in the still liquid lava within a flow are localized at a point, or sometimes along a line, for some tumuli are rather elongated.

Stony Rises   These are known as malpais in the USA, though the terms may not be entirely synonymous. Many widespread lava flows have a very irregular surface, though tending to a plain on a broad scale. Hummocks and depressions, ridges and blind channels, make a completely confused

Plate 5.7 Tumulus (lava blister), Wallacedale, Victoria, Australia. Note the layering formed by vesicles and discontinuous partings, and the columnar jointing formed perpendicular to the surface, apparently before doming of the lava surface into a tumulus (M. C. Brown)

topography called 'stony rises' in Australia, with relief usually about 10 m. There appear to be several varieties. Some are made of a coalescing group of narrow flows emerging from the base of a broad lava sheet. Good examples are found on the south side of Lake Corangamite, Victoria, Australia. In this case the bases of the depressions, being an old plain, have accordant levels, but the height of the ridges is variable. Another kind of stony rise is produced by draining of lava from beneath the skin of a partly congealed plateau. The crust then sags into a series of irregular hollows and channels, but the ridges in between tend to be flat-topped and of accordant level. Sometimes the depressions are predominant, and only a few flat-topped hills remain at a high level. Mt Violet, Victoria, Australia, is a flat-topped hill of this kind.

Depressions   When lava is drained from beneath the crust of an extensive lava sheet, large closed depressions may be formed. There are two such depressions about 1 km wide and 50 m deep near Exford, Victoria, Australia.

Small-scale Constructional Features

Lava Levees   In a gutter carrying water and fallen leaves it may be seen that the leaves tend to be pushed to the side, and a clear channel of water flows in the centre. In the same way a lava flow may run fastest in the centre and heap solidified fragments of crust at the side. Topographically the effect of two ridges and a central depression is similar to the lateral ridge situation, but heaps of irregular block are exposed rather than a neat cross-section of a single crust. Sparks et al. (1976) distinguish several stages (see figure 5.9): initial levees; accretionary levees (made by smearing clinkers on the sides and tops of initial levees); rubble levees (built by avalanching of steep flow fronts); and overflow levees (where successive flows drape over existing levees).

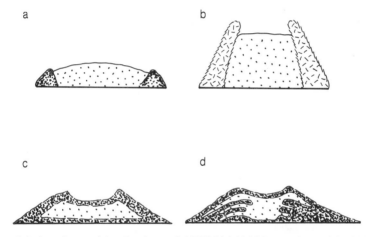

Figure 5.9   Lava levees (after Sparks, et al. 1976) (a) initial (b) accretionary (c) rubble (d) overflow

Spatter Ramparts   Parallel ridges of welded spatter on each side of a fissure eruption are known as spatter ramparts.

Spatter Cones   After the rampart stage described above, most of a fissure may seal, and agglutinated spatter may build up over a few points to make a spatter cone, sometimes called a cinder cone. Spatter cones differ from hornitos in being directly over a fissure, but some authors use the two synonymously.

Lava Rings   These are walls of spatter, similar to spatter ramparts, but built up around the edge of a lava lake. Examples are given by Wentworth and Macdonald (1953).

Hornitos   Spatter may be erupted through a crack in the surface of a pahoehoe flow, and build up a small cone or spire of scoria and driblets. This is called a hornito or driblet cone. The term is usually restricted to small features perhaps 5 m high, and larger cones built in this way (that is, not directly connected to any feeder pipe but deriving their lava within a flow) are called *adventitious cones*. Hornitos commonly have an open pipe at the centre. Parasitic cones are sometimes called 'adventive' or 'adventitious' cones and should not be confused with the type of landform described here.

Rootless Vents   Rootless vents are similar in some ways to hornitos, but are said to be produced when lava pours down earlier lava tunnels and reappears at the surface some distance away from the original source (Wentworth and Macdonald, 1953).

Squeeze-ups   These are somewhat similar to tumuli, but the crust has been cracked open and pasty lava has been squeezed through as a dyke-like auto-intrusion. Colton (1930) described squeeze-ups 2 km long and 20 m wide from Sunset Crater, Arizona. Nichols (1939) described bulbous squeeze-ups from New Mexico that spread slightly and are up to 5 m across. On aa flows, spines up to 30 m high are the equivalent of sqeeze-ups.

Grooved Lava   When semi-solid lava is extruded through a crack, as for instance in a squeeze-up, the edges may be scratched, slickensided, or grooved by projections on the solid lava at the edge of the crack. This is called grooved lava.

Miscellaneous Features

Open Fissures   Where lava sheets issue from rift zones, there may be open cracks along the line of the fissure. These are generally fairly small features, a metre or so wide and a few tens of metres long, but they sometimes attain much larger size when they may be termed 'rifts' (see p. 62, chapter 4).

Cave Lining   Many lava caves have a lining of basalt about 10 cm thick, which may cover roof and walls completely. Where it collapses, layered lava can be seen behind (see plate 5.6). The cave has an erosional contact with the layered lava, and the lining is plastered on roof and walls as the lava tube is drained.

Lava Stalactites and Stalagmites   The lava lining of a cave may be lique-fied, usually by hot gases filling the cave when the original contents are drained out. This liquid drips, and may freeze to form lava stalactites. These may be up to a metre long and may be smooth and shiny, or vesicular and rough. Lava that drips to the floor may form lava stalagmites, which are rarer than stalactites. The lava usually appears to solidify somewhat during its fall, and many lava stalagmites are made of agglutinated driplets, and do not become smooth. In many caves dripping lava probably falls on to a still liquid flow, and is simply incorporated into it.

Shark-tooth Projections   If two sheets of solidifying lava are pulled apart, liquid lava between the sheets may be drawn out into strands, as treacle in a sandwich may be pulled into strands if the two halves are pulled apart. The pointed projections thus formed have been termed shark-tooth projections, and are up to 25 cm long.

High-lava Marks   When very liquid lava stands for some time at a certain level it cools around the edges, and if the lava is then drained away to a lower level, a narrow shelf of lava may mark its former position. This is known as a high-lava mark. Some high-lava marks in Victorian lava caves have curved downwards while still plastic, and have been called benches (Skeats and James, 1937). In Staircase Cave, Byaduk, Victoria, there is a whole series of high-lava marks.

Lava Tree Moulds   When trees are buried by lava, their shape is often preserved in the lava, though the wood may be completely burned away. The hollows so produced are called tree moulds, and may be so numerous as to play a major part in determining the porosity of the rock.

Lava Blisters   Wentworth and Macdonald (1953) report lava blisters from Hawaii, consisting of shells a few centimetres thick around bubbles up to 1 m in diameter. So-called lava blisters in Victoria appear to be very exaggerated tumuli (Ollier, 1964a).

The Nature of Lava Flow

Some viscous lava flows as a pasty mass, moving slowly under a cover of blocky and scoriaceous debris. When such a flow comes to rest little internal structure is present and when the flow cools it will be a solid, more-or-less uniform mass, except for cooling structures. At the other extreme, some lava moves almost as a pure liquid to a position of rest and then solidifies. Such very fluid lava will also come to rest as a homogeneous mass, except perhaps at the surface, and will solidify into an apparently uniform rock except for cooling structures.

But in many instances the nature of lava flow is complex because lateral movement and solidification are occurring together. Little work has been done on the fundamental nature of liquid flow close to the melting point, and ideas are largely based on theory, analogy (such as experimental flows of kaolin), and interpretation of landforms.

The surface of the flow naturally cools faster than inner parts, so a crust is repeatedly formed only to be broken by further movement. In some flows blocks may be carried over the toe of the flow and buried beneath advancing lava, so that the flow moves almost like a caterpillar track, and the massive interior of an aa flow may be both underlain and overlain by clinkery boulders. Alternatively, the top of a flow may cool over, and then suddenly rupture so that liquid lava is extruded on tothe top of a flow through cracks in the surface, where it spreads out to form a flow unit.

Flows are deepest in the middle and so cool more slowly there. The centre is therefore more fluid than the edges, and remains mobile for longer. This gives rise to differential flow, fastest in the centre and slowest at the sides, which causes some of the small-scale features described earlier. Lava flows respond to topography flowing fastest down the steepest slopes, and at cliffs there may be lava-falls analogous to waterfalls. The more viscous lavas may override obstacles, but the fluid lavas flow around them, and may sometimes be diverted by quite small embankments.

Some lavas flow and solidify in a complicated manner beneath a crust, giving rise to various features such as layered lava and lava caves. Changes may also affect the surface of the flow, creating tumuli, lava blisters, and squeeze-ups; reduction in pressure leads to sagging, and the formation of lateral ridges, etc. Flow in lava tubes under a crust would very much reduce the thermal diffusivity and prolong the flow of lava. Swanson (1973) indicated that lava within tubes flowed virtually isothermally, cooling at a rate of only about $1\,°C/km$. Malin (1980) suggests that such tube-fed flows, if limited only by cooling, could possibly produce flows up to 200 km long, which is quite a reasonable approximation to the longest known, 160 km length of the Undara flow.

According to Walker (1973b) the most important factors affecting the length of lava flows are rate of extrusion, volume erupted, physical properties, environment into which erupted, and local topography.

Viscosity is the most important physical property. The silicon dioxide (SiO_2) and aluminium oxide (Al_2O_3) content is more important than SiO_2 alone in affecting viscosity (and explosivity) of eruptions, and basaltic lavas are more fluid than felsic types because of their lower SiO_2 and Al_2O_3 contents. A second factor is temperature, and the higher the temperature the lower the viscosity. Temperatures may fall rapidly away from an erupting vent except in the very large flows or when lava moves through tubes. Macdonald (1972) described a viscosity increase of only two times after almost 20 km flow from a vent on Mauna Loa. On the other hand, Walker (1967) reported an increase in viscosity from $0.4 \times 10^5 P$ to $1.5 \times 10^7 P$ within 500 m on a flow on Etna.

Long Lava Flows: Simple, Compound and Multiple Flows

Walker (1971) proposed the term compound lava for a lava which is divisible into flow units, and simple lava for one which is not so divisible. For units erupted so close together in time that the whole assemblage cools as a single cooling unit, the term multiple is applied. He suggests that the ability shown by some basalt lavas to flow long distances, generally attributed to the high fluidity of the basalt, may in fact be related to a high rate of effusion.

Walker's (1973a; 1973b) conclusions regarding relationship between flow type and flow length can be summarized as:

High effusion rate: long flow: simple flow: single flow unit.

Low effusion rate: short flow: compound, or: many flow units; multiple.

Malin (1980) examined the length, volume and effusion rate for 87 historic Hawaiian lava flows, and found there was little support for a direct relationship between flow length and effusion rate. A relationship between flow length and total volume extruded is statistically more significant. He notes that 'One reason for the observed relationships in Hawaii may be that tube-fed flows, with approximately constant cross-sectional area, advance farther than other types of flows for similar effusion rates and volumes.'

In reality many long flows consist of layered lava, including Undara flow, Queensland, Australia (160 km) and Tyrrendara, Victoria, Australia (30 km). Having layered lava or flow units these flows would be classed as *compound*. Since lava tubes in these flows cut across the earlier-formed layered lava we must assume a single cooling history, so they must also be described as *multiple*-type lava bodies. Such flows, far-reaching but composite and even multiple, may require a high effusion rate, but effusion rate may be less important than the duration and especially the continuity of flow. If an eruption ceases just long enough for lava to solidify, the lava tubes will be blocked. A subsequent eruption may invade some old tubes, but will essentially flow over the earlier lava flow, increasing its thickness but not its length. If, on the other hand, an equivalent volume of lava were erupted without interruption, a single very long flow is more likely to eventuate, with a continuous lava tube system operating for a longer period.

6 Pyroclastic Fall Deposits

Formation of Pyroclastics

Pyroclastic rocks are fragmentary rocks produced by volcanism, sometimes in great volume (table 6.1). Magma contains considerable quantities of dissolved gases or volatiles. In some conditions the gas may be suddenly released, with the explosive production of many gas bubbles that can shatter the lava into countless fragments of rock, mineral fragments, and glass shards. These produce deposits known as pyroclastics. An account of the physics of vesiculation is given by Williams and McBirney (1979).

Table 6.1 Volumes of pyroclastics produced in some eruptions

Eruption	Volume (km³)	Date
Toba (Indonesia)	2000	75000 BP[a]
Tambora (Indonesia)	100–300	AD 1815
Mt Mazama (USA)	30	6500 BP
Santorini (Greece)	30	1400 BP
Mt St Helens (USA)	1	19 May 1980

[a] BP = Before present.

Most kinds of magma may produce pyroclastics, but the majority of pyroclastics are of acid and intermediate composition, for such magmas are more viscous than basic ones. Basaltic lava commonly erupts as a fluid and allows gentle release of volatiles. But rhyolite tephra is produced even in oceanic volcanoes. The 1875 eruption of Askja (Iceland) produced 0.2 km² of rhyolite tephra.

Most pyroclastics are produced by the expansion of gas inherent in the parent magma, but gas may be produced by other means, as when an ascending magma hits a large body of groundwater and converts it into steam (a hydroclastic, phreatic or phreato-magmatic eruption). In this case a considerable amount of lithic (bedrock) ash may be expected, as is often found in maars.

A lava flow that enters water may be shattered by the explosive generation of steam. The underwater sediments that result are coarsely cross-bedded to form a foreset-bedded breccias dipping about 25° outwards and so indicating the direction of flow.

Submarine eruptions may produce pyroclastics, but at some depth the hydrostatic pressure is greater than the critical pressure of water, and it is impossible for volatiles to be discharged explosively. Steam blast eruptions and eruptions of pumice from submarine volcanoes must therefore take place at a lesser depth. The depth, called the volatile fragmentation depth, depends on magma type and the amount of dissolved volatiles, but is generally shallower than 500 m.

The terms palagonite and hydroclastic have been applied to many glassy pyroclastic deposits, especially brecciated products of underwater eruption of lava.

Lastly, lava may be erupted beneath ice sheets, as in Iceland, where once again steam generation produces pyroclastic deposits. Moberg is the name given to the hydroclastic deposits in the central graben of Iceland, which occasionally overspill onto the edge of the lava plateau.

There are two kinds of pyroclastic deposits: pyroclastic fall deposits, dealt with in this chapter, and pyroclastic flow deposits, which will be treated in chapter 7.

Tephra Fragments

Pyroclastic fall deposits are made up of fragments that have fallen through the air after a volcanic eruption. 'Tephra' is a convenient name that has been suggested as a collective term for all volcanic matter that falls through the air. 'Ash fall deposit' is another term sometimes used, though such deposits may contain particles of sizes other than ash (see below).

Tephra is a synonym for pyroclastic ejecta, originally used by Aristotle in the 4th Century BC and revived by Thorarinsson in 1954. Williams and McBirney (1979) use both 'pyroclastics' and 'tephra' and say that 'tephra . . . applies to all airborne pyroclastic ejecta whether loose or consolidated and excludes fragmental debris produced and laid down under water or in volcanic vents. It is not normally used for pyroclastic flows'. The broader term 'volcaniclastic' refers to a clastic rock containing volcanic material (any proportion) without regard to origin or environment (Bates and Jackson, 1980).

The fragments produced in pyroclastic eruption vary in size between wide limits, and are classified by size into the following divisions:

Blocks and bombs	64 mm
Lapilli	2–64 mm
Ash	2 mm

Volcanic bombs are commonly spindle-shaped with twisted 'tails' (see plate 6.1). They often contain a core of basalt, country rock, or peridotite

Plate 6.1 Olivine cored bi-polar bomb, Mt Noorat, Victoria, Australia: length 1 metre (A. A. Baker)

inside a wrapping of younger, often frothier, basalt. To some extent they may attain their shape by spinning through the air, but most seem to be shaped by the hurling of solid pieces of rock through liquid in the throat of the volcano (see figure 6.1), a process first described by Reck (1915).

Bombs may continue to expand after forming a first skin, which then cracks. The appearance of the split skin backed by frothy lava gives rise to the name 'breadcrust bomb'.

Most bombs vary from fist size to football size, but occasionally very much bigger ones are found. One on Mt Vulcano is said to be of 25 m³ and to weigh 65 tonnes. Asamayama (Japan) is said to have thrown out a bomb or block in 1783 that measured 75 × 40 m and formed a small island. In 1930 the usually moderate Stromboli threw blocks of up to 30 tonnes for 3 km, and Cotopaxi is said to have thrown a 200-tonne block for 14 km.

Blocks are irregular in shape, more angular than bombs, and often made of pre-existing rock, either volcanic or country rock, thrown out by a volcanic explosion but not made of the magma produced during the same eruption.

Dark, frothy, vesicular lapilli and small bombs of basic composition may be known as scoria or cinders. The names 'ash' and 'cinders', like the more scholarly term 'igneous', suggest fire and combustion, and derive from early beliefs that volcanoes were indeed the burning mountains that their heat, flame, and smoke suggested. The modern use of 'ash' and 'cinder' has no such implication.

The action of strong wind on a fountain of very liquid lava may blow it

Figure 6.1 Formation of volcanic bombs from a ribbon of lava with projected inclusions. The two-ended bombs are called bi-polar

into thin glass threads known as Pele's hair, Pele being the fire goddess of the Hawaiians. Pele's hair has been known to fall thickly in the streets of Hilo, Hawaii, and is used by local birds to build their nests. Acid and intermediate volcanoes tend to produce pyroclastics with many closely spaced bubbles making a rock foam that cools as pumice. This often has so much void space that the bulk density is less than that of water, so pumice will float. Continued expansion of gas bubbles can shatter ejecta into fragments of bubble walls (see figure 6.2), recognized under the microscope as curved splinters and fragments with concave edges. These shards are common in fine ash and tuff. Actually there is a wide range of shard types, discussed further by Fisher and Schmincke (1984); and Heiken and Wohletz (1984).

Pyroclastic Rocks

A rock made of consolidated and cemented pyroclastics is known as agglomerate or pyroclastic breccia if coarse, and as tuff if fine (see figure 6.3). Tuffs are further distinguished as lithic tuff if most fragments consist

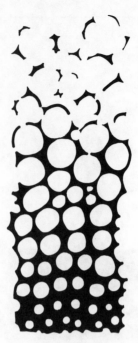

Figure 6.2 The formation of shards (bubble walls). Bubbles or vesicles in a lava expand to make a pumice, and when the bubbles burst the fragments of bubble walls are shards. They are commonly about 0.5 mm long

of comminuted old rock, vitric tuff if most fragments are of glass, and crystal tuff if well-formed crystals predominate. Augite crystal tuffs are found on Vesuvius, Monte Rossi (a parasitic cone on Etna), and Muhavura (Uganda). Vesuvius also produces leucite tuffs, while Mt Erebus in Antarctica produces anorthoclase crystals in abundance and Miyakijima in Japan produces anorthite. The terms lithic, crystal, or vitric can be applied to the unconsolidated ash and lapilli.

Sorting, Settling and Rock Structure

Although fragments produced in pyroclastic eruptions can vary greatly in shape, size, and weight, they tend to be somewhat separated or sorted as they fall. The coarsest material accumulates as a cone around the vent. This material is badly sorted and the space between large blocks and bombs is filled with finer material. With increasing distance from the cone the sorting becomes better, and the average grain size smaller. At some distance from the cone there is often an area which is well sorted but not too fine, and here there is a paucity of fine ash to make a 'matrix' so the

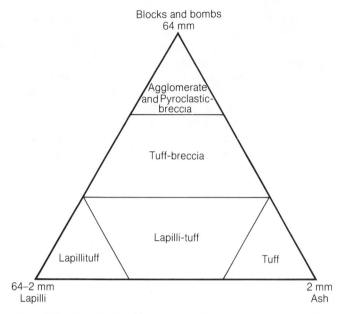

Figure 6.3 Classification of rocks formed from pyroclastic material

deposit has much void space. This is important in holding groundwater, and affects the future course of erosion. Beyond this porous zone the ash is very fine, but makes only a thin deposit, getting thinner with distance from the cone. Plate 1.2 shows the typically asymmetrical distribution of ash around a volcano due to the effects of wind on the finer particles.

Larger bombs and blocks are little affected by wind and so may be dispersed all around a cone, even though the finer material is confined to one flank. This was observed in the 1947 eruption of Hekla (Iceland).

The finest volcanic dust is almost impalpable and travels to great height and for great distances. Dust from the eruption of Krakatoa in 1883 travelled right around the world, and produced very spectacular sunsets for several years, illustrated in colour in Simkin and Fiske (1983).

During settling the coarse and heavy fragments fall most quickly and the fine dust most slowly, so that deposits from individual 'puffs' in an eruption may exhibit graded bedding, with coarse bombs or lapilli at the base and ash on the top. If there is a strong horizontal wind at the time of deposition, sorting may also result in aeolian cross-bedding. This may be due to a simple meteorological wind, but might also be caused by the blast of the volcanic eruption itself.

Details of the eruptive and erosional history of a volcano may be recorded in some detail in pyroclastic deposits, as for instance in the products of the Irazu eruption of 1963–5 in Costa Rica (Murata et al.,

1966). In sections, rainy season deposits could be distinguished from those of the dry season by their well-developed stratification. A zone with three persistent pumice horizons represents the climactic period of eruption. A highly rilled surface records a cloudburst of 10 December 1963, and a rilled lag deposit records the strong winds of the 1964 dry season.

Pyroclastic deposits at some distance from the cone are generally draped over pre-existing topography as a sheet that follows all the old topography, but in general makes it more subdued. This is known as mantle bedding (see plate 6.2). The topographic effect of an ash field has been likened to that of a blanket of loess. Around several East African volcanoes, including Kerimasi, Elgon, and Napak, there are beds of limestone that can be traced to the volcanoes and are often interbedded with ashes. These were once supposed to be lacustrine limestones, but Dawson (1964) suggested that they may be altered volcanic ash of carbonatite composition.

The welding together of fragments, very common in pyroclastic flow deposits, is generally absent in fall deposits, and welded scoria is found only in the immediate vicinity of vents, spatter cones, and hornitos.

Plate 6.2 Mantle bedding, Waiouru, New Zealand. An ash layer of uniform thickness overlies with angular unconformity eroded lahar deposits (C. D. Ollier)

Production and Distribution of Tephra

In many volcanoes tephra is the main product. In the great eruption of Coseguina (Nicaragua) in 1935, for example, almost all the ejecta were ash, thrown high into the air and falling as showers; there were a few pyroclastic flows towards the end of activity but no lava. The andesitic tephra was very finely divided; in most places only sand-size particles are found, and even close to the vent there is nothing larger than gravel. The ash was produced by sudden 'ultra-vesiculation' (Williams, 1952).

Tephra may be produced rapidly. Thorarinsson (1956) has calculated that the 1947 eruption of Hekla (Iceland) released ash at 100,000 m³/s for the first half hour, production later falling to about 30,000 m³/s. The total volume of ash erupted was 220,000,000 m³ of ash, equivalent to about 50,000,000 m³ of rock.

The distribution of tephra is commonly shown by isopach maps, which show the thickness of individual tephra layers. With the intensity of modern deep-sea coring, isopach maps can often be extended offshore, especially for major eruptions (see figure 6.4).

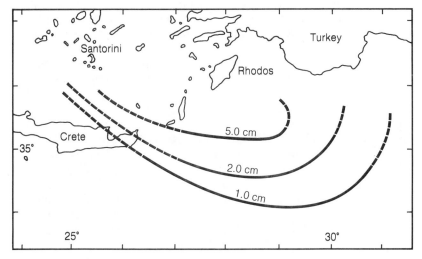

Figure 6.4 Isopach map of Minoan tephra in eastern Mediterranean cores, based on observed thickness (after Watkins, et al. 1978)

Tephrochronology

Some layers of tephra provide useful markers in stratigraphic correlation. For this purpose the ideal bed is distinctive in appearance, mineralogy and chemistry, and is widespread. In any stratigraphic section where the layer is found it clearly separates those beds older than the ash from those younger.

Where the ash lies over datable material, most commonly some charcoal that is suitable for carbon dating, then an absolute age can be used in the correlation of section and geological events. In New Zealand, for example, the Taupo rhyolite pumice overlies logs dated AD 130 and provides a marker between older and younger events. The method is made difficult by reworking of ash, by alteration with increasing age, and by the strong resemblance that is sometimes found between ash from different vents. Nevertheless some ash layers prove to be useful markers.

In Iceland, every eruption has left a layer of tephra, which in some instances covers the greater part of the country. Where not eroded by wind or water these layers make distinct horizons in soil profiles, and there may be up to 100 layers in a single profile. Thorarinsson's tephrochronological studies show that most activity of Hekla, Iceland, has been cyclic for 8000–9000 years. There have been five cycles, each starting with a basic mixed eruption, followed by a period of a couple of centuries of quiescence, followed by a purely explosive rhyolitic eruption.

Ash falls are of great importance in the North Island of New Zealand, where Holocene and Late Pleistocene ashes cover about half the island. Deposits of sixteen separate showers have been recognized in the surface soils, and areas with over 3 inches (7.6 cm) of each ash have been mapped during soil surveys (Gibbs and Wells, 1966). The tuff and lapilli distributed by the Tarawera eruption of 1886 form a recognizable layer over an area of 10,000 km^2.

A summary of the many geomorphic purposes to which tephro-chronology has been applied in New Zealand is provided by Pullar (1967). Ash layers can be used to determine rates of infilling of depositional basins. They are also useful markers for measuring the rate of alluvial fan building; for instance, the 80-year-old Tarawera ash is buried by 30 cm of alluvium on the fans at Whakatane. Where an ash layer is complete, there has been virtually no erosion since the time of its deposition, so the preservation of ash layers on hillsides provides a basis for the study of the distribution of erosion. Dated tephra layers mantle old dunes and beach ridges at Whakatane, Gisborne and elsewhere, and are useful in indicating the position of the shoreline in past time and the rate of progradation of the coast. Pullar also describes, with examples, the application of tephro-chronology to terrace correlation and chronology, archaeology, tectonics, and the study of sea level changes. Further examples of tephra studies are provided by Self and Sparks (1981).

From the stratigraphic viewpoint, it is important to distinguish indivi-dual beds of short-time range from larger units of tephra with a longer time range, but which may nevertheless prove useful in tephrochronology. Kaizuka (1965) has proposed the following categories:

(1) *Tephra bed or fall unit*; products of a single or continuous explosion (duration 10^{-2} years).

(2) *Tephra member or an eruptive cycle unit*: products of single eruptive cycle unit (10^1–10^2 years).

(3) *Tephra formation*: products of a polycyclic volcanic mass (10^3–10^4 years).

(4) *Tephra group*: products of a volcanic belt (10^6–10^7 years).

Deep-sea drilling was originally used for stratigraphic correlation, and has extended back to the Jurassic period. Most submarine tephra come from eruptions on land that were dispersed by wind. The specialized topic of submarine tephrochronology is discussed by Kennett (1981).

7 Pyroclastic Flow Deposits

Fluidization

A mixture of solid particles suspended in a gas can behave in many ways like a liquid, a principle used in industrial 'fluidization' for the transport of such materials as cement and coal dust through pipes. Fluidization can occur naturally in volcanic eruptions, when finely divided pyroclastics are suspended in volcanic gases. This natural fluidization is in many ways more active than the industrial process, for the suspended particles are themselves emitting gases. The fluidized ash moves like a fluid at very great speed even over very gentle slopes. Pyroclastic flow deposits are the results of deposition from such flows of hot fragmentary volcanic material made buoyant by hot gases. Components include crystals, shards, pumice and lithic fragments.

Active pyroclastic flows have the appearance of rapidly projected clouds of dust (see plate 7.1). They are generally dark, but sometimes, especially at night, incandescent material may be seen and gives rise to the common name for such emissions – nuée ardente, generally translated as glowing cloud or glowing avalanche.

The great mobility of pyroclastic flows is explained by several factors, including exsolution of gas, release of gas from broken fragments, and heating of engulfed air.

Origin of Pyroclastic Flows

Pyroclastic flows result from sudden and large eruptions of volcaniclastic or hydroclastic material together with large amounts of gas. Several types of formation are known (see figure 7.1):

- (a) by gravitational collapse of a vertical eruption column;
- (b) by 'boiling over' from a crater;
- (c) by explosion of a growing dome;
- (d) by an inclined blast from an emerging spine or dome;
- (e) by simple eruption of a magma highly charged in volatiles;
- (f) by reaction of ascending lava with water.

Plate 7.1   Nuée ardente, Manam, Papua New Guinea. 17 March 1960 (G. A. M. Taylor)

The idea of collapsing vertical eruption columns was regarded as a major – if not universal – process in the formation of pyroclastic flows and was widely held, but in some cases at least, flows have been observed before a vertical column was formed (Mt St Helens), or even without formation of a vertical ash column.

The most voluminous flows come from calderas. The formation of ignimbrite sheets from collapsed Plinian columns requires a central vent eruption. Maars are an obvious source, and may be related to fluidization. Foam lava and froth flows have been postulated to explain some problematic deposits that might be pyroclastic flow deposits.

Size and Classification of Pyroclastic Flow Deposits

The length of flows and the area of deposition depend to some extent on pre-existing topography, but some examples will give an idea of the size of pyroclastic flow deposits.

Flows in the Valles Mountains, New Mexico, are traceable for over 30 km. Some from Mt Mazama, Oregon, travelled for 70 km. The Valles Mountain flows cover over 900 km². The Lake Toba, Sumatra, ignimbrites cover 25,000 km², and the Taupo-Rotorua flows of New Zealand have an area of 26,000 km².

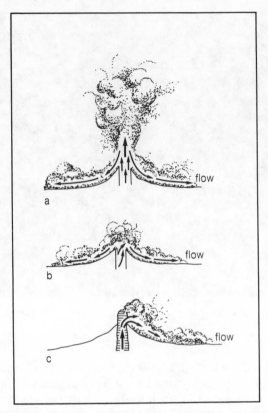

Figure 7.1 Some ways that pyroclastic flows can originate (a) collapse of vertical eruption column (e.g. Mayon) (b) low pressure boiling over (e.g. Mt Lamington) (c) directed blast or dome collapse (e.g Mt St Helens)

The thicknesses of flows vary from a few metres to 300 m in the Valles Mountains, and up to 500 m in some Soviet ignimbrites.

Calculated volumes of flows deposits ranges from 1 km³ or less from a small central vent, such as Mont Pelée or Mt St Helens, up to about 100 km³ for large strato-volcanoes such as Krakatau or Mt Mazama, to 1000 km³ for calderas such as Yellowstone, Taupo, or Toba. Whole pyroclastic flow provinces are even bigger. The New Zealand field has an estimated volume of 8300 km³, the San Juan flows of Colorado 9500 km³, and the North Queensland flows 2800 km³. Individual calderas also produce large amounts of material, ranging up to the 90 km³ Aira caldera, and the 80 km³ of Aso, both in Japan.

These vast volumes suggest that the magma chambers that produce them were originally close to the surface. This idea is supported by geophysical data, and by the discovery of old ignimbrites in the geological column which have been intruded by a related pluton.

The flows are evidently thick and have high momentum: an eruption at Ito (22000 BC) travelled 70 km and crossed barriers 600 m high (Yokoyama, 1974); the Taupo eruption (AD 186) crossed obstacles 1500 m above the source at a distance of 45 km (Walker, 1980).

Pyroclastic flows may be erupted very quickly. The Katmai eruption produced 28 km³ in 60 hours, and it is estimated that the 2800 km³ of Northern Queensland were produced in a few days (Branch, 1966). However, some flows, including those of New Zealand, may continue to be produced over a long period.

Yellowstone Park in the USA is an area of broad ignimbrite sheets produced in Eocene times, remarkably similar in many ways to the ignimbrite plateaus of the North Island of New Zealand. In the Lamar River area of Yellowstone Park some forest trees are preserved in an upright position, and there are the remains of 27 distinct forests, one on top of another, each in its turn buried by pyroclastics.

Classification of Pyroclastic Flows

Aramaki (1961) made a three-fold classification of pyroclastic flows based on viscosity and volume. Since the viscosity of old flows is difficult to estimate, this scheme was replaced by one using size of flow and the degree of vesiculation of the erupting magma, which is reflected in the bulk density of the products and is easily measured (Aramaki and Yamasaki, 1963):

Dense pyroclastic flows	(0.001–0.3 km³)
Intermediate pyroclastic flows	(0.05–1 km³)
Vesicular pyroclastic flows	(0.1–90 km³)

A somewhat similar scheme based on clast density was proposed by Wright et al. (1980).

Traditionally, different kinds of pyroclastic flow have been named after the volcano where they were observed. The following simple classification is based on Murai (1961), Macdonald (1972), and Williams and McBirney (1979):

(1) Pelée type, e.g. Mont Pelée (flow from the side of a dome)
(2) Merapi type, e.g. Lamington, Merapi, Hibok (flow from a collapsing dome)
(3) Lakurajima type, e.g. Lakurajima, Hambara (flow from an open crater)
(4) Asama type, e.g. Asama, Agatsuma (intermediate between Pelée and Krakatoa type)
(5) St Vincent type, e.g. St Vincent, Komagatake (collapse of vertical eruption column)
(6) Krakatau type, e.g. Krakatau (as St Vincent, but of greater magnitude)

107

(7) Valley of Ten Thousand, Smokes type, e.g. Valley of Ten Thousand Smokes (magma discharged mainly through fissures)
(8) Valles type (eruption from arcuate fissures over the roofs of rising magma; the volumes of ejecta are so great that the magma chamber roofs collapse along the fissures to produce calderas).

Column Collapse and Sedimentary Structures

Many pyroclastic flow deposits are thought to originate from the collapse of a vertical eruption column of pyroclastic fragments. The collapse, under gravity, leads to rapid spread of an ash cloud, which deposits particles in different ways depending on various factors.

There is variation from proximal (near source) deposits, which have more coarse fragments, to distal deposits which are finer and thinner. The bulk of pyroclastic flow deposits are homogeneous, but some have many bedding structures. These include massive graded bedding (with many variations), planar bedding, and cross-bedding (see plate 7.2). These can be interpreted in the manner of normal aqueous or aeolian sediments, for which a great deal of observational and experimental data are available. Allen (1982) criticized simple hydrodynamic interpretation of pyroclastic structures, as fragments are sticky and reactive.

Emplacement facies express the spatial relationships and internal structures within an eruptive unit. For example, collapse of a Plinian column

Plate 7.2 Cross-bedded ash, Purrumbete maar, Victoria, Australia (E. B. Joyce)

gives rise to a complex column of rock (see figure 7.2). Fluidization caused by ingestion of air occurs at the head of a flow and generates 'layer 1'. The bulk of the ashflow makes 'layer 2', and fallout tephra makes 'layer 3'. Furthermore there may be lateral variation in the Plinian unit from near the source to the distal end.

Fisher and Schmincke (1984, p. 206) write that 'Different kinds of pyroclastic flows, however, produce different vertical stratigraphic sequences ... there is no single standard flow unit to cover all types of eruption'. Nevertheless the study of pyroclastic sequences now promises to tell us more about the details of past eruptions than even eyewitness accounts could provide. The eruption of Vesuvius in AD 79 can now been seen as a sequence of flows and surges, often dated to the hour, which are in turn related to collapse of the eruption column, caldera collapse, and reaction with groundwater (Sigurdsson et al., 1985).

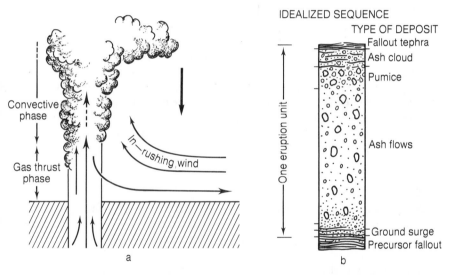

Figure 7.2 (a) Formation and collapse of an eruption column. The lower part of the column is caused by direct blast, but hot air causes convectional rising of the higher part of the column. The ash cloud cools and spreads. Coarser material falls close to the column forming pyroclastic flow. Ash fall deposits come later. (b) A typical sedimentary column associated with a pyroclastic flow caused by column collapse

The Base Surge

The base surge is not a separate kind of eruption, but is a phenomenon associated with various kinds of vertical explosion (Moore, 1967). A base surge is a ring-shaped basal cloud that sweeps outward as a density flow from the base of a vertical explosion column. Fisher and Schmincke (1984) think they are restricted to hydroclastic eruptions. The base surge may result from collapse of the vertical column of ash, or from atmospheric resistance to the rising column of gas and tephra. The initial velocity is commonly greater than 50 m/s, and it can carry clastic material for many kilometres. Ash, mud, lapilli, and blocks can all be transported. Trees, houses, and other obstacles may be knocked down by the surge, or sand-blasted on the side facing the volcano, and the blast side may also be coated by layers of ejecta. The base surge may deposit material beyond the range of ejecta that simply fall through the air. Near the source of the eruption it can erode channels, and can deposit material with dune-bedding. In the 1965 eruption of Taal, Philippines, the base surge obliterated all trees within 1 km and sandblasted objects up to 8 km away. Wood neither burns nor chars, and it is possible that the temperature in a basal surge is less than 100 °C. It must be remembered that the base surge contains no free oxygen.

Rock Types in Pyroclastic Flow Deposits

Many kinds of rock from basalts to rhyolites may give rise to pyroclastic flows, but silicic rocks are by far the most important. Nuée ardente and intermediate types of flow generally have silica percentages of from 55 to 65 per cent. Ash flow types are generally in the range of 60–75 per cent silica. The bulk density of the rock also appears to be related to type of flow. Nuée ardente types have a bulk density greater than 1.2; St Vincent-type flows are in the range of 0.7–1.2; Krakatau-type ash flows are in the range of 0.5–0.7.

Ignimbrite

Many names have been used for the deposits that result from pyroclastic flows, including ignimbrite, ash flow deposit, welded tuff, tuff flow deposit, nuée ardente deposit, and many others.

Ignimbrite will be used here in the sense of Cook (1966). This is a rock unit term, and should not be used as a petrological term; several petro-logical types can give rise to ignimbrites though rhyolite and andesite predominate. Neither does the term imply any post-depositional alteration such as welding, though this may be present. Thus one pyroclastic flow gives rise to one ignimbrite, which may or may not be welded, and may be of any petrological type.

As with pyroclastic fall deposits, it is important to distinguish between flow units and cooling units, which may consist of several flows that all cool together.

Homogeneity of Pyroclastic Flows

Ash flows are remarkably homogeneous, because fluidization causes intense mixing of material and there is little lateral or vertical variation (see plate 7.3). This homogeneity is present regardless of the magnitude of the flow, and is very different from the variability generally found in all parts of pyroclastic fall deposits. In some volcanoes there is not even variation with time, and similar material may be found in deposits discharged at different times from the same volcano. The material erupted from Komagatake, Japan, in 1929 was exactly like that of the previous eruption.

However, some studies (for example, Lipman, 1967) have shown a significant variation in chemistry and mineralogy from bottom to top of thick pyroclastic flow deposits. The changes in composition apparently reflect in inverse order a compositionally-zoned magma chamber, more silica rich at the top.

Kuno et al. (1964) have provided interesting data on the homogeneity of lithic and pumice content of pyroclastic flow in comparison to variation in pyroclastic fall deposits. In a pumice flow eruption of Towada caldera (North Honshu) the fragmental lithic material, but not the pumice, exhibits a systematic size variation with distance from the crater. In a pumice fall eruption from the same caldera all erupted material showed systematic variation. In the flow eruption most energy was used in shattering country

Plate 7.3 Homogeneous unbedded, unwelded, and highly porous ignimbrite near Otamarakau, New Zealand (C. D. Ollier)

rock, whereas during the pumic fall the energy was involved in explosive ejection of material to great heights.

Welding

Although flow material may be originally homogeneous, great apparent changes are caused by welding and compaction. Because pryoclastic flows move with great rapidity, the time for cooling is small, and so when the flows come to rest they retain a considerable amount of heat. Above a certain temperature the glass shards will adhere together, a process known as welding. Degrees of welding are marked by the amount of cohesion, deformation of shards, elimination of pore space, and even homogenization of the glass. Those parts of ignimbrites that are most welded are often known as welded tuffs.

The degree of welding depends on the initial temperature of the magma, the quantity and composition of the volatiles, the chemical composition of the ash, the pressure of the superincumbent load, and the speed of cooling (itself affected by the thickness of the flow, since ash is a good insulator). Normally there will be a systematic variation in thickness and degree of welding (see figure 7.3). In some sheets the degree of welding varies over short distances, which later leads to differential erosion.

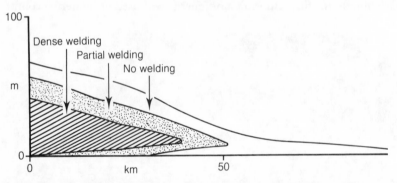

Figure 7.3 Idealized lateral and vertical variation in a welded pyroclastic flow

Ignimbrites are often zoned, especially if thick, the main zones being a thin unwelded layer at the base (where cooling was rapid), a welded zone in the middle, and a thicker, unwelded zone (see plate 7.4). The welded zone has a fairly sharp boundary with the lower layer, but merges into the upper zone. Welding and compaction cause a change in the shape and colour of pumice fragments. Fresh pumice is white or grey, and it changes through shades of brown to dense black obsidian-like material in the strongly welded zones. Compaction flattening gives a foliate structure to welded tuff, and the compaction of pumice results in a relative increase in

Plate 7.4 Base of ignimbrite at Matahina dam, New Zealand. Strongly welded zone over less welded zone (C. D. Ollier)

the content of crystals per unit volume which can be most striking in tuffs with an initially high crystal content.

Vapour squeezed out of the welded zone during compaction may react in the porous zones and give rise to the growth of crystals of feldspar and tridymite, a process known as vapour phase crystallization. The welded zone may eventually devitrify to form aggregates of feldspar and cristobalite, resulting in a rock that closely resembles a lava flow.

Jointing and weathering may further enhance the differences between the zones, and often give the impression that an ignimbrite is made up of many distinct flows and ashfall layers when in fact it is one depositional unit.

Jointing

Columnar jointing is common in many welded tuffs, but joints seldom extend into the non-welded zones. Joint spacing varies from a few centimetres to over a metre, the closest joints being associated with the most intense welding. Like joint-columns in lava flows, the columns in welded tuffs are generally vertical, but are occasionally fanned or curved. The joint pattern is irregular, tending to be rectangular or square in plan rather than the roughly hexagonal jointing of lava flows.

The zone of maximum compaction often has horizontal platy jointing as well as vertical joints. This should not be confused with the platy structure developed by weathering of foliation planes in the zone of partial welding.

The Flat Top of Pyroclastic Flow Deposits

Because pyroclastic flows move almost like a liquid they can spread out over great distances as fairly thin sheets. They can move over very low gradients and even flow uphill over considerable obstacles; they fill in hollows, and flow around obstacles. When they settle they have a very flat top, however rugged the pre-existing scenery may have been. In this they are markedly different from pyroclastic fall deposits which are draped over the topography fairly evenly. The zones of welding and compaction are roughly parallel to the flat upper surface.

When an ignimbrite sheet is thin relative to the available relief of pre-existing topography, it will follow the old valleys and will inherit the drainage pattern. This kind of deposition simply makes the old valleys flat bottomed but the pyroclastic flow may drain back from upper slopes leaving levees or 'high-water marks'.

Thick multiple sheets on the other hand can obliterate pre-existing topography and produce extensive plateaus such as the Mamaku Plateau, New Zealand.

Other Kinds of Pyroclastic Flow Deposits

Although ignimbrites are by far the dominant kind of pyroclastic flow deposit, two other kinds of deposit may be regarded as belonging to this category. Basic agglomerates are not definitely known to be flow deposits, but many of their features indicate that such an origin is probable. Lahars are flows of pyroclastic material mobilized by water.

Basic agglomerates

Mt Elgon on the border of Kenya and Uganda is about 50 km across and over 3000 m above its base. It is built up of a large number of layers of volcanic agglomerate, each marking a separate eruption (Davies, 1952). After each eruption there was evidently a period of quiescence when soil was formed and trees grew. Fossil trees are found in the thin layer of ash that marks the start of each new eruption, and which flattened them. Despite the size of the pile that makes up Elgon, there is virtually no change in the petrology, which is basaltic, and little sorting of the agglomerate. This suggests that some kind of pyroclastic flow may be responsible.

Exactly the same conditions of deposition of agglomerate layers, ash layers, and moulds of fallen trees are found in the Sogeri Plateau near Port Moresby, Papua. There is no cone here and the source of the agglomerates has not yet been identified.

In both Elgon and the Sogeri Plateau, the agglomerate tends to make flat-topped plateaus or steps, with widely spaced vertical jointing giving rise to steep cliffs, often undercut at the base by erosion of the less resistant thin ash layer.

Lahars

Lahars are landslides or debris flows of volcanic debris mixed with water. They may be divided into hot mudflows of fresh ejecta mixed with water, and cold mudflows caused by the mixture of rain or surface water with a mass of unconsolidated and unstable ash.

Macdonald (1972) classifies them into:

(a) direct result of eruption;
(b) those occurring soon after eruption, triggered by earthquakes, etc.;
(c) those unrelated to contemporary volcanic activity, brought about by heavy rain, collapse of frozen ground, etc.

Many occur on strato-volcanoes, to which they add considerable bulk. Many are limited to valleys, but in geological time there have been some that covered thousands of square kilometres. Most are less than 5 m thick, but some are up to 200 m (see table 7.1). They travel tens or even hundreds of kilometres.

Most lahars are very mobile, travelling rapidly down valleys or hillsides and doing great damage in inhabited areas, though some cold mudflows can spread fairly slowly as rather stiff lobes. In the eruption of Vesuvius in AD 79 the town of Herculaneum was buried under 20 m of mud, which crushed houses and knocked down walls, but the absence of skeletons shows that people had time to get out of the way. Some lahars do not seem to erode their beds, despite huge boulders in load, and the base may be carpeted by grass or pine needles.

115

Table 7.1 Dimensions of some lahars

Name of lahar, volcano or formation	Date of eruption	Distance travelled (km)	Thickness (m)	Area (km²)	Volume (km³)
Yatsuga-dake, Japan	Pleistocene	24			9.6
Osceola, Mt Rainier, USA (Crandell, 1971)	5700 BP	110	6 (av.) 60 (max.)	260	>2.0
Electron, Mt Rainier, USA	600 BP	50	4.5 (av.)	36	0.15
Cotopaxi, Ecuador	1877	>240			
Kelut, Java	1919	40	50 (max.)	130	
Santa Maria, Guatemala	1929	100		15	
Mt St Helens, North Fork Toutle River, USA	18 May 1980	>120	1–2		>0.36

Source: Fisher and Schmincke (1984).

Displacement of a crater lake is very likely to cause lahars. One of the best known examples of this is Kelut, Indonesia, where the 1919 eruption displaced a crater lake estimated at 38,000,000 m³, and killed 5500 people. Ruapehu, New Zealand, has also produced many lahars in the past that were probably started by displacement of the crater lake.

Lahars carry material for long distances; Cotton (1944) describes a boulder of about 37 tonnes transported 75 km by a lahar from Ruapehu. Lahar debris is deposited as large sheets of crudely bedded, ill-sorted sediment with occasional layers of cross-bedded sands (see plate 7.5). Large boulders are scattered randomly in the deposit and give rise to the typical lahar landscape of moundfields with hundreds of hillocks from a few metres to several tens of metres high, each having a core of boulders. Although hummocky in detail the surface tends to be flat over wide areas.

The 1888 volcanic explosion of Bandaisan, Japan, was a very exceptional kind of eruption (see p. 00) in which a large part of the mountain, estimated at 1.2 km³, was blasted away and descended as a huge avalanche or mudflow. A moundfield was formed that was similar in all respects to those produced by smaller lahars.

Galunggung, Indonesia, is an amphitheatre-shaped volcano and on a gentle plain below the breach are the Ten Thousand Hills of Tasik Malaha (actually fewer than 4000), ranging from 3 to 70 m high. This vast mound-field covers an area of about 250 km², but its estimated volume is only one-twentieth of the missing sector of the volcano.

Plate 7.5 Typical lahar deposit, Waiouru, New Zealand (C. D. Ollier)

8 Intrusive Igneous Rocks

The magma that erupts in volcanoes originates deep in the earth's crust and reaches the surface through fissures and pipes. Igneous rocks that cool in the feeding channels or other weaknesses in the crustal rocks are called intrusive or hypabysall rocks, and they occur in a few fairly well-defined forms (see figure 8.1).

Intrusive igneous rocks cool more slowly than effusive ones, so are more coarsely crystalline and the crystals can usually be seen with a hand-lens. The commonest intrusive rock associated with basic volcanoes is dolerite.

The slow cooling of intrusive rocks often gives rise to well developed jointing due to shrinkage. Columnar jointing is the commonest type, and the columns are usually vertical in sills and horizontal in dykes. Jointing is explained in chapter 5.

When erosion has removed upper portions of volcanoes and neighbouring rocks, the intrusive igneous bodies give rise to landforms due to differential erosion.

Volcanic Necks

Volcanic necks are the cylindrical feeders of volcanoes which are filled with solidified lava, or with tuff-breccia and agglomerate, depending on the nature of the original eruption and magma type. Volcanic necks may also be referred to as plugs. The term 'neck' suggests a lava column joining the head of the active volcano to the body of the magma chamber, but some necks may never reach the ground surface and never give rise to active volcanoes.

The numerous plugs of the Fitzroy Basin in Western Australia provide an interesting sequence where, by carefully comparing the rocks in many plugs, Prider (1960) concluded that they were sections at different levels in similar pipes. A typical plug is shown in figure 8.2 and examples of hills at different levels can be seen. Some pipes did not reach the surface, but may have had crypto-volcanic features above the pipe, as at Mt Abbott. Other pipes reach the surface and gave rise to surface volcanoes such as Mt North. Two distinct joint patterns seem to occur in lava-filled volcanic

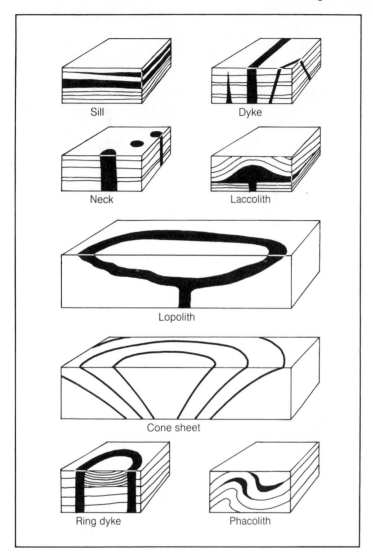

Figure 8.1 Diagrammatic representation of igneous intrusive bodies

necks. Where the conduit has been deeply eroded there is a rosette with horizontal columns radiating out from the axis, perpendicular to the walls. In others, such as the famous Devil's Tower, Wyoming, the columns make an inverted fan. This is an anomalous pattern that probably forms at a high level in the neck (Hunt, 1938; Spry, 1962).

Williams (1936) distinguished two types of volcanic necks (see figure 8.3). The first, called the Hopi type (from the Hopi Buttes of New Mexico),

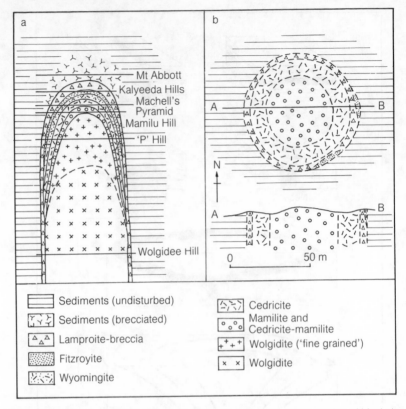

Figure 8.2 Plugs in the Fitzroy area, Western Australia (a) vertical section of ideal plug, showing the level exposed in several actual plugs (b) plan and cross section of Mamilu (after Prider, 1960)

is near the very top of the original volcanic pipe, and is virtually a crater fill. The columns of lava may rest upon inward dipping tuffs. The second type, called the Navajo type, is formed by erosion to a lower level, and is at a section far below the original ground surface. Most necks are of the second type, but in younger volcanic areas examples of Hopi necks can be found. Saddle Hill, Dunedin, New Zealand, is a Pliocene volcano of Hopi type (Benson and Turner, 1940).

Volcanic necks often rise abruptly from the surrounding country, as in the Warrumbungles, New South Wales (see plate 8.1). and the Glasshouse Mountains of Queensland, where the necks rise for hundreds of metres from the coastal plain.

It is also possible for the volcanic rock in a pipe to weather faster than the surrounding rock, creating a hollow. In parts of New South Wales necks give rise to many remarkable amphitheaters bounded by sandstone cliffs

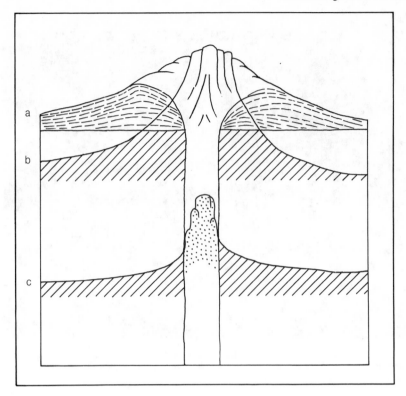

Figure 8.3 Types of volcanic neck. The original volcano was at level **a** a Hopi-type neck is poroduced by erosion to **b** and erosion to **c** produces a Navajo-type neck

more than a hundred metres high forming unbroken circular walls, except when streams leave them through clefts in their lower rims (see plate 8.2).

Dykes

Most volcanoes are fed through vertical fissures which give rise to vertical sheets of igneous rock called dykes. Sometimes a dyke splits up near the surface into a number of pipes. Some dykes are seen to thin out towards the surface, suggesting that the lava is emplaced by wedging aside the bounding rocks.

Dykes vary in thickness from a few decimetres to hundreds of metres, but widths of 1–10 m are commonest. In length they can be many kilometres long, or only a few metres. They commonly occur in swarms (see figure 8.4) or in radiating patterns around a volcanic centre (figure 8.5).

Parallel swarms of dykes are thought to be formed deep in the crust,

Plate 8.1 Volcanic neck. Crater Bluff (foreground) and Mt Tonduron (background), Warrumbungles, New South Wales, Australia (New South Wales Government Tourist Bureau)

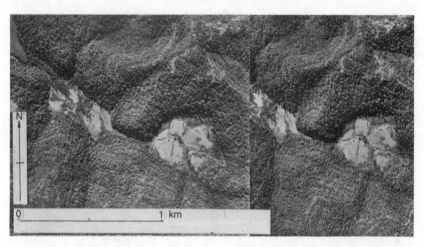

Plate 8.2 Eroded volcanic necks making basins below the general level of the surrounding sandstone country, Hawkesbury River, New South Wales, Australia (Courtesy of the Department of Lands, New South Wales, Australia)

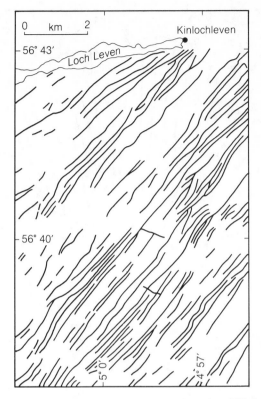

Figure 8.4 Dyke swarm near Loch Leven, Scotland (based on HM Geological Survey maps)

while radial dykes and concentric fractures (see figure 8.5) are produced in the upper layers around pipes or domes of rising lava. Even without erosion the radial pattern of feeders can sometimes be determined from the pattern of satellite or parasitic volcanoes. The giant basaltic volcano, Klutchevskoi, in Kamchatka, has twelve lines of vents 6–18 km long, radiating down the slopes from the summit crater, the number of vents along each line ranging from three to eleven.

Dykes give rise to wall-like ridges, such as the Breadknife in the Warrumbungles (see plate 8.3). More commonly, dykes give more subdued ridges, and occasionally the rock of the dyke weathers faster than the surrounding rock, forming a trench or depression that will often be followed by a watercourse. The island of Arran, Scotland, provides examples of three relationships between dyke and landform: in the north, dykes give rise to trenches in high-grade metamorphic rocks; in the south they form walls in the weak sedimentary rock, except where the margins of the dyke have been baked to an even harder state when double walls are produced. Dykes usually fill

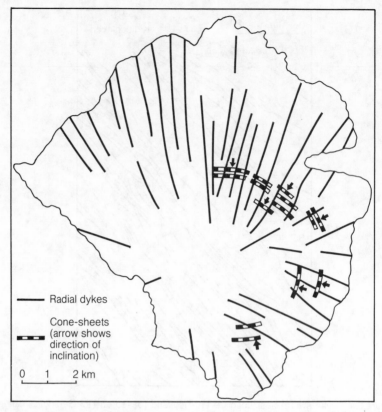

Figure 8.5 Radial dykes, Island of Rum, Scotland (based on HM Geological Survey maps)

gaps in the crust caused by tension, and the aggregate thickness of dyke swarms indicates the total extension of the crust. The Mull (Scotland) swarm has a total thickness of over 1000 m and indicates a stretching of the crust in the affected region of 3.8 per cent; the Arran swarm shows an extension of 7 per cent.

Although most dykes are intruded into bedrock, some actually penetrate into the volcanic pile above, and may even reach the surface exposed in a crater wall like that of Red Crater, Tongariro, New Zealand (see plate 8.4). This dyke reveals a most interesting history: evidently the lava rose in the dyke, the edges were chilled and solidified, and then the lava drained away leaving the present hollow dyke.

Plate 8.3 Dyke: The Breadknife, Warrumbungles, New South Wales, Australia (New South Wales Government Tourist Bureau)

Sills

Intrusive rock may form nearly horizontal tabular bodies of rock called sills. These commonly follow the bedding of enclosing sedimentary rocks for considerable distances and are said to be concordant intrusions (see plate 8.5). Few remain concordant for their entire extent, however, and are locally transgressive where they cut across a bed and then spread along another bedding plane. Sills are particularly abundant in basins of thick, unfolded sediments such as those of South Africa, Tasmania, Antarctica and Brazil, where conditions are ideal for widespread lateral intrusion. Intrusion of sills appears to lift the overlying sediments, which are floated up to make room for the intrusion, presumably causing considerable uplift at the ground surface.

Plateau basalt fields are built largely of innumerable lava flows, but also often contain thick sills of similar material intruded between previously erupted flows. Sills may be injected between earlier layers of a strato-volcano; one such sill exposed in the crater of La Soufrière, St Vincent, is said to be many tens of metres thick and to have a columnar jointing.

Sills can be of very large dimensions, like the Jurassic sills of Tasmania

Plate 8.4 Dyke exposed inside crater and partially drained, Red Crater, Tongariro, New Zealand (C. D. Ollier)

Plate 8.5 Jurassic sill of dolerite, maximum thickness 210 m, in sandstone of Devonian age, forming part of West Beacon Mount, Antarctica (C. T. McElroy)

which are up to 700 m thick. The sills in the Karroo of South Africa extend over an area of 500,000 km^2 and make up 15–25 per cent of the geological column in the area. The Whin Sill in northern England underlies an area of 40,000 km^2.

Because their heat alters the enclosing rock both above and below, whereas lava flows only bake underlying rocks, sills can be distinguished from thick lava flows. Sills also have chilled edges on both upper and lower surfaces while flows have distinct scoriaceous upper surfaces. When eroded, sills behave like any other body of hard rock in a sequence of layered rocks, and commonly give rise to a landscape of plateaus and cliffs. The very good jointing helps in maintaining steep, often vertical, escarpments.

In Tasmania the Jurassic dolerite mostly appears as a single body made up of interconnected sheets which resists erosion and tends to dominate the landscape; dolerite caps most of the highest mountains and underlies the great Central Plateau. In some parts of South Africa great mesas of intrusive dolerite are prominent in the scenery. The intrusion of these sills is thought to have occurred at the same time as the outpouring of the plateau basalts.

A special kind of small sill is the phacolith, a concordant igneous intrusion in the crest of an anticline or the trough of a syncline. Phacoliths (and many stranger intrusions for which names have been coined) are rather rare.

Cone Sheets

Cone sheets are curved concentric assemblages of dykes inclined inwards towards a common centre of eruption. They are inverted cones, becoming successively flatter away from the centre (see figure 8.1), and the outermost cones also flatten towards the surface like an inverted trumpet. Presumably cones of country rock are displaced to allow the intrusion of the cone sheets. Individual cone sheets may be about 10 m thick.

Hotz (1952) and Walker (1958) have shown that the cone sheets of the Palisades (USA) and the Karroo (South Africa) have an inward dip of about 20° and an average diameter of 8–16 km, so if conical their apices would be at depths of about 3.5 km.

Ring Dykes

Ring dykes are structures which are circular in plan and dip vertically or outwards at high angles. They appear to be filling a cylindrical fissure around a subsided cylinder or slightly conical mass. The material inside is generally (but not always) of volcanic origin and has inward dips, possibly due to drag caused by its downward movement. Subsidence of this kind is called cauldron subsidence, and is often associated with caldera collapse. A present-day example of the surface expression of a ring dyke is provided by the island of Niuafo'ou near Tonga. This is a basalt dome with a caldera surrounded by a complex of fissures 5 km across which has erupted lavas during the present century (Cotton, 1944).

Most ring dykes are revealed only after considerable erosion, and stand as arcuate ridges above the surrounding country. These are known from many parts of the world, and often have diameters of up to 25 km.

Laccoliths

A body of intrusive rock that has a flat base but pushes overlying strata into a dome is called a laccolith. Many bodies originally thought to be laccoliths have since been shown to be other kinds of intrusions. The type area for them is the Henry Mountains of Utah (USA) intruded beneath 800 m of overlying sediment. However, they have been shown to be fed laterally from a central stock, not from below. Edwards (1941) described two laccoliths from Stanley and Wynyard in Northern Tasmania, but later workers interpret them as steep-sided bodies intruding horizontal Tertiary lavas and pyroclastics (Spry and Banks, 1962, p. 272).

However, there appear to be plenty of true laccoliths. Carne (1903) described a series of twelve laccoliths from the Barigan district in New South Wales. The largest has a basal area of 5 km² and is at least 300 m thick. All have arched the overlying strata.

Lopoliths

Enormous saucer-shaped intrusions are called lopoliths. Like laccoliths, they are becoming less common with further work, and the best-known examples are proving to be structures of different form. The Sudbury Complex in Ontario is now thought to be a ring complex, and the Bushveld Complex of South Africa is now considered to be a number of separate bodies, with thick dyke-like feeders.

Tasmanian dolerite sills are locally transgressive and on the broad scale form a lopolith. Carey (1958) showed that regionally the bodies have the form of large cone sheets, but on a very large scale. On reaching the base of the horizontal Permian and Triassic sediments, the magma has spread out laterally as a transgressive sheet, lifting and floating its roof of sediments. The dolerite in doing so has formed a number of very large shallow saucers, each cradling a raft of sediments.

Batholiths and Stocks

Batholiths and stocks are large bodies of igneous rock which are formed deep in the earth's crust, and are plutonic rather than volcanic. Stocks are small (generally a few kilometres across) and batholiths are large (tens or hundreds of kilometres across).

Batholiths are generally granitic and batholiths of basalt are unknown. Stocks are the solidified remains of magma chambers at fairly shallow depth. In Hawaii some have been identified geophysically; the largest is 20 × 12 km and extends from 1 km below ground surface to a depth of 23 km. Most batholiths are only exposed after deep erosion, and have no place in a book on volcanoes, but others are very closely related to their volcanic products.

One of the surprises of modern work is the height that plutons can reach in the crust. It appears that some plutons at depth give rise to volcanoes at the surface, and then continue to rise until they eat into their own volcanic products. The rise appears to be largely diapiric, as a blob of light material rising through denser material, and a ring shaped trough develops around the rising pluton in compensation. This trough is filled with debris derived from erosion of the volcano, and even the pluton itself. An example is Mt Duval in Australia (Korsch, 1982), where a Permian pluton has risen into its own prior volcano, rising above the surrounding ground level. Permian volcanic and plutonic debris was deposited in the surrounding trough by penecontemporaneous erosion. The present shape of Mt Duval is essentially the shape of the original pluton.

North of Mt Duval is the Mole Plateau, which is a flat-topped, mushroom shaped pluton that has spread out a short distance below the ground surface, at the base of its own volcanic products. Geophysical and geochemical data suggest that the top of the pluton was not more than half a kilometre below the ground surface.

In New Guinea some plutons are found in the cores of active gneissmantled domes, which appear to be emplaced above the surrounding

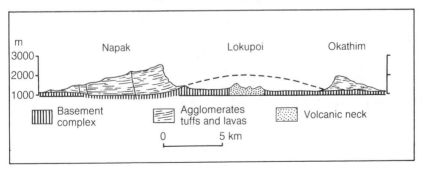

Figure 8.6 Cross-section of Napak, Uganda (after King, 1949)

general ground surface. These sometimes have volcanic activity associated with the edge of the gneiss dome. Several plutons of this type are very young, of Pleistocene age (Ollier and Pain, 1981).

Many large terrestrial volcanoes are underlain by a dome in the bedrock (see figures 3.2, 8.6). It is most improbable that volcanoes could consistently erupt on pre-existing domes that happen to be about the same diameter as the volcano, so intrusive activity probably inflates the basement under the centre of eruption.

9 Hydrology and Drainage of Volcanic Areas

Groundwater

The water-holding spaces in a rock, such as joints, cracks, and the interstices between rock fragments, will generally form an interconnecting mesh of channels through which water can move. The percentage of total space in a rock is a measure of its porosity. The rate at which water can move through a rock is its permeability.

Some water is held by molecular attraction on to surfaces of rock fragments, and such water cannot flow freely. If the rock porosity is made up of many very small pores, as in fine ash, most of the water is held in this way and permeability will be very low. If the pores are large, as in blocky lava, the greater part of the water will be unaffected by molecular attraction and can flow freely.

A laboratory specimen of fresh, dense basalt or rhyolite may show virtually no porosity, and the only water it could retain would be that wetting the surface of the block. Small specimens of such rock therefore indicate no water-holding capacity at all. In the field, however, such rocks may hold water in joints, cooling fractures, rubbly layers or other features, and they often contain a lot of water. The hydrological properties of a rock therefore depend on structure and field relationships as well as petrological type, though some generalizations can be made.

A rock with spaces that hold water is called an aquifer; and impermeable rock that may hold up or dam back water is called an aquiclude. The surface of the groundwater in an aquifer is known as the water table. Where the water table intersects the groundsurface, groundwater will emerge at a spring.

Water-bearing Properties of Igneous Rocks

Most massive basalt flows are permeable, and usually the most significant hydrological feature of basalt is its great permeability. Cavities that hold water in basalt include interstitial spaces in clinker or flow breccia, cavities between flows, joints, gas vesicles, lava tubes, and tree-mould holes. A major exception to the general permeability of basalt may be provided by the basalts of the Deccan Plateau. Certainly in the area behind Bombay the basalts have very low permeability, although the shape of the major valleys

131

with steep sides and flat bottoms suggest that basal sapping may be important. Pillow lava is usually very permeable except where the interstices have been filled by secondary minerals, and most of the great springs of the Snake River Canyon near Twin Falls, Idaho (USA), issue from pillow lava. Acid lava flows generally have low permeability because they are massive, though if they have a deep blocky layer on the surface this will be very permeable.

Pyroclastic fall deposits are very permeable, except for the finest ash. The permeability of the younger volcanoes of Hawaii is so great that no runoff occurs, and no well-defined stream channels exist even where the rainfall exceeds 5000 mm (Stearns, 1966).

The coarsest scoria is found close to vents and is, of course, extremely permeable, though the porosity may be reduced by lack of sorting of the deposit and the presence of fine material in the interstices. Some distance from the vent, moderately coarse, well-sorted lapilli and scoria are found, producing an excellent water-holding rock. Further still from the vent the ash is well sorted and fine. Pore spaces are small, so water is held by molecular attraction, and though porosity may be high, permeability is low. Fine ash is prone to fairly rapid weathering, alteration, and compaction, which tend to reduce permeability further.

Thus on a pyroclastic cone the upper and middle slopes tend to be very porous and good water-holders, but the lower slopes tend to be more impermeable, so springs arise on the lower slopes at the top of the impermeable deposit.

Downstream of springs there is a simple stream erosion, and basal sapping by the spring causes steepening of the headwall and gully retreat.

Pyroclastic flow deposits vary greatly in permeability. Unconsolidated pumice is extremely permeable. Welded zones of ignimbrites may also be sufficiently cracked to yield water freely, but may also be so massive as to be aquicludes considered safe even for dam foundations.

The Water Table

The water table is at its simplest on wide lava plains, where it is generally very flat with gradients of less than 1 : 1000. Because basalt is so permeable the level of the water table is rapidly adjusted to the level of the lowest outlet, and so if the lava is thick there may be a considerable depth to the water table. In the Snake River lava plain the depth of the water table is generally over 150 m. Because of the flatness of the water table, a few wells usually provide enough information to predict water levels over a considerable area, though complications can occur. Some complications are caused by perched water tables, the water being held up by sheets of impervious alluvium on top of the lava plain or interbedded with lava flows. Another complication occurs when the lava plain is divided into compartments by ridges of bedrock or by impermeable dykes. Such divisions may be quite invisible at the surface, for a lava flow may have a very smooth top but a quite irregular base.

Vertical dykes, especially if arranged in several directions, divide the intervening volcanic rocks into separate groundwater compartments. The water table in each is largely independent of the rest and is controlled by the height of the lowest point on the dyke barrier, where overflow occurs. For water supply purposes, the dykes act as dams, and if a tunnel is bored through the dyke it taps a large supply of groundwater. This technique is used for town water supply in Hawaii. If the overflow is at the ground surface, soft rock on the downstream side may be worn away leaving the dyke as a cliff, over which water flows from the lowest point. In time, the overflow point will be lowered by erosion, making a notch in the dyke, and lowering the water table in the compartment behind the dyke. The Heart-Shaped Waterfall on the island of St Helena is a classic example (see figure 9.1). This is upstream of the main town, Jamestown, which sometimes suffers drought. In the past, authorities have tried to improve the water supply by damming *above* the falls, which is of course above the water table. Abundant groundwater could be obtained from bores located upstream of the falls, or from a tunnel near their base.

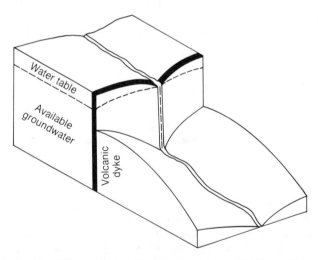

Figure 9.1 The Heart-Shaped Waterfall behind Jamestown, St. Helena. Abundant fresh water for Jamestown could be obtained by drilling into the groundwater impounded by the dyke over which the stream falls (after Wace and Ollier, 1984)

Many rivers flowing from impermeable rocks will sink underground as soon as they reach a porous lava plain. If the river is carrying considerable sediment this will be deposited on the lava, and will slowly fill up the crevices and reduce the porosity of its bed. By continually silting its channel a river may extend across a permeable lava plain and deposit a veneer of sediment that can hold up surface water, which is said to be perched. A very good example of this is Mud Lake, Idaho (see figure 9.2). On the north side of the lake there is only one water table, but on the south side there is a perched water table over the main water table, which here shows an exceptionally steep gradient.

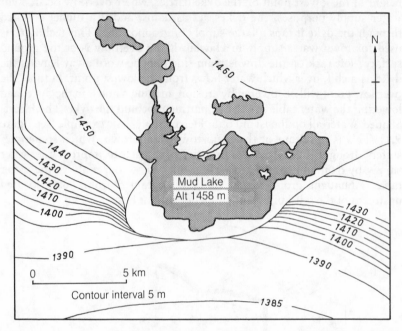

Figure 9.2 Water table map, Mud Lake, Idaho. The lake is perched on clay beds on flat land, and the main water table is below with a groundwater cascade (after Stearns, 1942)

In a simple volcanic island of perfect permeability, the water table would rise slowly from sea level at the coast to a point beneath the wettest part of the island. Volcanic cones on land have a more irregular base, but in principle the situation is the same. The water table rises slowly from the level of springs around the base. The spring may be controlled by the contact with impermeable bedrock, by impermeable ash, or by other volcanic features such as dykes or impermeable flows.

Returning to the situation in volcanic islands, these hold a lens of fresh water within the rock, virtually floating on salt water. Like an iceberg, the floating water has a much greater part below sea level than projecting above. Water leaks out at springs at about sea level (see figure 9.3), though more complicated situations are common where impervious sediments accumulate around the shore, as in Hawaii (see figure 9.4). Springs may be due merely to variations in topography, as in ignimbrite regions, but they are found more commonly where an impermeable bed crops out at the

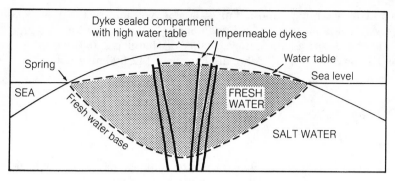

Figure 9.3   Fresh water distribution in a volcanic island

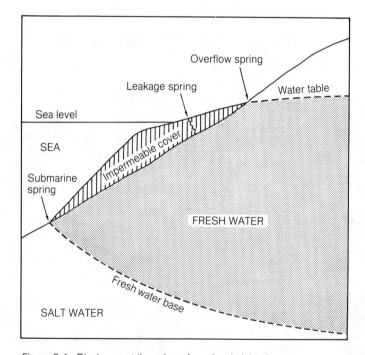

Figure 9.4   Discharge at the edge of a volcanic island

surface. Lava flows, welded ignimbrite zones, or dense, impermeable pyroclastics are the commonest aquicludes. Composite cones, with their many alternations of porous and impermeable layers, lead to the common occurrence of springs, as for instance on the flanks of Tongariro and Ruapehu in New Zealand.

Some of the springs arising in volcanic country are extremely large, and according to Meinzer (1949) 38 of the 65 first-magnitude springs in the world (discharging almost 3 m³/s) are in volcanic rocks or associated gravel. These include Sheep Bridge Spring, Oregon, with a discharge of 791 m³ a day; Malade Springs, Idaho, discharging 2,761,000 m³ a day; and Thousand Springs, Idaho, discharging 2,112,000 m³ a day.

Drainage of Volcanic Areas

Drainage Patterns

Volcanoes have some very characteristic drainage patterns, of which the most obvious is the radial drainage pattern on volcanic cones. The streams originate some distance below the rim and run with little sinuosity down the flanks (see plates 9.1, 9.2). Even actively growing volcanoes of fine

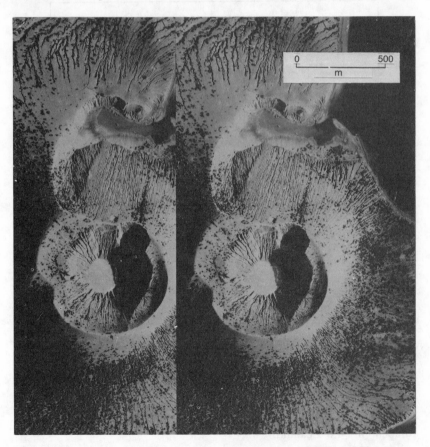

Plate 9.1 Stero-pair of Vulcan, Rabaul, Papua New Guinea, showing radial drainage, and centripetal drainage inside the crater (Illinois Committee on Aerial Photography)

Plate 9.2 Radial drainage on Mt Egmont, New Zealand. The parasitic cone of Fantham Peak to the south has its own radial pattern. To the north the deeply dissected older volcano, Poukai, still has radial drainage. Typical 'gutter' drainage runs between the two cones (The circle marks the limit of the National Park and forest clearance.) (Department of Lands & Survey, New Zealand)

scoria and lapilli are commonly dissected by numerous ravines, for example, Ngauruhoe, New Zealand, and Matupi, New Guinea.

When several volcanic cones erupt close together their drainage patterns interfere, giving several sectors of radial drainage with another drainage line along the gutter between adjacent cones. A good example from Gough Island is illustrated in figure 9.5.

When volcanic eruption is intermittent, ravines may be cut while the volcano is dormant; these are filled with tongues of lava when activity is renewed. The tongues then become divided and new valleys are excavated along their sides on the sites of earlier ridges. This is simply an example of inversion of relief on the flanks of an active cone.

137

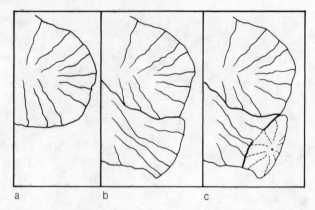

a b c

Figure 9.5 Drainage pattern evolution in SE Gough Island (a) radial drainage on South Peak (b) Green Hill erupts and blocks the southern streams, forming a new stream (thick line) between the two volcanoes (c) eruption of Richmond Hill blocks Green Hill drainage, resulting in two new streams (thick lines) between the volcanoes (after Ollier, 1984b)

Inside craters and calderas the streams run from some distance below the rim towards the centre in a centripetal pattern. If a former crater lake overflows, the originally centripetal drainage becomes a mere appendage at the head of a main stream that drains the crater through a breach (see figure 9.6).

Alternatively the crater may be breached by headward erosion of one of the radial streams, which captures the drainage of the crater and any lake it may have contained.

Volcanic plains of large size will develop an insequent drainage on their surface that follows irregularities of the type described in chapter 5. However, most of the drainage on lava plains is due to drainage displacement, as will be described later.

On ignimbrite plateaus the upper zone of unwelded pumice is very porous, but water flows over the welded zone if one is present. This also tends to be flat (like the surface of the ignimbrite itself) and a more or less insequent pattern may be expected. However, many ignimbrite areas have a markedly parallel drainage pattern (see figure 9.7). This is presumably due to long and uniform slopes on uniform material.

Drainage Density

Lava plains are often highly porous, especially at the base of flows, and layers of alluvium between flows may also provide aquifers. For this reason surface drainage is usually scarce on lava plains, and drainage density is low. For 320 km along the northern edge of the Snake River Plain, Idaho, all the rivers descending from the mountains sink into the porous lava, and at the end of the plain, great springs discharge groundwater from the old

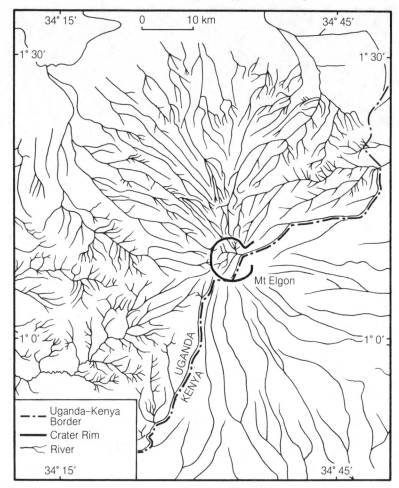

Figure 9.6 Mt Elgon, East Africa. Radial drainage pattern and breached crater

lava-filled canyons. Only two rivers cross the Western District volcanic plains of Victoria from north to south.

One might expect that ignimbrite plains, having high porosity, should have a low drainage density, but this does not seem to be the case. To some extent this is because the welded zone of ignimbrites is relatively impermeable and holds up groundwater, and to some extent due to the mechanism of valley formation on ignimbrite plains. Many of the valleys are dry for long periods, and occasional floods, accompanied by much tunnelling and mass movement as well as normal erosion, may be largely responsible for the relatively high drainage density of valleys.

139

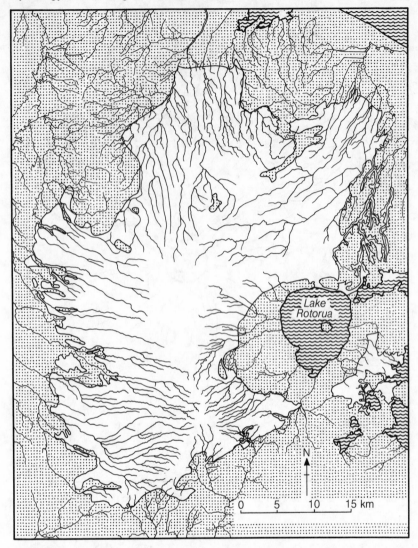

Figure 9.7 Mamaku ignimbrite plateau, New Zealand. The drainage pattern is radial overall, made up of a number of sectors with parallel drainage

Further generalizations about drainage density are hardly warranted, since it depends on so many factors, including amount and distribution of rainfall, permeability of rock, erodibility of rock, and topographic situations.

Drainage Diversion

Volcanic activity has a marked effect, sometimes utterly catastrophic, on pre-existing drainage. If only small cones and flows are produced, streams may flow around them with but little shift from their old courses, but if enough lava is produced, all pre-existing topography may be obliterated and a completely new drainage pattern initiated on the volcanic cones and lava plains.

A fairly simple example of drainage diversion is provided by Mt Etna (see figure 9.8). Prevolcanic rivers flowed to the south-east, but after being blocked by the volcano the drainage now flows via the River Alcantara in the north and the River Simeto to the south. The details of the blocking and the interaction of fluvial and volcanic features over the past 300,000 years are given by Chester and Duncan (1982).

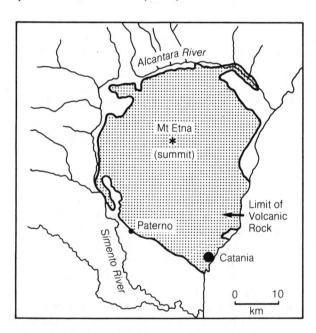

Figure 9.8 Drainage diversion around Mt Etna, Sicily

Lava flows displace rivers from their beds, and the water they carried must be accounted for in some other way. The various kinds of drainage diversion that can be caused by lava are shown diagrammatically in figure 9.9.

For a time the river may flow over the lava in an ill-defined course depending on minor irregularities in the lava surface. At this stage a thin layer of alluvium may be deposited haphazardly on the basalt, and this may

141

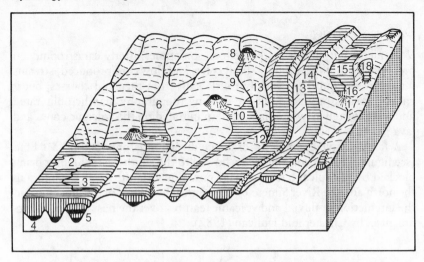

Figure 9.9 Drainage and landforms associated with lava flows **1** river diverted by lava plain **2** insequent lake on lava surface **3** insequent stream on lava surface **4** deep lead **5** multiple lava flows and deep leads **6** lava dammed lake (main valley) **7** lava dammed lake **8** stream flowing beneath cone and flow **9** spring **10** flow diverting river into next valley **11** lava diverted stream **12** probable site of gorge **13** twin lateral streams **14** inversion of relief **15** insequent stream on valley flow **16** waterfall **17** alluvial fan **18** residuals of older lava flow

account for the plentiful quartz and other unlikely minerals found in some 'basalt' soils. Eventually, however, the river will incise a well-defined valley either across the lava or around it.

Many lava flows are slightly convex so there is a shallow trench where the lava meets the old valley wall. This is commonly the place where diverted water flows, in what is called a lateral stream (see figure 9.10).

A simple example of drainage diversion is shown in figure 9.11. The ancestral Mt Emu Creek, Victoria, flowed southwards, with a number of tributaries from the east, one from the north, and one from the north-west. The course of this river was then blocked by extensive flows from Mt Hamilton and The Peak. Mt Emu Creek then flowed along the eastern edge of the flow, following the edge very faithfully, even where lobes from the lava flow extend up tributary valleys. The stream from the north now disappears in a series of swamps, some of which may overflow occasionally into some insequent lakes on the surface of the lava flow. The tributary from the north-west has been diverted to Lake Bolac, and then to Salt Creek, which is itself a lateral stream bounding an earlier flow. When a lava flow occupies a broad valley with tributaries on each side, lateral streams may develop on both sides of the flow as twin lateral streams.

A slightly more complex example is shown in figure 9.12a, with drainage largely bordering the rather complicated flows from Mt Rouse which flowed through several valleys to the sea more than 60 km from the

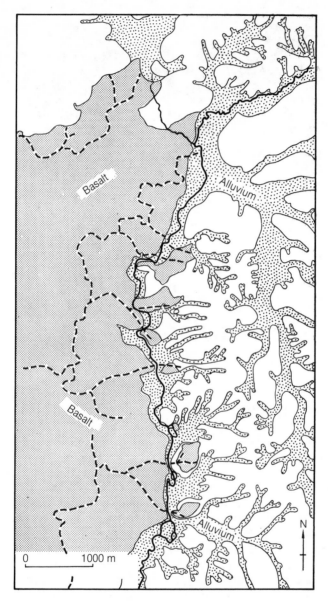

Figure 9.10   Lateral stream, deep leads and aggraded lava-blocked valleys near Ballarat, Victoria, Australia

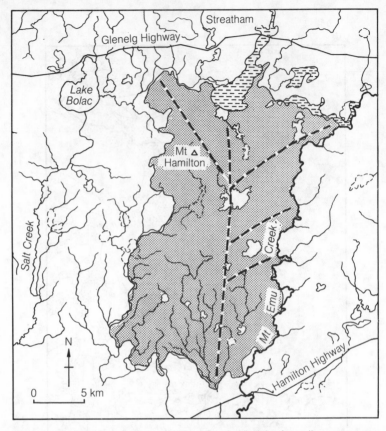

Figure 9.11 Drainage diversion, Mt Emu Creek, Victoria, Australia

vent. The distribution of lava and the river pattern enables quite detailed reconstruction of the pre-volcanic drainage (see figure 9.12b).

Thick flows of lava may reach or overtop the old interfluve ridges, and streams may then be displaced entirely from their old valleys. Very large sheet flows of basalt may divert rivers completely from their course so that they flow for many miles around the lava edge. The River Wannon in Victoria may provide an example.

Alluvial deposits in valley bottoms that are buried beneath lava flows are known as deep leads. Some contain economic placer deposits, such as tin and gold. Deep lead mining has provided a lot of information about pre-basaltic drainage patterns, even when lava plain formation has completely obliterated pre-existing topography.

The drainage pattern of deep leads may contain stream channels of several different ages, possibly reflecting lava diversion at several times, but nevertheless the drainage pattern revealed by deep lead maps is a useful

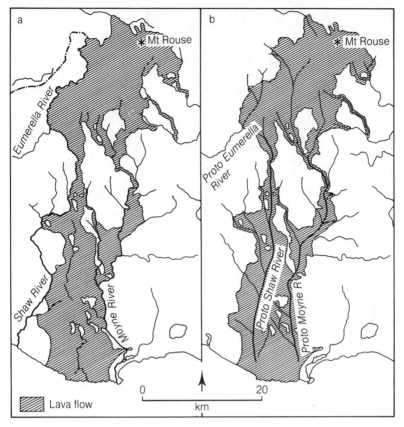

Figure 9.12 (a) Lava flows from Mt Rouse, Victoria, Australia and associated drainage (b) palaeodrainage reconstructed from map **a** (after Ollier, 1985)

tool for working out details of geomorphic histories. It may be compared with maps of modern drainage to see what changes have taken place since lava modified the drainage pattern. West of Ballarat, for instance, it can be seen that the position of the main divide has moved as much as 20 km to the north (see figure 9.13).

In some circumstances the direction of drainage may be completely reversed, usually in association with lake formation. In New Zealand, the upper Waitangi valley has been dammed by lava to form Lake Omapere, which has a westward overflow now, although the original Waitangi drainage was to the east. In Nicaragua volcanoes have ponded and reversed drainage so that water now flows eastward across a former continental divide.

Drainage can be disrupted catastrophically during actual eruptions. A lake that occupied the crater of La Soufrière, St Vincent, was thrown out of

145

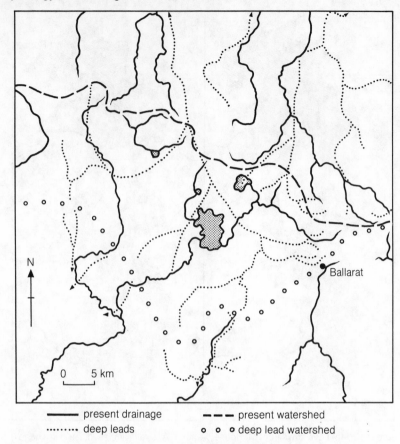

present drainage   — — — present watershed
········· deep leads   o o o deep lead watershed

Figure 9.13   Change of position of watershed near Ballarat, Victoria, Australia

the crater during the first phase of the eruption in 1902, producing extensive hot mudflows that rushed down the mountain into the sea. The crater lake in Kelut, Indonesia, used to be similarly displaced during eruptions producing dangerous lahars.

Some of the ice-caps (jokulls) of Iceland cover hundreds of square kilometres, and they may be partly melted from beneath by volcanic action to produce vast quantities of water in the so-called jokulhlaup (glacier burst) which devastates affected country and leaves the landscape unrecognizable.

Estimates of the discharge rates of water in a jokulhlaup are almost incredible. The Grimsvotn jokulhlaup of 1934 discharged at an average rate of 100,000 m³/s for two days, and the jokulhlaup of Katla in 1918 discharged at the rate of 400,000 m³/s, also for a two-day period. This is more than ten times the discharge rate of the Mississippi and four times that of the Amazon. Katla produces the most dangerous and unpredictable hlaups because it has a greater gradient than others. The hlaups carry huge boulders; one of 400 m^3 was carried 14 km by the hlaup of 1918.

Lakes

Crater Lakes, Caldera Lakes and Maars

Closed depressions on impermeable rock may hold lakes. These of course are specially prominent in craters and calderas (see plate 9.3). Mahavura in Uganda is a symmetrical scoria volcano rising about 3000 m above the local bedrock, with a tiny but perfect crater lake at the top of about 10 m across. Most crater lakes are considerably larger than this, though their importance in the overall hydrology of volcanic areas is still slight. Caldera lakes, such as Crater Lake (Oregon) and Taal (Philippines) are substantial bodies of water and important in regional hydrology.

Plate 9.3 Crater Lake, Mt Raupehu, New Zealand (New Zealand Geological Survey)

Maars typically hold water and usually give rise to strikingly circular lakes such as Pulvermaar (see plate 3.4). Where the maars are formed through irregular topography they may have more irregular outlines, like the Rubirizi volcanic lakes of Uganda. Others may be irregular due to the close eruption of several maars, as is the case at Tower Hill (see plate 1.2). Some maars are almost perfect funnels, like Pulvermaar, but others have broad, very flat bottoms. The flat floor is probably made of pyroclastics that have fallen back into the crater, modified to some extent by alluvial fill.

Few crater lakes, caldera lakes, or maars have active overflow channels, for if overflow persisted for very long it would soon cut a channel that could drain the lake. A few have small overflow channels that are only used on rare occasions of high water.

Some maars may reflect the local groundwater level, but others are obviously isolated water bodies, and it is possible for two lakes only a few hundred metres apart to have completely different levels and different salinities, showing that the water bodies are not connected.

Lakes Formed by Volcanic Damming

When volcanic products pile up in a valley they create a dam that holds back drainage and produces a lake.

On the largest scale a drainage system may be blocked by a whole volcanic field, to form a huge lake like Lake Kivu which occupies a high valley that originally drained to the north, and so to the Nile. The eruption of the Birunga volcanic field dammed back the water to form Lake Kivu, and now the drainage flows to the south through an older and lower volcanic barrier and eventually to Lake Tanganyika.

On a much smaller scale a single small volcanic cone may block a valley, as Le Tartaret in the Auvergne blocked the River Couze to form the Lac de Chambon, only 5.8 m deep.

More lakes are dammed back by lava flows than by cones. A main valley may be blocked by lava flows along its course forming a lake on the upstream side like Lake Bunyoni, Uganda, or lava may flow down a main valley and create many lakes where it blocks tributary valleys. The lakes accumulate silt which remains as alluvial flats when the lakes are drained, as they inevitably are, by cutting down of the overflow channel.

Lakes are normally drained by overflow as described above, but if evaporation removes most of the water, a salt lake will be formed such as Lake Baringo in the Kenya Rift on the site of the much larger lava-dammed, Pleistocene Lake Kamasai.

On complex initial topography more elaborate lakes may be formed. An example is Lake Lanao on Mindanao in the Philippines. Here the initial topography was an upland plateau cut by a deep ravine. A lava dam caused water to fill the ravine and spread out on to the plateau, so the lake now has a large expanse of water of 4–10 m deep with a trough of about 300 m deep on the site of the old ravine.

Lakes may form in valleys blocked by volcanic mudflows, as at Bandaisan, Japan. Ponding may also be due to river aggradation of volcanic fragments as in the Waikato valley, New Zealand. Great eruptions of pumice fragments added easily transportable material to the River Waikato, which rapidly aggraded its bed along a 130 km stretch. Tributary valleys, not supplied with sufficient volcanic fragments, were unable to build up their beds to the same level, and so formed shallow lakes (McCraw, 1967).

Volcanic activity is frequently accompanied by earth movements, and lakes may be caused by a combination of both effects; they are known as volcano-tectonic lakes. In New Zealand there is a large complex of volcano-tectonic depressions in the North Island, containing Lakes Rotorua and Taupo. Lake Toba in Sumatra, Indonesia, is of similar origin, and the many lakes of the Valley of Mexico are possibly volcano-tectonic too.

The surface of lava flows may have many minor features and irregularities, described in chapter 5, and the drainage on some flows is insequent or almost random, with many small and shallow pools in irregularities of the surface. The volcanic plains of western Victoria contain many such lakes. Occasionally large but shallow lakes are maintained on the surface of volcanic flows, like Yellowstone Lake in Yellowstone Park, and Myvatn in Iceland which has an area of 27 km^2 and a maximum depth of only 2.3 m.

Hydrology and Geothermal Energy

As explained in chapter 1, there is a growing interest in geothermal energy, which has environmental advantages over other forms of energy such as fossil fuel or nuclear energy.

Most modern production of commercial geothermal energy requires high-pressure steam (see plate 1.2), which is only produced under special circumstances. The conditions required for geothermal energy fields are an efficient caprock, to seal the steam in; an underlying permeable aquifer in which hot water and steam may be stored; a substantial thermal anomaly, to provide heat; and of course an adequate supply of water. This situation is illustrated at Wairakei, New Zealand (see figure 9.14) where the caprock consists of the shales of the Huka Falls formation and the aquifer is the Waiora pumice breccia. In practice, although steam can be obtained almost anywhere from the breccia, power-producing hot water is obtained from deeper drills that tap fissures in the underlying ignimbrite. The water reaches the surface at a temperature of about 200°C where it is separated from steam (which is allowed to blow off), the superheated water is piped to the power station and there 'flashed' into steam which drives the generators. Use of the water is complicated because of the corrosive chemicals dissolved in it.

In New Zealand there are geothermal areas and geysers of great attraction to tourists. Tapping the steam reservoir for geothermal energy appears to affect the natural displays adversely and there is some danger that they may be destroyed. In any costing of geothermal energy the potential loss of tourism should be taken into account as well as the cost of the energy,

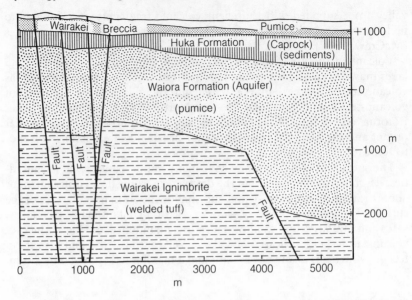

Figure 9.14 Simplified geological section of Wairakei geothermal area, New Zealand, showing caprock, aquifer, and heat source

though so far there appears to be little concern in New Zealand. Rotorua, for example, depends very much upon tourism, but there appears to be a *laissez-faire* attitude to tapping of steam for domestic use. With continued development it is possible that the town will eventually have abundant hot water in every house, at the expense of declining geyser activity and a declining tourist trade.

10 Weathering and Soils

Weathering

The normal processes of weathering affect volcanic rocks much as any others, but the basic factors are the nature of the material, climate, drainage (itself dependent on topographic site) and time. Acid volcanic rocks contain quartz, and are non-extreme or 'normal' parent material except that they may also contain the very weatherable material volcanic glass. Basalts are not a 'normal' parent material, because they have no quartz and can weather without producing sand. Both feldspars and ferro-magnesian minerals are easily altered to clay minerals, with silica and bases lost in solution.

In tropical climates and in very leached sites, kaolin is the common end-product, accompanied by iron oxides. Tropical red earths are the commonest soils. Ferricrete (hard vesicular or nodular iron oxide) or 'laterite' may be formed. In extreme cases bauxite can be produced. Raggatt et al. (1945) showed that bauxite could be derived from basalt by nothing more than addition of water and removal of salts and silica in solution.

In temperate climates and in badly-drained sites where bases are retained, montmorillonite clay is often produced. Where leaching is limited, carbonate may be precipitated in various parts of the weathering profile. The ultimate product is often a brown, base-rich, heavy soil.

Montmorillonite clays swell and shrink, so many basalt soils have this property. Swelling can cause severe foundation problems for buildings, so is of considerable practical importance. The swelling and shrinking breaks up soil by deep cracks, improving soil structure for agricultural purposes. Swelling properties result in basalt soils often having patterned ground, commonly known as gilgai. Many different patterns are found, but they all have a basic style of 'subsoil' material, with carbonate, appearing at the ground surface on the high parts, and thick black clay overlying the carbonate-rich B horizon in the lowest parts.

Weathering profiles on old volcanic rocks can be very deep, sometimes over 100 m in depth. Many deep profiles in places like Australia formed in the past when the climate was very different from that of today. Some of these have been dated by palaeomagnetism to Tertiary and even Cretaceous times.

Weathering follows joints, and then attacks the individual joint blocks between. Successive layers of weathering are preserved as concentric shells around the central core of the joint block. This feature is called spheroidal weathering, and it is very common in well-jointed basalts and dolerites (see plate 10.1). Deep within weathering profiles the joint pattern of the rock is preserved in the weathered rock or saprolite. Alteration is commonly isovolumetric, that is, there has been chemical and mineralogical change with no change in volume. Occasional cores of joint blocks are preserved in unaltered rock, completely surrounded by totally altered rock. Such remnants are called corestones. Besides the well-rounded corestones, weathered basalt profiles occasionally contain irregular pieces of basalt, sometimes known as floaters.

Plate 10.1 Spheroidal weathering in basalt. Cooma, Australia (C. D. Ollier)

Weathering does not always decrease systematically down the profile. In some lava flows both the top and the bottom of the flow are more porous, because of accumulation of scoriaceous lava, than the dense centre, and both top and bottom weather faster than the middle of the flow (see plate 10.2).

Basalt can affect the weathering rate of adjacent rock – an example of 'incompatibility' of rocks. Schmidt et al. (1976) found several examples at dam sites in Victoria, Australia, where weathering of Ordovician bedrock is intense where it is overlain by basalt, even though the basalt is little

Plate 10.2 Weathered lava flow, Tumut, Australia. Note increasing weathering at depth, presumably caused by groundwater movement along joints. Also, slight weathering and organic matter accumulation to form the soil at the surface (C. D. Ollier)

weathered. The situation is shown in figure 10.1, and two possibilities may be envisaged to account for the distribution of weathered rock beneath the basalt:

(1) There has been an increase in the weathering of Ordovician rocks beneath the basalt.
(2) The Ordivician rock was weathered in low areas and then covered by basalt.

The junction between weathered and fresh bedrock is sharp, and dips steeply from the original position of the basalt edge, at a gradient that is not parallel to an earlier valley side or to any rock structure. Since the weathered rock is found under all areas ever covered by basalt, and is absent from all valley sides that never had a basalt cover, it seems most probable that the intense weathering is post-basaltic.

In regions of plateau basalt, successive widespread flows may each have

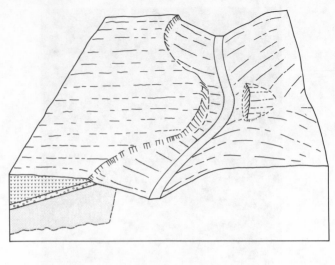

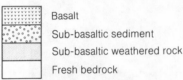

Basalt

Sub-basaltic sediment

Sub-basaltic weathered rock

Fresh bedrock

Figure 10.1 Sub-basaltic weathering, Eppalock, Victoria, Australia. Weathered shale (stippled) extends to the original edge of the lava flow

a weathered zone. In Australia this is known as a bole. Normally it is red clay, but occasionally it may be weathered to a more extreme degree. Some of the weathered basalt in the Tertiary basalts of Northern Ireland has even been worked economically for bauxite. It would seem perfectly natural for a lava flow surface to become altered in time into a weathering profile or bole, but detailed studies in Australia and in the Deccan of India have suggested that it may be a layer of volcanic ash that is altered to the bole.

The weathered horizons affect the hydrology of the region, being generally less permeable than the unweathered basalt. They also affect the course of erosion, acting as a soft, erodible layer between tough basalt sheets which may also have vertical jointing. This is quite likely to result in a stepped landscape as a result of differential erosion.

Silica dissolved out of weathering basalt may be re-precipitated in the underlying material as nodules or sheets of crypto-crystalline silica known as silcrete. This may be sufficiently massive to produce landforms of its own during later erosion, and silcrete may be used to deduce the former presence of lava cover even when no trace of igneous rock remains. Unfortunately silcrete is also produced by weathering mechanisms totally unconnected with vulcanicity, and there are many problems with its interpretation (Langford-Smith, 1980).

154

Weathering can produce peculiar landscapes under certain conditions. One such landscape is that developed on kaolinized pyroxene andesites of the Caliman Massif, Eastern Carpathians (Naum et al., 1962). The landscape has many pseudo-karst features similar to those developed in areas of massive limestone, including lapies and dolines, and stalactites, stalagmites and even flowstone have been formed from limonite. The name 'volcano-karst' was proposed for this kind of scenery. The 'stone forest' near Huaron, Peru, is a rugged topography of towers similar to some tropical karsts, but is produced by frost action on Tertiary ignimbrite (Tricart et al., 1962).

Soil

There is a considerable range of volcanic soils, depending on soil-forming factors (parent material, climate, topography, time, organism). The main volcanic factor is the nature of the parent material – whether lava or ash, and whether acid (quartz rich) or basic.

Basalt commonly gives rise to very productive soils of high fertility, though sometimes the physical properties of the soils are not good, especially on ill-drained lava plains. In general the more acid the soil the lower the fertility, but the quartz content of acid and intermediate volcanics can help improve soil structure.

Well-drained, leached sites will usually have a soil dominated by kaolin and iron oxides, such as a red or brown earth; poorly drained sites will usually have montmorillonite-rich soils, with black cracking clays as in vertisols.

The actual soil formed depends on several factors including climate and position on a slope, for upper slopes are relatively arid and leached, and lower slopes are relatively moist and potentially sites for chemical precipitation.

A number of soil types with a regular relationship to slopes is called a catena. For example, in New South Wales on basalt slopes, if the rainfall is over 150 cm krasnozems cover the entire slope. Where the rainfall is about 100 cm, krasnozems are found on upper slopes, chocolate soils on middle slopes, and prairie soils on lower slopes. In areas receiving 70 cm rainfall, the catena consists of chocolate soils on upper slopes, prairie soils on mid slopes, and black earths on lower slopes. In areas with only 50 cm rainfall, black earths occupy the whole slope.

Volcanic ash give rise to a different range of soils. Basic pyroclastics can give rise to very fertile soil, as the distribution of cultivation around Tower Hill clearly shows (see plate 1.2). Pyroclastics, with their high porosity, weather very much faster than solid rocks of the same composition, especially if they contain large amounts of glass.

Andesitic volcanic ash often produced the most distinctive of volcanic

155

Plate 10.3 Andosol soil profile formed on siliceous pyroclastics, Rabaul, Papua New Guinea. The dark A horizon is rich in clay and organic matter. Below is a zone of yellow staining, and then unweathered ash (C. D. Ollier)

soils called an andosol (plate 10.3), from the Japanese *an* (dark) and *do* (soil). These consist of a black or dark topsoil (A horizon) over white ash (C horizon) with little development of a B horizon. The soil profile differs from most common soil profiles in having more clay in the topsoil than in the subsoil. The dark A horizon has low density, clay dominated by amorphous material (allophane) and high organic content (Ugolini and Zasoski, 1979). Phosphorous is the main elemental deficiency.

A volume devoted to soils on tephra and basalt is provided by Fernandez Candas and Yaalon (1985). Most of the papers are very technical, but a few are on soil genesis and there are four papers on andosols. The emphasis on andosols in soils literature should not obscure the fact that many different soils are formed on volcanic products, ranging from tropical red earths in Hawaii, Samoa and Mauritius, to red-brown earths and vertisols in Australia and podzols in New Zealand.

Rates of Weathering and Soil Formation

Volcanic eruptions produce fresh parent material that provides excellent material for rate studies of weathering. Ash weathers rather quickly.

In St Vincent, West Indies, it was found that a fertile soil had formed within twenty years of eruption on andesitic ash, and some plants can grow almost as soon as the ash is cold.

The rate of weathering of andesitic ash was studied in detail in St Vincent by Hay (1960), who found that a 4000-year-old ash had weathered to form a clayey soil 2 m thick. The soil was formed at a rate of 0.45–0.6 m in 1000 years. Glass decomposed at a rate of 15 $g/cm^2/1000$ years.

A 6000-year-old ash from South Australia had lost up to 80 per cent of its calcium, magnesium and sodium, but there was essentially no loss of titanium, silicon or aluminium.

Ruxton (1968) worked on the weathering rates of some ash layers in Papua that could be carbon dated. The ash layers are nearly all derived by ash fall from Mt Lamington, 20–28 km to the north-west, at a fairly uniform accumulation rate beteen 12 and 19 cm/1000 years over the last 90,000 years. By analysis and calculation of the loss of mobile elements, principally silica, it was shown that the weathering rate decreased exponentially and the average rate of weathering is halved about every 5000 years. The rate of clay formation, up to 14 $g/cm^2/1000$ years, is similar to that calculated by Hay from St Vincent.

On a longer time scale Ruxton (1968) determined rates of weathering of rocks of The Hydrographers strato-volcano, Papua, potassium/argon dated at 650,000 years. The weathering profiles on sites with little or no erosion have an upper zone of 1.5–7.5 m of silty clay over a lower zone of 15–30 m of clayey silt with rock structure preserved. The average loss of silica per unit area is 4–6 $g/cm^2/1000$ years, which compares with 3.8 $g/cm^2/1000$ years in Oahu, Hawaii, and 4 $g/cm^2/1000$ years, in St Vincent (Ruxton, 1968).

In Victoria, Australia, lava flows of up to 20,000 years old have virtually no soil; flows of up to hundreds of thousands years old have red earths sometimes over a metre deep, and flows of over about a million years old have deep profiles with pallid zones at depth and ferricrete crusts.

11   Erosion in Volcanic Areas

Erosion of Cones

Many young scoria cones are so porous that they suffer virtually no erosion, and Stearns (1966) notes that the younger scoria cones of Hawaii are not eroded even under a rainfall of 5000 mm annually. On older volcanoes the weathering of ash and the formation of soil increases the clay content, lowers permeability, and thus leads eventually to erosion. On some volcanoes, however, erosion apparently sets in despite the porosity of the material: the small cone of Vulcan, New Guinea, for instance, is only 50 years old and made entirely of very porous pumice and ash, yet is already well gullied (see plate 9.1). In complete contrast there are many scoria cones in Victoria of considerable age – perhaps half a million years or more old – that have not been gullied and undergo only slow rounding and reduction by weathering, mass movement, and sheet wash.

Lava cones, though not necessarily very permeable (see chapter 9), will generally be more susceptible to erosion than scoria cones, and impermeable layers in the strato-volcanoes will tend to make them somewhat prone to erosion also.

Larger volcanoes will be more liable to erosion than small volcanoes made of the same material, for they have a larger catchment area and so water can more often accumulate to the stage of runoff, whereas small volcanoes may remain entirely within the hydrological limits of 'no erosion'.

Theoretically, when drainage is first initiated on a cone, there will be little erosion near the crater rim because there is no catchment for water collection, and also because the rim is often extremely porous. Somewhere on the mid-slopes of the cone erosion will be at a maximum, and will fall off towards the lower slopes because of declining gradient and deposition of material around the base of the volcano. Gullies will therefore be deepest on the mid-slopes, and when these coalesce to form valleys they will produce a concave long profile.

Larger valleys on volcanoes of fairly uniform rock will tend to be typically V-shaped in cross-section. On some volcanoes such valleys run almost from top to bottom of the slopes, with the valley sides intersecting in sharp-edged ridges. The radial pattern of uniform sized valleys, with regularly spaced ribs between them, gives rise to what has been called 'parasol ribbing'.

There appear to be two erosional mechanisms that can cause parasol ribbing. According to Cotton (1944), parasol ribbing is caused not by normal erosion but by an avalanching process associated with hot ash. The grooves formed by avalanching are entirely due to gravity and not to any explosive propulsion, although avalanching takes place while the ash is still hot. Each groove can carry many slides and the ash comes to rest in fans or irregular heaps around the base of the cone.

But some examples of parasol ribbing appear to be definitely due to fluvial erosion by radial ravines, including those on Batok (see figure 11.1) and Bromo in Indonesia.

Figure 11.1   Parasol ribbing, Mt Batok (2420 m), Java

Perhaps the two types of parasol ribbing may be distinguished by the valley pattern. From the pictures of the avalanche-formed grooves on Vesuvius shown by Cotton (1944, p. 238) it seems that all grooves originate at the crater rim. Photographs of Batok show shorter valleys on the lower slopes that appear as if inserted between the longer valleys, and originating in the middle and lower slopes.

In lava cones and strato-volcanoes, structural control by hard lava beds will commonly lead to steep-sided, gorge-like valleys. One distinctive variety of valley of this kind is known as an amphitheatre-headed valley (Stearns, 1966) and is found on most of the larger islands of Hawaii and on many other volcanoes, including those of Vanuatu (as shown on figure 11.2).

Alternate resistant and non-resistant beds, usually dipping downstream,

159

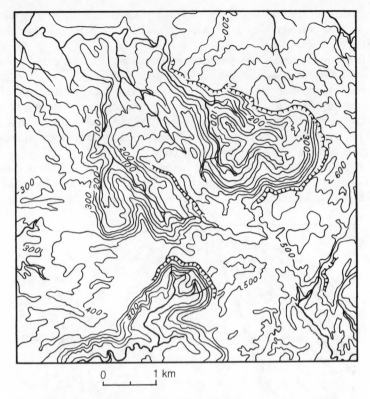

Figure 11.2 Amphitheatre valleys, Efate, Vanuatu

are especially favourable for the development of these valleys. The non-resistant beds are undercut and give rise to waterfalls. As such falls erode headwards they tend to coalesce into one big fall. Eventually the streams reach the stage where they have a 'fall point', above which the stream continues to cut down, and below which lateral erosion is dominant. Haiku Stream, Oahu, has a gradient of 2° below the fall point and a gradient 41° above. River capture on upper slopes of a volcano, where the streams are converging upwards, helps the valley to enlarge into an amphitheatre near its source. Captured tributaries form coalescing plunge pools, with narrow ridges in between which are easily undercut.

According to Stearns (1966) such amphitheatre valleys do not develop where the original slope of the groundsurface was 3° or less. The steep headwall and sides of the amphitheatre valleys are dissected into many spurs by close-set ravines, chutes, or 'flutes' so precipitous that they are sometimes called 'vertical valleys'. At a later stage of denudation, the side and head walls of the valleys retreat, and the lower gentler slopes come to occupy a large part of the landscape. The steeper upper slopes are still dissected by many steep gullies, but at this stage they will no longer be eroded by plunge pools and collapse. However, according to Wentworth (1943), they will be eroded by a process of shallow landsliding which periodically, during very heavy rains, cleans out each gully as a 'soil avalanche'. When the steep edges of neighbouring valleys retreat far enough they will intersect to form steep ridges, which will eventually be consumed. On the north-eastern, most rapidly eroded side of Oahu, former ridges have apparently been reduced in this way. The ridges between the lower valleys have been destroyed, but the valley heads, which are still very steep, coalesce to make a continuous cliff. This cliff, or 'pali' as it is called, is still retreating and consuming what is left of the earlier dome.

Occasionally one amphitheatre valley may grow to enormous size, far outstripping its neighbours. This is especially probable if it breaches a crater and thus extends its catchment. Such enormous valleys are then bordering on the scale of so-called 'erosion calderas'. The Caldera of La Palma (Canary Islands), which supplied the general term for great depressions, appears to be of this kind. A number of amphitheatre valleys are combining to erode an interior lowland in Réunion. The so-called 'crater' or 'caldera' of Haleakala on the island of Maui (Hawaiian Islands) is formed basically by the meeting of two amphitheatre valleys, Kaupo valley and Keanae valley, working backwards from opposite sides of the island.

It is of great significance that the drainage pattern on cones is radial, and the valley heads converge towards the top of the cone (see figure 11.3). As they erode headwards they come closer together, and eventually stream abstraction and river capture are inevitable. This process is particularly effective on those cones of sufficient size to induce orographic rainfall, for the upper slopes will of course receive more water, increasing the drainage density and thus the incidence of abstraction and river capture. Since this process is most effective on the upper slopes it is there that the original surface of the volcano is first removed. On lower slopes the valley sides have not met, and large triangular facets of the original volcano surface are preserved, often for considerable periods of time. These triangular facets of original volcano surface are called planezes (see figure 11.4). Of course the surface of a planeze will seldom be completely uneroded, but such gullies as dissect it are very much smaller than the large valleys between planezes. Some of them may be small channels which flowed before stream abstraction and capture; others are small channels which developed later to carry run-off from the planeze surface itself.

A secondary cone on the slopes of a large volcanic dome deflects drainage to form two main channels, one on each side. These concentrate the drainage and give rise to valleys larger than unconcentrated radial valleys. After considerable erosion a wedge-shaped remnant of the secondary cone remains, and even if it should be entirely eroded, the drainage pattern will continue to indicate its former presence. A lava fill in the crater of a scoria cone can affect the course of subsequent erosion. The

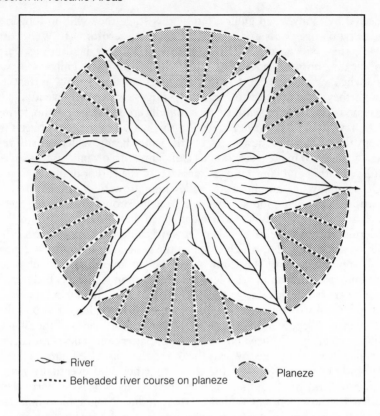

River
Beheaded river course on planeze
Planeze

Figure 11.3 Planeze formation by stream abstraction of radial drainage

'Mount Holden' type of volcano in Victoria (Australia) refers to a group of such volcanoes, which have a flat top and one flank of lava, the rest of the volcano being of scoria. It is thought that these volcanoes were scoria cones with breached craters from which a lava flow issued, and then by a kind of inversion of relief caused by sheet erosion of the scoria, the lava became a caprock.

In those volcanoes with closed craters, erosion will eventually lead to breaching of the crater. This erosion may be brought about by overflow from a crater lake, or by headward erosion of a radial valley. The first radial valley to notch the crater thereby increases its catchment, which consequently increases its erosion rate. This valley therefore becomes much larger than the other valleys on the cone, and the eroded volcano thus becomes typically horseshoe-shaped.

Centripetal drainage of the crater also erodes, making the crater even larger. In the course of time a large erosional basin takes the place of the crater, surrounded by remnants of the old volcano flanks. These basins,

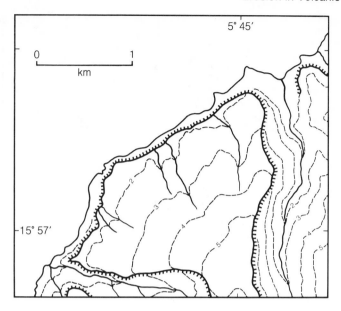

Figure 11.4 A planeze on St Helena, a dissected volcano in the Atlantic

which may be several kilometres in diameter, are called erosional calderas, a term not in favour as the term caldera has come to have more specific usage as described in chapter 4, but no alternative has been proposed.

The Banks Peninsula, New Zealand, provides an excellent example. It is made up of two shield volcanoes, Lyttleton which was active between 10 and 12 million years ago, and Akaroa which was active between 7.5 and 9.5 million years ago (Stipp and McDougall, 1969). The central regions of both volcanoes have been very deeply eroded and subsequently drowned to form the harbours of Lyttleton and Akaroa.

A volcano may go through a number of stages during the course of erosion (figure 11.5). Starting from a complete volcano, the next stage would be a gullied volcano, followed by a volcano dissected by large valleys with planezes around the edge. Eventually all the planezes would be eroded away, leaving an irregular hilly mass that may be termed a residual volcano, and after further erosion only a few necks, dykes, and sills would rise much above the general level of erosion. This may be called the skeleton stage.

In New Zealand, Kear (1957) believed that the difficult states of dissection could be related to the length of time since the volcano erupted, and the different states indicated the following ages:

Volcano – Holocene
    Planeze – Middle Pleistocene to Holocene
    Residual – Plio-Pleistocene
    Skeleton – Upper Miocene

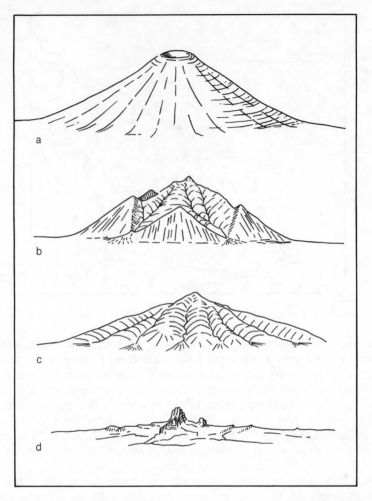

Figure 11.5 Stages in erosion of a volcano (a) intact volcano (b) planeze stage (c) residual volcano (d) volcanic skeleton

It must be realized that this idealized sequence of erosional forms does not hold in all, or even in most cases. The course of erosion depends on many factors including the size and structure of the volcano, climate, vegetation, and setting. The style of erosion varies from place to place, for reasons we do not always fully understand.

In some volcanoes, a small number of main valleys are responsible for most of the erosion, and such circumstances lead to the preservation of planezes. On the other hand, it is possible for many valleys to be eroded simultaneously, producing the parasol-ribbing effect when a planeze stage would be virtually non-existent. In some volcanoes practically all the volcanic edifice is removed before the intrusive necks and dykes are exposed, in others, they may be exposed by erosion of the heart of the volcano while extensive planeze remnants are preserved.

It is thus possible for different parts of a large volcanic mass to be at different stages of erosion – some parts may be completely removed exposing underlying bedrock, elsewhere, intrusive rocks may be exposed, while in some places considerable remnants of the volcano may be preserved.

The large Tertiary Napak volcano of Uganda still has planeze-like remnants (see figure 8.6) even though it is estimated that no less than 97 per cent of the original volcano has been removed by erosion, together with a large quantity of bedrock (King, 1949).

Erosion of geologically much older volcanic complexes can produce topography similar in a general way to that of a younger complex. In the Mullaley area of New South Wales, for instance, Dulhunty (1967) has described a Mesozoic volcanic complex where streams have excavated valleys exposing up to 300 m of lava flows, and eroded plugs now stand up to 450 m above the valley floors. Despite the age of these volcanics, erosion has reached the underlying sediments in only a few places within the volcanic area (see figure 11.6).

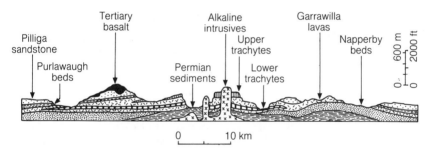

Figure 11.6 Generalized geological section in the Mullaley area, New South Wales, Australia (after Dulhunty, 1967)

The course of erosion becomes especially complicated when the volcano continues to be active during erosion, or resumes activity after a period of erosion, which can of course happen many times. A sequence of erosion and later eruption appears to be typical of some of the volcanic masses of New South Wales. At Canobolas, for instance, there is an approximately level plateau of Silurian and Devonian rocks about 1000 m high on which stands a pile of Tertiary 'earlier lavas' and tuffs rising to a height of about 500 m above the plateau (Old Man Canobolas). The 'earlier lavas' are not found below the plateau level at 1000 m. A later period of erosion reduced the volcanic pile and cut valleys into the plateau. 'Later basalts' then flowed down these valleys at altitudes below 1000 m, sometimes filling them

165

completely and overflowing on to the tableland and lapping around the old volcano.

Aspect is very important in controlling the degree of erosion of slopes. The north-eastern slopes of the larger Hawaiian islands may be incised by deep canyons because of the high rainfall, whereas leeward slopes remain relatively undissected, provided they have both been eroded for the same length of time. However, on the Waianae Range, Oahu, the leeward slope is older and hence much more eroded than the windward side. The rate of erosion on a volcano may be reduced by the growth of another volcano to the windward, as happened when the Koolau dome cut off the trade winds from the Waianae dome.

Large volcanoes have significant climatic changes at different altitudes and on different aspects, which affect the type and degree of erosion. On El Misti, Peru, for example, a composite cone of lava and ash, there are larger and more persistent snowfields on the western side, and consequently a much more advanced state of erosion (Bullard, 1962).

Kilimanjaro, Tanzania, shows a whole range of glacial erosion forms, including cirques, U-shaped valleys, pavements, striations, roches mouton-nées, lateral moraines, kettle holes, and crag-and-tail (Downie, 1964). Six episodes of glaciation are recognized, of which the last two are post-Pleistocene.

A glacier that taps the crater of a large volcano, as does the Weyprecht Glacier on the Beerenberg, Jan Mayen, obtains a big advantage over other glaciers because of its increased area for neve accumulation. The Weyprecht valley is much deeper than that of other glaciers on the mountain as a result.

The planezes that extend up to about 3000 m on glaciated Mt Rainier, USA, are known as 'wedges'. On higher slopes, between 3000 m and 4000 m, the wedges are replaced by long walls of rock arranged radially from the summit known as 'cleavers', for they split the descending ice into lobes (see figure 11.7). The cleavers appear to be remnants of the original volcano surface, for although their walls can be over 300 m high, their upper surfaces are uneroded dip slopes (Coombs, 1936).

There may be interaction of vulcanicity and glaciation as described from the Santiago Basin of Chile by Tricart (1965). Glaciers were already in decay at the end of the last glaciation, but ash eruptions catastrophically increased the rate of deglaciation, and a very large area is covered by ashes that were transported by the water so produced.

Periglacial action, with frost and solifluction causing screes and block-fields, can occur on volcanics in suitable locations, as for instance in the Ardeche, France (Bozon, 1963).

Occasionally a number of different modes of erosion combine to dissect a volcano and provide a measure of the effectiveness of different agents under the prevailing conditions. An example is provided by Ross volcano in the Auckland Islands, about 400 km south of the South Island of New

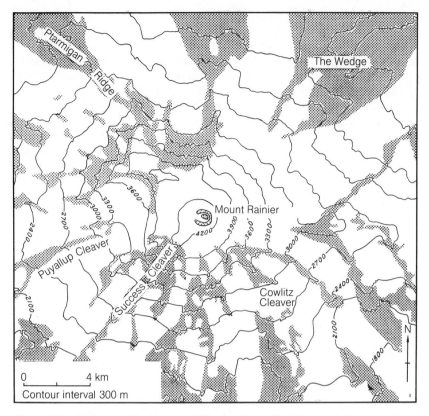

Figure 11.7 Mt Rainier, Washington, USA, showing radial ridges and cleavers of rock (stippled) separated by glaciers

Zealand. Ross volcano was originally dissected by a typical radial series of valleys. Most of these were later glaciated, and some were truncated by marine erosion which produced precipitous cliffs of up to 500 m high on the west coast. Some of the ridges were reduced to saddles by the erosion of tributaries. In unglaciated areas the interfluves are strongly dissected, but where interfluves were covered by snow they have been protected and remain as gentle-sloping undissected ridges between glaciated troughs (Wright, 1967).

The Piton des Neiges forms the north-west part of the island of Réunion, and overall is a shield 50 km across at sea level. The amount of erosion varies enormously from place to place on this volcano, and while many young flows and pyroclastics are preserved on its flank, elsewhere there are deep gorges with amphitheatre-shaped heads exposing sections of the lava succession of up to 2500 m high. On this volcano there is considerable erosion even of the summit, and it is probable that a summit cone rose

300 m higher than the present summit at the time when activity ceased (Upton and Wadsworth, 1966).

Many strato-volcanoes have a very long active life, and their story is usually one of gullying, then filling the gully with a flow, and later formation of new gullies, the sequence being repeated many times and varied periodically by occasional pyroclastic deposits or parasitic cone formation. In this type of volcano a species of steady state is achieved; so long as the volcano remains active no major change of form will be produced by erosion.

In eastern Australia a great escarpment has cut back from the continental edge (Ollier, 1982a), in places cutting across volcanoes. The best example is the Miocene Ebor Volcano (Ollier, 1982b). Scarp retreat has moved past the centre of eruption, but the radial drainage is preserved on both the remains of the cone, and on Palaeozoic bedrock on which it was superimposed (see figure 11.8).

Erosion of Lava Flows and Lava Plains

The streams that drain lava plains, whether insequent, lateral, or complex types, will erode their valleys and modify the landscape. In many instances the basalt is harder than the surrounding bedrock, so the latter is eroded fastest. The amount of incision of lateral streams will depend on the size of the catchment, amount of runoff, hardness of rock, age and other factors. When there is sufficient available relief, lateral streams may incise valleys hundreds of metres deep. This process can eventually lead to 'inversion of relief' whereby the lava flow which originally occupied a valley bottom comes to mark a ridge top (see figure 11.9). Eventually a string of basalt-capped hills may be all that remains to indicate the early drainage system.

An excellent example is shown in plate 11.1. El Capitan is a hill 50 km north-east of Cobar, New South Wales, capped by fine-grained basalt. The shape of the hill in plan clearly indicates the remains of a main valley with a tributary, and indeed river deposits have been found below the basalt. The lava is of Miocene age, and the surrounding plain is eroded across Silurian sedimentary rocks. Another very small example is shown in plate 11.2.

By using such hills, and also deep lead information, early drainage can often be worked out, and the course of erosion determined in some detail. Thus figure 11.10 shows part of the course of the Loddon River, Victoria and its associated outcrops of basalt. Near the headwaters in the south the old valley is still filled with basalt, and the deep lead has been mapped, predictably, along the centre of the flow. The present river is here a lateral stream, with tributaries flowing over the basalt. Further downstream to the north the river originally meandered over the lava surface, but it has now cut down to a level below the deep lead, leaving remnants of lava as flat-topped hills in meander cores.

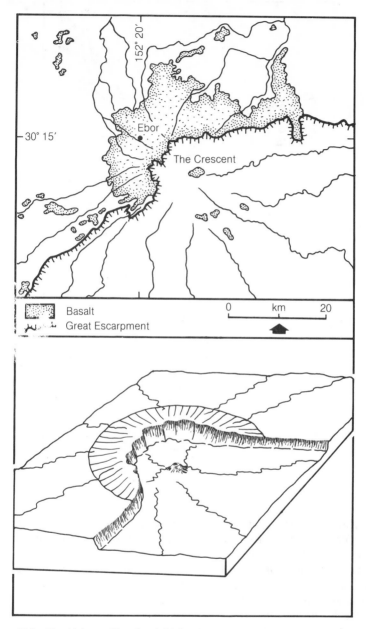

Figure 11.8 Ebor Volcano, New South Wales, Australia *top* map showing radial drainage on both volcano remnant and superimposed on bedrock below Great Escarpment *bottom* block diagram of the same

169

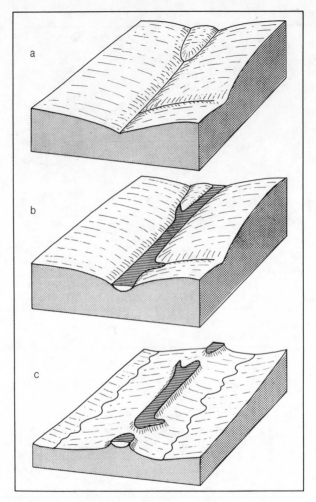

Figure 11.9 Inversion of relief

The area shown in figure 11.11 was originally drained by the Campaspe River, Victoria, which took most drainage, and by the small Coliban river in the north. The old courses can be traced from the deep leads. After the valleys were filled with lava, no tributaries from the west seemed able to cross the basalt to join the Campaspe; they were diverted north as a lateral stream, and eventually joined the Coliban which became much larger and cut deeply through its lava. The Campaspe, deprived of its tributaries, failed to cut down very much and still flows over the basalt in most of its upper reaches, occasionally crossing on to bedrock.

Lava diversion and stream incision may be repeated many times in areas of continuing volcanic activity, as exemplified by the Snake River in

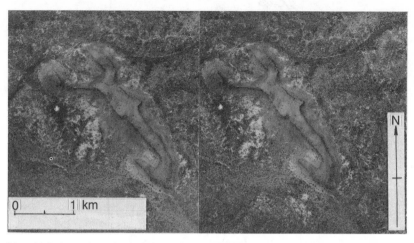

Plate 11.1 Inversion of relief. Stero-pair showing the basalt-capped El Capitan, near Cobar, New South Wales, Australia which was originally a valley flow (Crown copyright. Courtesy of the Director of National Mapping, Department of National Mapping, Canberra)

Plate 11.2 Inversion of relief, Cima volcanic field, Mojave Desert, California, USA. 0.67 m.y. vent and flow overlying weakly indurated mid-Tertiary gravels (J. Dohrenwend)

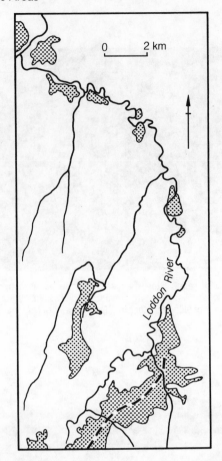

0   2 km

Loddon River

Figure 11.10 Deep lead (dash line) and lava residuals, showing drainage modifications on the Loddon River, Victoria, Australia

southern Idaho. The Snake River first cut a canyon at least 30 m deep. Then came the Malad basalt, entirely filling the canyon for at least 16 km of its length and displacing the river south-westwards. The river then cut a canyon about 70 m deep, which was interrupted by the outpouring of the Thousand Springs basalt and further displacement to the south-west. The next canyon was eroded to a depth of over 170 m and then blocked by three further flows. The river flowed around the south-west of the latest barrier, and tumbled back into its old course at Thousand Springs.

The many changes in drainage that accompany volcanic action and the repeated damming and downcutting of rivers leads to the formation of many alluvial and lacustrine terraces. When a diverted stream falls back into its old channel the sudden decrease in gradient causes deposition of an

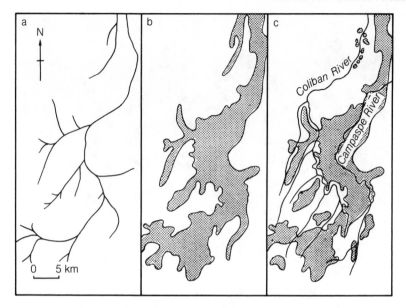

Figure 11.11 Drainage modifications of the Campaspe River, Victoria, Australia (a) original drainage as indicated by deep leads (b) maximum extent of lava (c) present-day drainage

alluvial fan, which is itself destroyed as the river continues its vertical erosion.

Basalt often gives rise to very steep, frequently vertical slopes, because it is hard rock and commonly has vertical joints. Where a stream leaves a basalt flow or sheet there is often a waterfall (see plate 11.3). The edges of lava plateaus frequently stand out as vertical escarpments, especially where the underlying material is softer sedimentary rock. Vertical jointing in other igneous rocks – agglomerate, dolerite, and the welded zone of ignimbrites for instance, can give rise to similar escarpments.

Basalt sheets are often superimposed one upon another, with zones of weathering, alluvial deposition, or pyroclastic deposits in between. In this case the interbedded soft material is a line of weakness attacked by erosion, spring sapping, and undercutting. The landscape comes to look like a series of giant steps, each flow producing a steep escarpment and a flat top. A splendid example of stepped topography is provided by Mount Elgon on the Kenya-Uganda border. It consists very simply of a series of thick, horizontal agglomerate flows separated by ash bands, and each ash band crops out at the foot of a steep cliff in agglomerate. Step topography is known as 'treppen' in German, from which comes the word 'trap', once used to mean basalt, as in the Deccan Traps. Many eroded lava plains or flows often retain a flat top making typical mesas and buttes capped with basalt.

173

Plate 11.3 Waterfall at the edge of a basalt flow, Campaspe River, Victoria, Australia (C. D. Ollier)

The many joints in basalt render it permeable and springs emerge at the base where it overlies impermeable bedrock. These springs erode head-words, and in the Snake River region give rise to typical 'alcoves', vertical-sided, round-ended side valleys, at the head of which issues a large spring (see figure 11.12). Similar sapping occurs round many lava sheets in other parts of the world, but is seldom so spectacular.

Valleys in lava plains are commonly modified by landslides. In Iceland, where landslides (mainly slumps and rock slides) are particularly common, they attain dimensions of up to 2 km broad, and most of them appear to be about 9000 years old. In most valleys there is some initial dip on the layers of plateau basalt exposed on valley walls, and landslides are confined to the side of the valley where the layers dip towards the valley. The slides have typical cirque-like scars, and moraine-like debris heaps of up to 70 m thick. It seems that initial valleys were cut by water erosion, and then glacial erosion over-steepened the valley sides. When the ice melted the unstable valley sides collapsed, possibly triggered by earth movements of post-glacial isostatic uplift. Landslides and avalanches are found in Hawaii, but are not as common as might perhaps be expected from the steep slopes. The relative stability is largely due to the low angles of dip of the beds and the scarcity of slippery ash beds and clays between lava beds.

The McPherson Range in the south of Queensland, Australia, consists largely of flat-topped spurs radiating to the north and separated by valleys

174

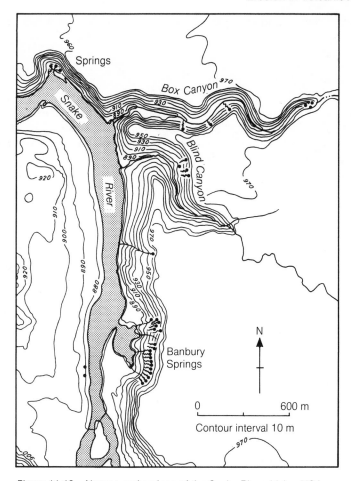

Figure 11.12 Alcoves and springs of the Snake River, Idaho, USA

which in some places are gorges some hundreds of metres deep. A feature of the physiography is the presence along the sides of these valleys of enormous old landslides now established by vegetation. Irregular terraces, more or less flat topped, have thus been formed at various levels (Stephenson et al., 1960).

The Tamar River, Tasmania, is an example of a river that closely follows its pre-basaltic course, and is superimposed on the basalt filling its old channel. As a result, the base of the basalt slopes downward towards the river on both sides of the valley. Columns tend to be normal to the base, and so are slightly overhanging. The downward slope of sheet jointing parallel to the base also helps to provide conditions extremely favourable for sliding. Failure takes place both by backward rotational sliding and by

175

forward toppling, and valley sides have widespread mantles of basalt fragments (Sutherland, 1966).

Erosion of Pyroclastic Deposits

There is a very marked differential erosion between the welded and non-welded parts of a pyroclastic flow. The welded zone is generally resistant to erosion and stands out as a prominent landscape feature, and the vertical jointing assists the general resistance to erosion in forming vertical cliffs. These may be undermined by the washing out of material from the underlying unwelded zone.

The unwelded parts of flows may weather to release silica solutions that can be reprecipitated at the ground surface causing case hardening; in other words a crust forms at the ground surface that is harder than the rock behind. In some areas, such as the Bandelier area of New Mexico, this gives rise to a 'Swiss cheese' effect, when the skin is broken at weak spots and the softer material behind removed to form cavities of up to cave size, possibly assisted by wind erosion.

A feature described from the New Mexico flows is the formation of tent hills, conical hills resembling wigwams. These are closely packed, and are in fact the interfluves between closely spaced gullies. Blocks in the ash may act as caprocks, and give rise to earth pillars, steep-sided columns of soft ash protected from erosion by a large rock on top. Well-known examples include The Pinnacles in Crater Lake National Park, USA, and the fields of huge earth pillars in Cappadocia in Turkey, famous for the villages, monasteries, and churches carved in them (see plate 1.3).

In New Zealand, thick pumice deposits produce a distinctive kind of scenery with well-rounded hills as seen in plate 11.4. When a welded zone is exposed, however, it gives rise to vertical cliffs of bare rock often following joint patterns. These are often found on mid-slopes, but in many places the upper pumice has been completely removed so that the welded ignimbrite makes a caprock. Here it gives rise to plateaus, mesas, and buttes very similar to those produced by basalt. However, these buttes seem to be able to withstand reduction to a very small size without collapse and to produce the ignimbrite tors, typical of parts of the North Island. A typical tor is shown in plate 11.5. It can be seen that no fallen columns of welded ignimbrite accumulate around the base of the tors; some are buried by later ash falls, but they presumably weather away much faster once they have fallen. Some tor topography may result from original variability in the welded zone, which can change rapidly over a short distance and is therefore susceptible to differential erosion.

In hard welded ignimbrites the valleys are steep-sided, and if narrow may be gorge-like. Where welding is not so intense, resistant slopes may have angles of about 30–35° and have a thin soil cover. These slopes often have

Plate 11.4 Rounded hills on eroded pumice deposits, near Lake Rotoiti, New Zealand (C. D. Ollier)

Plate 11.5 Ignimbrite tor. A small remnant of welded zone over rounded lower slopes on unwelded Mamaku ignimbrite, 25 km north-west of Rotorua, New Zealand (C. D. Ollier)

ribs of more resistant rock that look like dykes, but are usually the hardened rock formed along a cooling joint.

In the conversion of land into pasture in the pumic lands of central North Island the yellow-brown pumice soils lose their structure, become less able to retain moisture, runoff increases, and erosion is accelerated forming gullies of up to 25 m deep and 150 m long (Selby, 1966).

Gullies cut in the pumice are characterized by vertical headcuts and side-walls. They are commonly discontinuous in their early stages, each short length of gully having a very low fan at its downstream end. With time, such gullies coalesce to form continuous gullies (Blong, 1966).

Marine Erosion

Most of the normal coastal landforms can be produced on volcanic rocks. Hard rocks commonly produce cliffs, which can be especially steep and spectacular if there is vertical jointing, as on the Island of Staffa, Scotland, with the famous Fingal's Cave. Differential erosion of hard and soft volcanics can produce capes and bays, and intrusive plugs often give rise to steep-sided rock stacks. Shore platforms may be created, and are especially wide on pre-weathered basalt. Experimental evidence shows that basalt is considerably more soluble in sea water than in fresh water.

Marine erosion trims back an exposed volcano, making a cliff. Streams draining the volcano are cutting down their valley floors, but very often they cannot keep pace with marine erosion, so the valleys 'hang' over the coastal plain, and the streams descend at coastal waterfalls (see plate 11.6). If, for some reason, the coast is protected (as by eruption of new volcanoes at sea level), the descending streams may build up large, steep alluvial fans, as behind the settlement plains on Tristan da Cunha (Ollier, 1984a). Individual lava flows that reach the sea are rapidly trimmed back.

In time a volcano may be reduced to a tiny remnant of the original by marine erosion. The final shape will depend on the dominant direction of wave attack, and so on winds and currents, more than on volcanic structure (see plate 11.7).

Erosional Caves

Erosional caves in volcanic rocks are generally easy to recognize and pose no special problems. Sea caves are common, such as the celebrated Fingal's Cave, Scotland, which is typical of sea caves in columnar jointed lava. Some caves are enlarged where groundwater issues from springs in volcanic rock. Some volcanic caves are not quite so easy to interpret, such as the caves of Mt Elgon on the borders of Kenya and Uganda. These have some-times been attributed to human excavation, but Ollier and Harrop (1958)

Plate 11.6 Coastal erosion of a volcano. When marine erosion cuts cliff back faster than rivers can erode their beds, the rivers plunge to the sea in coastal waterfalls. Kohala Volcano, Hawaii. Rainfall along the 1000–1700 m high crest of this volcano (on the skyline) is about 5 m/y. (J. Dohrenwend)

believe they were formed by emergent springs washing out ash layers interbedded between resistant layers of volcanic agglomerate. Caves in acid rocks are rare, but an example is Gulemwawaya on Fergusson Island, Papua New Guinea, where suffosion has removed pumice from beneath a welded cave roof (Ollier, 1981). Small caves at Mt Gisborne, Victoria, Australia, have been described as 'fossorial' caves, meaning that they were burrowed out by animals long ago.

Rates of Erosion

Volcanoes provide some good opportunities for quantitative studies on rates of erosion.

Some rates can be determined by direct observation of processes on recently produced deposits. Others can be determined from a study of historically active volcanoes for which the date of eruption is known. For yet others it may be possible to determine the age of volcanic deposits by other means. The age may be determined stratigraphically, from the age of fossils found underneath the volcanics. For deposits of up to about 40,000 years old it is often possible to use carbon dating. It is not uncommon to find charcoal beneath volcanic deposits, charred by the volcanic heat, and this carbon can provide a date for the volcanic event itself. Vegetation

Plate 11.7 Ball's Pyramid, Lord Howe Island, New South Wales, Australia. This island, 551 m high with a base of 1.1 × 0.4 km is the erosional remnant of a volcano at least 6 km across. The island consists of almost level flows on a base of older lavas intruded by many dykes (C. D. Ollier)

carbonized by the most recent lava flow from Puy de la Vache, Auvergne, France, gave a date of 7650 ± 350 years. The eruption that produced the caldera of Crater Lake, Arizona, took place about 6600 years ago. Pyroclastics of Mt Gambier, South Australia, overlie carbon that gave a date of 6000 years, proving it to be the youngest volcano in Australia.

For older volcanoes the potassium/argon method may be used, and this method can be applied to whole rock samples. Potassium/argon dating can be applied to very old rocks and can be used on rocks as young as perhaps 20,000 yars, and to any age further back. Palaeomagnetism, fission track dating, and other methods are also available.

The rate of erosion immediately after an eruption can be found by direct observation. There do not appear to be any quantitative results available from such observations, but qualitative observations give some idea of the obviously rapid erosion rates in the early stages of dissection of newly deposited volcanic material. As an example, the erosion of deposits laid down by Barcena, Mexico, has been reported by Richards (1965). The eruption of Barcena started on 1 August 1952, and covered Isla San Benedicto with tephra. Until mid-September wind erosion was dominant, but then the first rain came, which formed a crust when the tephra dried out. The ash mantled pre-existing valleys, and later erosion caused gullies to appear, the formation of which can be dated

12 September 1952: there was no evidence of drainage on the island;
20 September 1952: a number of gullies were present, with irregular courses, and dry waterfalls of up to 10 m high;
May 1955: the gullies were now well established, with fairly smooth long profiles, and few waterfalls remained.

The rim of the crater also showed rates of erosion. It was at first a sharp, knife-like rim, and could only be traversed by straddling it up to December 1952, but by March 1953 it was well rounded. Tholoids appeared in the crater in November and December 1952, creating a V-sectioned fosse between the tholoid and the crater wall. By 1954 this had been filled in by erosion of the crater wall.

To obtain quantitative erosion rates, the original form of a landsurface, the present form, and the time that has elapsed between the two surfaces need to be known. Volcanoes have particularly simple original forms in many instances, and so provide an excellent starting point for such calculations.

A simple example is provided by the scoria cone Vulcan near Rabaul, New Guinea (Ollier and Brown, 1971). It is known that the volcano was originally smooth, and indeed much of the original surface is preserved. The cross-sectional area of all the gullies in a section is calculated, and if this is averaged out along the total length of the section, an average amount of surface lowering is obtained. In this instance the average amount of surface lowering was as much as 101 cm. The volcano erupted in 1937, and the survey was carried out in 1967, so this amount of lowering took 30 years.

Erosion rates are conventionally expressed in Bubnoff units, symbolized B. One Bubnoff unit is equivalent to 1 mm in 1000 years, or 1 m in a million years. The maximum rate for Vulcan works out at over 30,000 B. The average rate of erosion, world-wide, in mountainous country is 500 B, so the Vulcan has an extremely high rate. The result suggests that at the start of erosion the rate is very high and falls off later on.

A similar technique using a longer time scale has been used by Ruxton and McDougall (1967) to measure the rate of erosion of The Hydrographers, an andesitic strato-volcano in north-east Papua. This volcano is in a late planeze stage of dissection, and the original surface can be reconstructed for the eastern flanks by drawing generalized contours. The amount of ground lowering of concentric sectors was measured as the difference between the present cross-sectional areas of the sectors and the original cross-section. The volcano was dated by the potassium/argon method, and assuming an age of 650,000 (the youngest date obtained) for the beginning of dissection, denudation rates range from 80 B years at a relief of 60 m to 750 B years at a relief of 760 m. There is a linear correlation between the rate of denudation and the relief, the average maximum slope angle, and the average slope length. The range of variation is generally similar to that found on other rocks in similar climatic environments.

Rates of marine erosion can be measured on volcanic rocks, and provide interesting information on erosion rates on newly formed land masses, uncomplicated by previous geomorphic history. The eruption of Barcena, Mexico, extended the shoreline 275 m seaward between 1 and 11 August 1952 (Richards, 1965). Erosion then set in, and was at a rate of 90 cm/day between 11 August and 15 November. From then until 10 December the rate averaged 170 cm/day. In February 1953 a lava flow put an end to this rapid erosion, and provided a new datum for measuring erosion rates. Erosion of the flow between 16 April and 20 May was 21–46 cm/day, but by September the rate had dropped to 12 cm/day.

The speed with which erosion can reduce a volcano to a flat-topped shoal like a guyot has been demonstrated by many 'hide and seek' volcanoes. Grahams Island, which appeared between Sicily and Africa in 1931, was reduced very rapidly. Bogoslov in the Behring Sea has a long history of dome building and erosion. Falcon Island, Tonga, has a remarkable history of eruption and erosion, which may be summarized as follows:

1867	a new shoal reported;
1877	smoke seen to rise;
1885	an island appeared, and reached a height of 80 m;
1895	the island was reduced to 8 m in height;
1898	the island once more became a shoal;
1913	the shoal disappeared;
1927	renewed eruption, and a cone 100 m high built.

Volcanic activity may be sometimes useful in measuring erosion rates of neighbouring rocks. In the Massif Central, France, for instance, vulcanicity in Villafranchian times partially buried pre-existing topography and provided a datum to measure subsequent erosion. Slopes on crystalline rocks have retreated only a few metres, whereas calcareous marls are much dissected and have been lowered by about 100 m (Bout et al., 1960).

Another way to determine rates of erosion is to determine the rates of infilling of a sedimentary basins. If the catchment has remained the same, then changes in rates of sedimentation will correspond roughly to changes in rate of erosion. Pullar (1967) has used layers of volcanic ash and buried soils to date rates of infilling of the Gisborne Plains, New Zealand. As there are five different marker beds he was able to work out accumulation for five different periods, going back to 1400 BC as shown in table 11.1 below.

Table 11.1 Rate of accumulation of volcanic ash on the Gisborne Plains, New Zealand

Stage	Marker bed	Infilling rate (million m^3/year)
1932–1950	Matawhero soils	1.14
1820–1932	Matawhero friable soils	0.13
1650–1820	Waihirere soils	0.17
130–1650	Taupo pumice	0.11
1400 BC–AD 130	Waimihia lapilli	0.21

The rate of present sedimentation is 5–10 times that of previous stages and is attributed to accelerated erosion following large-scale deforestation at the time of European settlement. Sedimentation during stage 1650–1820 is attributed to catastrophic storm damage about 1650, and that during stage 1400 BC–AD 130 is attributed to tectonics shortly before the Taupo pumice eruptions.

12 Patterns of Volcanic Distribution

When the distribution of volcanoes is examined, either in detail or on the world scale, several significant patterns are revealed. Some result from local structural controls, and some relate to morphotectonics and earth evolution at the largest, global scale.

Lineaments

A lineament is a significant line in the earth's surface which is expressed topographically by valleys, ridges, or in the present case by lines of volcanoes. Aligned volcanoes immediately suggest fissures through which lava has emerged. In some instances there is observational proof that this is the case. Many fissure eruptions have started as a curtain of fire fissure eruption, of up to 22 km long. Usually, the fissure is reduced to a few points of eruption within a day, but the points remain on a line.

Lava shields are typically built over fissures, which are concentrated in narrow zones called rift zones. Most Hawaiian islands have two or three rift zones, from 100 m to 3 km wide. Rift zones are marked at the surface by lines of cinder cones, pit craters, lava cones, and open fissures. Working back from volcanic patterns to determine the underlying fracture patterns is not always easy, especially where there are many closely spaced volcanoes and a number of different lineaments can be inferred. Figure 12.1a shows a number of volcanoes in central Victoria, Australia and by experiment Ollier and Joyce (1964) found little agreement between the interpretations of different people. However, once the lineaments are drawn in as by Coulson (1953) the map (figure 12.1b) looks quite convincing. Such interpretations are always open to question, and it is a matter of judgement how far they should be pursued.

An interesting pattern was presented by Shand (1938) for the Galapagos Islands (see figure 12.2). The intersecting lineaments, possibly fissures, divide the crust of the earth into blocks. Shand reasons that these blocks have a distinctive size depending on the thickness of the crust. Just as in breaking a slab of chocolate or toffee, there is a smallest size that can be broken, approximately equal to the thickness of the slab, so one might

184

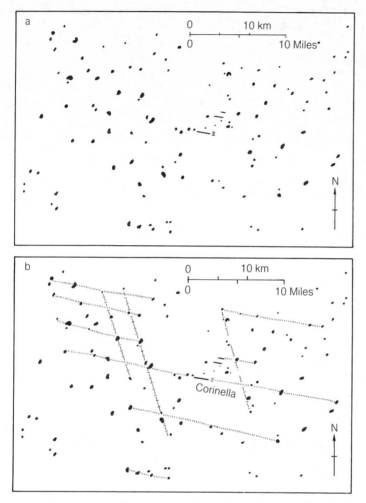

Figure 12.1 (a) volcanoes of central Victoria, Australia (b) lineaments of central Victoria (after Coulson, 1953)

conclude that the distance across the Galapagos blocks is approximately the same as the thickness of the earth's crust.

Volcanoes of Mexico fall in two lineaments. One is east–west, possibly an extension of the Clarion Fracture Zone, a zone of transverse faulting that can be traced for 3000 km into the Pacific. Popocatepetl, Colima, and Barcena (born 1952) are on this line. The second lineament is NNW to SSW parallel to the structural trend of the Mexican plateau, and Jorullo and Paricutin are on this line.

The Azores show three structural trends: a dominant east–west trend along one of the transverse zones; a pattern of concentric faults; and a

185

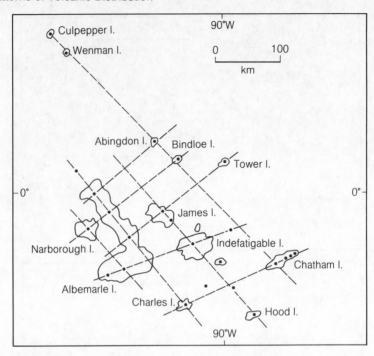

Figure 12.2   Spacing of Volcanoes in the Galapagos Islands

pattern of radial faults. Minor eruption centres often occur at the intersection of concentric and radial faults.

The Andes chain of volcanoes provides a remarkable example of a long chain of central volcanoes, which turns into a double chain north of 30 °S and has a gap between 8 ° and 18 °S for no known reason.

Although fault lines would seem to be likely lineaments for volcanoes to follow, volcanoes often fall a little to one side on either the upthrown or downthrown block. Along the fault bounding the Western Rift Valley in Uganda, for example, there are volcanoes both in the graben and on the upthrown block, but not actually on the line of the fault. Possibly the fault line is a zone of local shearing and compression, while on each side is a zone of slight tension.

The western volcanic district of Victoria, Australia, considered as a whole exhibits a similar pattern. Figure 12.3 shows that the Western Plains cover a relatively downwarped area, a Tertiary syncline. On the upthrown block there are many volcanoes, there are few volcanoes around the edge of the syncline, and there is another maximum along the deepest part of the syncline. No explanation so far has been offered for the occurrence of many volcanoes along the line of the syncline.

Distribution patterns may be accompanied by petrological and structural

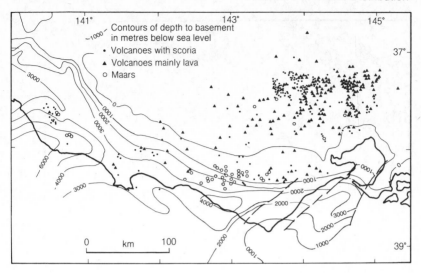

Figure 12.3 Distribution by type of volcanoes in south-eastern Australia, showing relation to basement contours (after Joyce, 1975)

contrasts among volcanoes within quite small areas. In Guatemala, there is a line of large, composite, andesite cones in the west, parallel to the coast, but in the east a scattered line of smaller, basaltic volcanoes (Williams and McBirney, 1964). The Cameroon line in West Africa consists of silicic volcanoes which erupted between 65 and 10 million years ago and basaltic volcanoes which erupted in large quantities only in the last 10 million years. The line is partly in the ocean (mainly basaltic) and partly on land where volcanism was accompanied by uplift of about 1 km. There is no regular trend in age along the line.

Global Patterns

Continents and Oceans

The active volcanoes of the world are shown on figure 12.4, and are related to distribution of earthquake activity (see figure 12.5). In order to explain that distribution it is necessary to consider other major features of the earth's crust.

The most obvious single feature is the division of the earth's surface into land and sea, continents and oceans. This is no mere accidental distribution, with water filling chance depressions on an otherwise continuous earth crust, but a reflection of a fundamental division between continents and oceans.

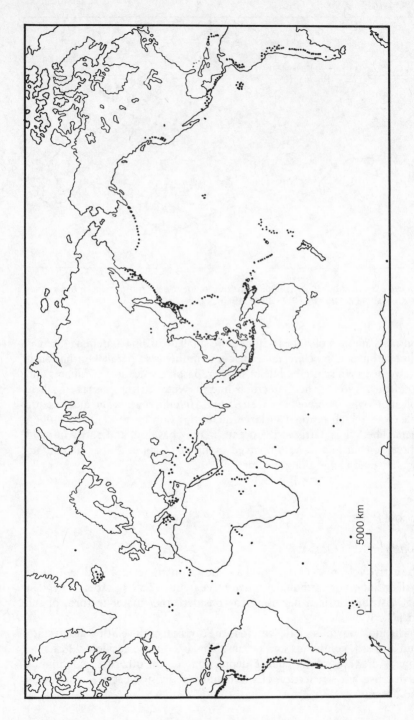

5000 km

Figure 12.4 Distribution of active volcanoes of the world

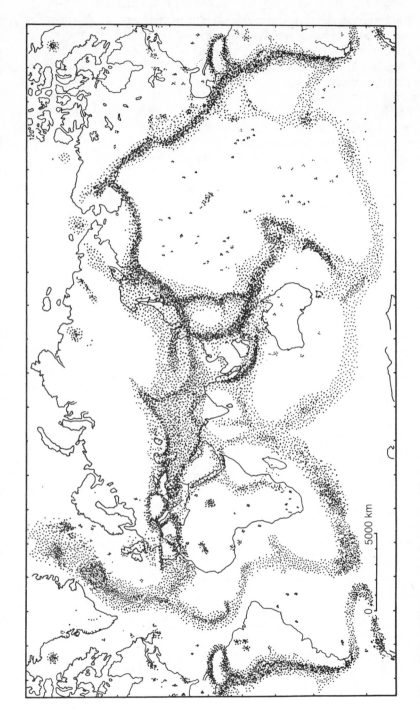

Figure 12.5   Distribution of earthquake activity

The continents are predominantly granitic in composition, and float like rafts on a layer of basalt which forms the solid surface beneath the oceans, and also underlies the continents (see figure 12.6). The granitic continents, consisting largely of silica and alumina, are said to form the sial layer: the basalt layer, rich in silica and magnesia, is part of a sima layer. The sial and sima together form the crust.

The base of the sima layer is marked by a sudden change in seismic velocities known as the Mohorivicic discontinuity (the Moho), which separates the crust from the mantle. The Moho may mark a change in chemical composition, or a phase change (change in physical properties

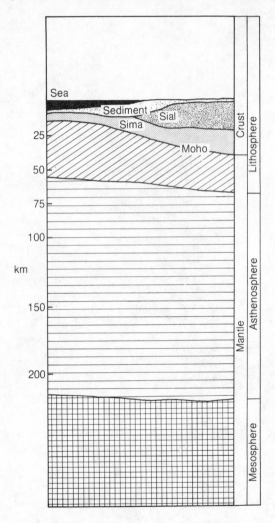

Figure 12.6 Layers in the earth's crust and mantle

without a change in chemistry, as from basalt to peridotite). An important layer from about 50 km to 250 km is the asthenosphere, or low-velocity layer, which underlies both continent and ocean. This layer is thought to be relatively plastic, and so is important in large scale movements of the rigid lithosphere above.

Pure oceanic volcanoes are almost entirely basaltic, being derived directly from the sima basalt. Continental volcanoes may be of all kinds: basaltic if deep-seated basalt manages to reach the surface without contamination, or various kinds of intermediate or acid rocks either if basalt is contaminated by admixture with continental rocks, or if a magma is produced by actual melting of continental rocks.

Around the Pacific it is possible to draw a line called the Andesite Line (see figure 12.7) that separates the central area of basaltic volcanoes from the surrounding area characterized by highly explosive andesitic volcanoes. The Pacific is ringed by volcanoes as well as having numerous volcanic chains in mid-ocean. Of the approximately 450 volcanoes that have been

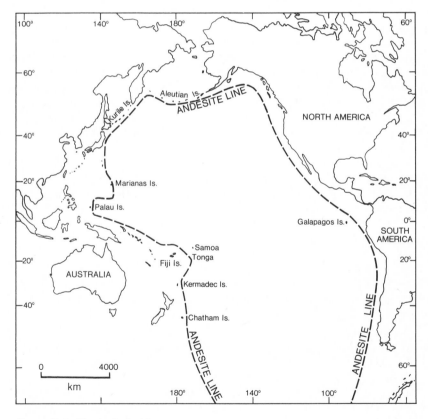

Figure 12.7 The Andesite Line

191

active in historical times, about 350 are in the Pacific hemisphere and of about 2500 recorded eruptions, over 2000 took place in the Pacific.

Plate Tectonics

Not only are continents different from oceans, but some of them have shapes which suggest that they may fit together like pieces of a jig-saw puzzle, a suggestion that is often reinforced by geological and bio-geographical considerations. Earlier in this century these features were explained by the hypothesis of continental drift, which was generally regarded as very improbable by most earth scientists. A series of discoveries in the 1960s led to its widespread acceptance in a new form known as Plate Tectonics.

In brief, it was found that there are major lines in the ocean, such as the Mid-Atlantic Ridge, from which the new sea floor is generated. Older ocean floor moves away from the ridge to make space, so the youngest sea floor is at the ridge, the oldest is furthest away. In fact there is no ocean floor anywhere on Earth which is older than about 200 million years. The continents move aside as the seafloor spreads. Thus, as the North Atlantic Ocean was created by seafloor spreading, Europe and America drifted apart; as the Southern Ocean was created by seafloor spreading, Australia and Antarctica drifted apart. But if the Atlantic Ocean is growing, the Pacific should be shrinking, as Eurasia and the Americas drift towards the Pacific from both sides. However the Pacific is itself spreading from the Pacific Rise. How can this happen? The answer lies in subduction, in which some of the earth's crust is consumed by moving under another part of the crust when two moving pieces of crust collide.

In plate tectonic theory the earth is seen to consist of a number of 'plates' bounded by spreading sites and subduction sites (see figure 12.8). Most of the 'action' takes place at the edges of plates. Examples are the distribution of earthquake activity (see figure 12.5) and the distribution of volcanoes (see figure 12.4). There is only one kind of spreading site but there are several kinds of collision site, many of them associated with volcanoes.

Spreading Sites

Running down the centre of both the North and South Atlantic Ocean is a ridge, submarine for most of its length. Iceland may be considered as an emergent portion of the ridge and so offers clues as to its nature. The island is traversed by a rift zone of young volcanic rocks which runs between areas of Tertiary plateau basalt. However, the neo-volcanic zone is quite wide and sinuous, and eruptions take place over a wider area than the central part of the ridge. The Atlantic Ridge is remarkably situated half-way between opposing land masses, and so is sometimes known as a mid-ocean ridge. The ridge is, however, only part of a world-wide system of ocean ridges,

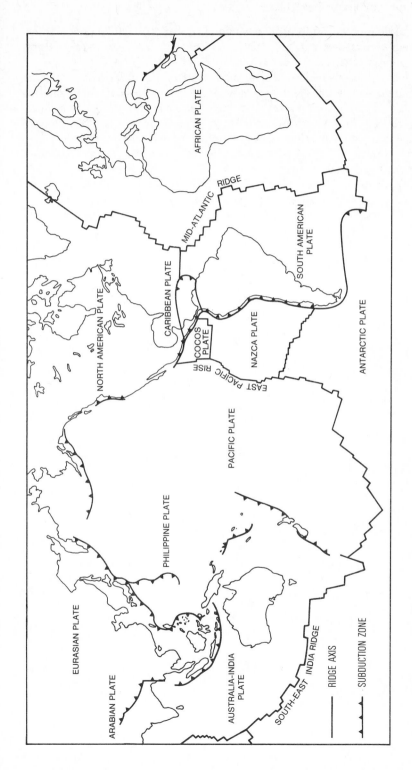

Figure 12.8 The major plates, ridges and subduction zones of plate tectonics

and although many appear to be equidistant from pairs of landmasses, the system breaks down in the Pacific, so the term mid-ocean ridge is not always appropriate.

One hypothesis is that volcanoes originate on the mid-ocean ridge and then drift away with seafloor spreading (Wilson, 1963). Evidence from the Tristan da Cunha group shows the situation to be more complicated. Since Gough Island is 450 km from the ridge, Tristan 200 km and Nightingale and Inaccessible slightly less than 200 km from the ridge, there is every chance for them to show progressive change in age, but the repeated eruptions on every island make Wilson's hypothesis improbable.

Supporting evidence for the spreading of ocean floors comes from modern studies of palaeomagnetism. The earth's polarity has reversed many times in earth history as shown in figure 12.9. Work on ocean ridges has revealed that this same pattern is found symmetrically on each side of

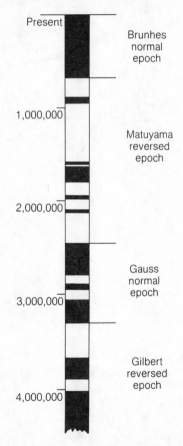

Figure 12.9 Reversals of the earth's magnetic field over the past 4 million years. Black is normal polarity, white is reversed polarity

the ridge (see figure 12.10), suggesting that new basalt has been injected at the centre, taking on the polarity prevailing at the time, and then drifted away to be replaced by a new line of injected basalt. By dating the rocks (by the potassium/argon method) and measuring the distance apart of corresponding bands of sea floor, it is even possible to work out the rate of ocean floor spreading.

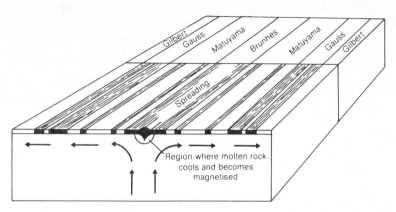

Figure 12.10 Seafloor spreading, showing symmetry of magnetic signature on the sea floor

Magnetic patterns over the Pacific ridge suggest that the Pacific expanded at 4.5 cm/year for ten million years, making a total of 45 km of movement. This may be compared with 1–2 cm/year for the North Atlantic and 2–3 cm/year for the South Atlantic and the Indian Ocean.

Several ocean ridges tend to be equidistant between landmasses, but some, like the Carlsbad Ridge in the Indian Ocean heads right into land. The Carlsbad Ridge is continuous with the Red Sea. Geophysical work has shown that the Red Sea has a high positive gravity anomaly, and is probably floored by sima. The Red Sea may represent a very early stage of ocean spreading when sima has reached the surface, but the land masses have only just started to drift apart. The continuation of the same line into the ocean marks the line from which India and the Horn of Africa have drifted. The Red Sea rift is accompanied by vulcanicity in neighbouring land areas.

Another branch of the system can be traced through Abyssinia into the rift valley system of Africa. The rift valleys are long fault troughs (grabens) with fault movement of several thousand metres. The fault troughs are filled with great thicknesses of sediment so they have a negative gravity anomaly (unlike the Red Sea), and the rift valleys may mark an even earlier stage in the dismemberment of continents. They are accompanied by vulcanicity, of basic type but different from oceanic basalt in being of alkaline rather than of calc-alkaline suites. The basalts of the Columbia River

195

volcanic province are possibly related to a spreading site under the western USA.

Triple Junctions and Aulacogens

If a flat plate is pushed up in the middle a dome may form, which will tend to crack in a Y-shaped pattern. Triple junctions are the Y-shaped junctions where three plates came together, and where three spreading sites join. New plate boundaries are commonly associated with triple junctions, but in many instances two arms become dominant and the third dies out. The 'failed arm' is called an aulacogen.

Figure 12.11 shows the break-up of the Atlantic interpreted in terms of

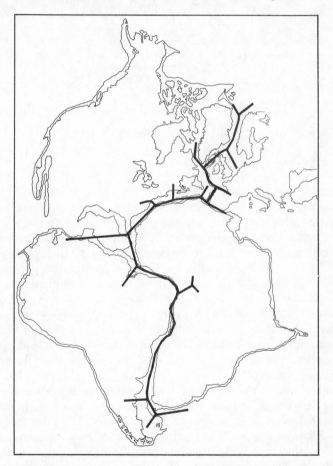

Figure 12.11 Triple junctions around the Atlantic. Most rifts are part of the major separation between America and Europe-Africa, but the failed arms are preserved on the continents as aulacogens

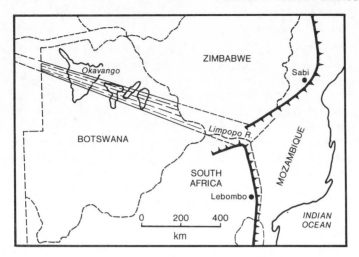

Figure 12.12 The Limpopo aulacogen, followed by a dyke-swarm. The other limbs are the Sabi and Lebombo monoclines (after Reeves, 1978)

triple junctions. An aulacogen is shown in figure 12.12, and is followed by a dyke swarm.

Hot Spots

In the Pacific there is another pattern of volcanic distribution, first discovered by Chubb (1957), which may have some bearing on ideas of sea-flooring spreading. Many Pacific volcanoes have a linear arrangement and there is a progressive change in age along the line. Thus in the Hawaiian Islands the most active vulcanicity is to the east on the island of Hawaii itself. The centre of activity appears to be still moving and there are active submarine volcanoes further east. To the west of Hawaii are older islands which are extinct volcanoes. These show progressively more erosion and subsidence, with drowned valley coasts. Fringing coral reefs come in next and beyond the chain of volcanic islands there are coral atolls further to the west built on volcanoes now sunk below sea level.

These observations fully support Darwin's theory of atoll formation by simultaneous coral growth and subsidence. Each volcano in turn appears to move through a sequence of eruption, erosion, coral growth, and subsidence.

Island chains are explained in plate tectonics as the result of an oceanic plate passing over a hot spot fixed in the mantle, which results in periodical eruptions. The rate of migration of the islands matches the rate of sea floor spreading, and the direction of the island chain matches the direction of movement of the plate.

Collision Sites

Andes Type Subduction   This is typified by the plate junction on the west of the southern half of South America. The sea floor is thought to be thrust down under the continental plate, the site being marked by a deep trench just off the continent. The down-going slab melts to produce andesitic magma which is intruded and erupted as andesitic volcanoes. The course of the slab's downward progress is marked by a series of earthquakes which get deeper away from the ocean, making an inclined zone of earthquakes called the Benioff zone. The continental edge is uplifted to form mountains (the Andes).

Island Arc Subduction   Off the east coast of the Asian mainland there are many islands arranged in festoons, convex to the east. These are the so-called island arcs (see figure 12.13) which run from the Aleutians, through Kamchatka, the Kuriles, Japan, etc., to New Guinea. In the Aleutians the simplest kind of arc is found. In Indonesia there are complicated double arcs.

The American coast of the Pacific does not have island arcs, but two notable arcs appear to have been pushed from the Pacific beyond the

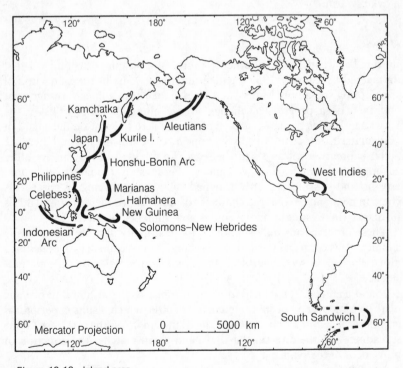

Figure 12.13   Island arcs

American continents. These are the Caribbean arcs and the South Sand-wich Island arc.

Island arcs are the site of many large deep-seated earthquakes, and a Benioff zone dips towards the continent at 30–35°, to depths of 700 km, that is, one-tenth of the earth's radius. The plate tectonics explanation for this is that Benioff zones are major fault planes, and movement along them causes earthquakes, pushes the continent towards the ocean (or the ocean under the continent) and topographically gives rise to the arc (see figure 12.14). The ocean floor is thought to be subducted under the arc, but the arc is separated from the continent by a back-arc basin, which is itself a spreading site. Geometrical considerations show that a plane surface at the angle of dip determined from earthquake plots would intersect the earth's curved surface in a much broader arc than the island arcs actually have. To account for the curvature of the arcs one must presume that the fault planes or Benioff zones are actually parts of conic surfaces. On the outside of island arcs the greatest ocean depths are found, rather suggesting that the ocean is being dragged or pushed down.

Volcanoes are active on many arcs. They are usually andesitic, and often violent as at Krakatau and Mont Pelée. Volcanoes tend to make a petro-logical series across island arcs, with more alkaline volcanoes (more potassium rich) to the back. There may also be a correlation of magma type with depth to the Benioff zone. Several mechanisms have been suggested to derive the different types, including contamination of basaltic parent material with siallic crust or sediment; differentiation of a primary magma; or partial melting of oceanic crust or its high pressure equivalent. For further details see Ollier (1981) and Aramaki and Kushiro (1983).

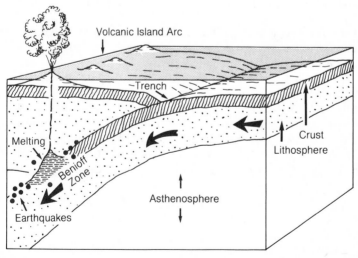

Figure 12.14 Diagram of plate tectonic explanation of subduction, the Benioff zone, and volcanoes

Other Types of Plate Collision

(1) Continent–continent collision. If two continental plates collide they may make a plate of extra thickness, and perhaps mountains. The Himalaya mountains are thought by some to be formed by collision of India and Asia. Such zones are generally devoid of volcanoes.

(2) Continent–ocean collision. In a few places ocean floor is thought to have been thrust over continent. In Papua New Guinea a slab of rock with structure and composition like oceanic crust forms the Papuan Ultramafic Belt. The Troodos Mountains of Cyprus are another example.

(3) Ocean–ocean collision. The Scotia arc seems to be formed by collision between a projection of the Pacific into the Atlantic, the contact being marked by a trench, earthquake zone and active volcanoes. The Caribbean arc is similar.

(4) Arc–arc collision. Two pre-existing arcs may collide, an example being the Philippines.

Volcanoes and Earthquakes

Both volcanoes and earthquakes tend to occur on plate boundaries, both spreading and collisional, but there are also some ultra-plate volcanoes.

To a large extent the patterns of distribution of volcanoes and earthquakes coincide, and indeed observation of earthquakes and tremors is one of the main tools the vulcanologist uses to predict eruptions. There are, however, some notable exceptions where vulcanicity and earthquakes do not occur together, as can be seen by comparing figure 12.7 and figure 12.8.

The circum-Pacific belt is followed by both earthquakes and volcanoes, as are the island arcs. The ocean ridges and the rift valleys are also lines of volcanic eruption and earthquake activity. Another notable earthquake zone is the Mediterranean area. The Himalaya may be an area where the Asian block overlies the Indian block, and this double thickness of crust is too great for penetration by ascending magma.

Antarctica is remarkably devoid of earthquakes, yet does have a small amount of vulcanicity, notably the active Mt Erebus. Some major eruptions, such as that of Coseguina in Nicaragua in 1835, appear to have taken place with little or no forewarning from earthquake activity.

13　Volcanic Rocks

Volcanoes differ from other landforms because they are built up of liquid ejected from deep below the earth's surface which cools to form new rock. The landforms are controlled to a large extent by the kind of volcanic rock involved. The correlation between rock type and landform is indeed so great that it is impossible to understand volcanic physiography without some knowledge of volcanic rocks. This chapter presents a simple outline of volcanic petrology and explains the rock terms used earlier in the book.

Igneous rocks are those that have cooled from a molten state, and the igneous rocks produced by volcanoes are often referred to loosely as 'volcanics'. The molten parent material is called magma which becomes lava when it erupts at the earth's surface. Magma and lava are not quite synonymous because gases (the volatile constituents) dissolved in the magma tend to be lost from the lava. Magma is volcanic material before separation into solid, liquid, and gas phases. The term lava is also commonly applied to the rock formed when liquid lava cools.

The classification of volcanic rocks is not standard, and there is still considerable disagreement amongst igneous petrologists (geologists who study igneous rocks) on the basis of classification and the terms to be used. The following statements provide a simple guide.

One classification uses the proportions of light- and dark-coloured minerals in the rock to give the felsic (light), intermediate, and mafic (dark) groups.

Another system is based on the amount of silica in the rock. Those rich in silica may be termed 'siliceous', but more commonly magmas with 66 per cent or more silica are called acid, and give rise to acid lavas and acid rocks. Intermediate rocks have 66–52 per cent silica. Rocks with 52–45 per cent silica are called basic rocks. Ultrabasic rocks have less than 45 per cent silica. This terminology is apparently based on the erroneous premise that SiO_2 reacts with H_2O to form acid, and it must be stressed that silica-rich rocks are not acid in the common sense of the term.

A related concept is that of 'saturated' rocks. A lava with insufficient silica has no quartz, as the silica is used in the crystallization of silicate minerals. An oversaturated lava, having formed its silicate minerals has silica left over which crystallizes as quartz. When a magma cools it crystallizes and a number of different minerals are formed.

Quartz, a mineral made of SiO_2, is commonly present in acid and some intermediate rocks. The total amount of silica in a rock is not necessarily reflected in the amount of quartz present, and rocks with quartz contents as different as 0 per cent and 35 per cent may have the same total amount of silica. The feldspars, which are complex alumino-silicates, are an important mineral group. The *plagioclase* feldspars are a continuous series of minerals varying in composition between two end members – *albite*, the sodium feldspar and *anorthite*, the calcium feldspar. The variation is shown in figure 13.1.

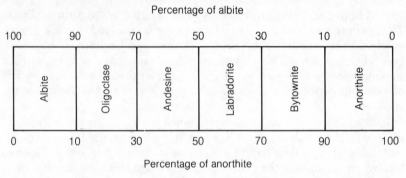

Figure 13.1 Composition of the plagioclase feldspar series

Oligoclase and *and andesine* are common in intermediate lavas, *labradorite* is common in basalts. Potassium-rich feldspars include *orthoclase* and *microcline*. A variety of orthoclase called sanidine is the dominant potash feldspar in volcanic rocks.

Corresponding to the feldspars, but with less silica in the mineral structure, are the *feldspathoids*. These are not found in acid rocks. *Nepheline* is the sodium feldspathoid, and *leucite* is the potassium one.

The *mica* group of minerals are also alumino-silicates. The two main minerals in the mica group are *muscovite* which is potassium rich, and *biotite* which contains magnesium and iron as well as potassium in its crystal structure.

The *ferro-magnesian* minerals are rich in iron and magnesium and include *biotite*, *pyroxenes*, *amphiboles*, and *olivine*. *Augite* is the commonest pyroxene and *enstatite* and *hypersthene* are fairly common.

Hornblende is the commonest amphibole. *Olivine* has less silica than pyroxenes or amphiboles, and only occurs in basic and ultrabasic rocks. The opaque minerals *magnetite* (Fe_3O_4) and *ilmenite* (Fe Ti O_3) occur in small quantities in volcanic rocks. Figure 13.2 shows the proportions of minerals in common igneous rocks. Another feature used to classify rocks is

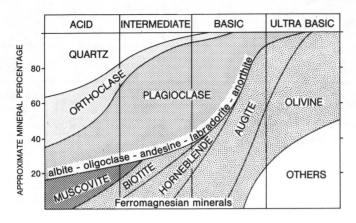

Figure 13.2 Mineral composition of common volcanic rocks

the texture, which refers mainly to the grain size, that is the size of individual mineral grains in the rock. Subdivisions include:

Glassy;
fine-grained (<1 mm);
medium-grained (1–5 mm);
coarse-grained (>5 mm);
poryphyritic (mixed, with some coarse grains (phenocrysts) in a finer-grained matrix).

The texture reflects the cooling history of the lava. If it cools slowly large mineral grains may form; if it cools quickly only small grains will form; if it cools very rapidly (as when quenched by entering water) no minerals form and a glass results. In porphyries the large crystals reflect an earlier episode of slow cooling followed by more rapid cooling when the fine-grained groundmass crystallized.

Another textural term is vesicular, referring to the property of having vesicles, formed by glass bubbles. Pyroclastic rocks have their own set of distinctive fragmental textures.

Table 13.1 summarizes igneous rock textures. The mineral composition and texture provide the basis for a simple classification of igneous rocks shown in table 13.2.

With lavas, the main concern is with fine-grained rock, of which basalt and andesite are of major importance. Most 'rhyolite' is in face ignimbritic, and not simply derived by cooling of liquid lava, as explained in chapter 7.

Amongst the intermediate rocks, the feldspar type is used as the basis for distinguishing different varieties. Andesite and diorite have potash feldspar making up less than one-third of the total feldspar content. In trachytes and syenites, potash feldspar makes up over two-thirds of the total feldspar

Table 13.1 Igneous rock textures

Texture	Description	Interpretation	Rock examples
Coarse-grained (>5mm)	Grains clearly visible to naked eye	Relatively slow cooling, usually intrusive	Granite Gabbro
Fine-grained (<1mm)	Many grains not visible to naked eye	Relatively fast cooling; usually extrusive but may form in shallow intrusives or at chilled margins of plutons	Basalt Andesite
Porphyritic	Some grains coarse (phenocrysts) most grains fine (ground-mass)	Two cooling rates; phenocrysts crystalized more slowly than finer-grained groundmass	Porphyry
Glassy	No minerals formed	Extremely rapid cooling (quenching) at surface	Obsidian Tachylite
Vesicular	Porous, bubbles	Rapid surface cooling with release of gases	Pumice
Pyroclastic	Fragmental	Explosive eruption	Tuff

Table 13.2 Simple classification of igneous rocks

	Acid	Intermediate	Basic	Ultrabasic
Coarse-grained	Granite	Syenite Diorite	Gabbro	Periodotite
Medium-grained	Microgranite	Porphry	Dolerite	Monchiquite
Fine-grained	Rhyolite	Trachyte Andesite	Basalt	Limburgite
Glass	Obsidian Pitchstone Pumice	Pitchstone	Tachylite	

content. Between these two groups, but not shown on table 13.2, are trachyandesites and monzonites.

Basalts may be divided into several varieties. Those rich in olivine (more than 5 per cent) and augite are called olivine basalts. Tholeiitic basalts (tholeiites) are relatively poor in alkalies and high in silica: the groundmass is commonly glassy, or if crystallized, usually contains quartz. Alkali basalts are relatively rich in alkalis and low in silica, and contain alkali feldspar. An overwhelming proportion of all basalts are tholeiitic, including the great volume produced at ocean ridges, and some of the great volcanic provinces such as the Deccan of India and the Snake River province of the USA. Alkali basalt may be erupted from the same source as tholeiitic basalt, late in the sequence, but makes up only about one per cent of the total volcanic rocks produced. This sequence is common in Hawaii and other volcanic islands. Deep submarine eruptions may produce a basalt rich in sodium known as spilite. This often takes the form of pillow lava and is frequently associated with serpentine and chert.

Dolerite (called diabase in American literature) is the commonest intrusive igneous rock associated with volcanoes. Coarse-grained rocks are of little direct importance in vulcanology, being formed deep below the earth's surface, but they are of course related to eruptive igneous rocks.

The rock types discussed so far are the fairly common ones, but there are many other, rarer types. One that may be mentioned is carbonatite, an igneous rock composed mainly of the carbonate mineral calcite and containing little or no silica (Tuttle and Gittins, 1966). Carbonatites are mostly found in intrusive igneous rocks associated with ring complexes, but may be erupted as pyroclastics or as lavas (Dawson, 1964). In 1960 Oldoinyo Lengai, Tanzania, erupted a soda-rich carbonatite lava, virtually free from silica, which simulated in detail the features of normal lava flows, and took both pahoehoe and aa forms (Dawson, 1962). At El Laco volcano in Chile there are lava flows of up to 20 m thick consisting essentially of magnetite, Fe_3O_4, with pahoehoe surfaces (Parks, 1961). On Siretoko-Iosan volcano, Japan, a flow of molten sulphur was erupted from a steam vent and produced a flow 2 km long and 5 m deep (Watanabe, 1940).

Violent explosions may so break up erupting lava that it comes to rest as fragmental rocks rather than as more or less massive lava. Such fragmental rocks include volcanic ash, scoria, pumice, palagonite (an altered basaltic ash), and others, which are collectively known as pyroclastic rocks, or simply as pyroclastics. These are described further in chapters 6 and 7.

Formation of Igneous Rock Varieties

Differentiation

There are a number of mechanisms by which an originally uniform magma may be differentiated into fractions having different composition. The simplest mechanism is gravity separation of heavy minerals. Suppose a basalt magma starts to crystallize. The first mineral grains to crystallize will be olivine, and as these mineral grains are denser than the melt they will sink, producing an olivine-enriched magma at the base of the magma chamber and a more acid, olivine-depleted magma at the top. The material at the top of the chamber is virtually a fresh non-crystalline magma of different composition from the original, and will itself then continue to crystallize. Under favourable circumstances a variety of differentiates may be erupted at the surface from a single magma chamber giving rise to a series of related (comagmatic) rocks. The area in which such related rocks occur is called a petrographic province.

Assimilation

Magma reacts with the rocks that make up the wall and roof of the magma chamber. The bounding rocks may be merely altered by heat, subjected to chemical alteration (contact metamorphism), or even totally dissolved and assimilated by the magma. Assimilation of sandstone, for example, adds silica to the magma, making it more acid; feldspathoids would be converted to feldspars, olivine to pyroxene. Assimilation of dolomite or limestone by a trachytic magma could produce a leucite-bearing magma. This has been suggested as a possible origin of the leucitic rocks of the Mediterranean.

Anatexis

Complete melting of formerly solid rocks of the earth's crust to form a new magma is called anatexis. Anatexis would normally produce acid magmas.

Volcanic Rock Suites

Although neighbouring volcanoes may produce different lavas it has become clear that many areas are characterized by assemblages of related rocks known collectively as suites. Suites are characteristic of petrographic provinces in which certain rocks are frequently associated, and others are absent.

There are two main suites:

(1) *Calc-alkaline suite*. These rocks are relatively rich in calcium, and are also relatively acid rocks. Rhyolites and andesites are included in this suite but the commonest rock is basaltic andesite. The calc-alkaline suite is found in the volcanoes of island arcs and the Pacific borders of North and South America. Since these areas are associated with mountain building, this suite is sometimes called the 'orgenic' suite.

(2) *Alkaline suite*. These are basic rock, relatively rich in alkalis (especially sodium) ranging from nepheline-bearing rocks to olivine-basalt. This suite is also known as the 'non-orogenic' suite.

Current theories of plate tectonics place much emphasis on the distribution of these two main rock suites. To indulge in great over-simplification, the alkaline suite can be regarded as being derived by differentiation of primary basalt magma (sima), and the calc-alkaline suite as being formed by the melting of crustal rocks to form a magma (anatexis), followed by assimilation and differentiation.

This chapter gives only an elementary and incomplete account of volcanic rocks. For a fuller and more accurate account of rocks and their classification, reference should be made to standard books on petrology, such as those by Middlemost (1985); Nockolds et al. (1978); or Carmichael et al. (1974).

Further Reading

The scientific literature on volcanoes is scattered through a wide range of books and journals.

A gazetteer of all the world's volcanoes and their activity is: Simkin, T. et al. 1981: *Volcanoes of the world*. Stroudsburg, Pennsylvania: Smithsonian Institution, Hutchinson Ross.

The *Catalogue of the Active Volcanoes of the World*, published by the International Association of Volcanology, consists of a number of volumes, each devoted to a particular area, in which brief accounts of all volcanoes regarded as active are catalogued and described.

Standard books on volcanoes include:
Bullard, F. M. 1977: *Volcanoes of the Earth*. Austin: University of Texas Press.
Decker, R. and Decker, B. 1981: *Volcanoes*. San Francisco: Freeman.
Francis, P. 1976: *Volcanoes*. Harmondsworth: Penguin.
Macdonald, G. A. 1972: *Volcanoes*. Englewood Cliffs, NJ: Prentice Hall.

The only book mainly concerned with the geomorphology of volcanoes is: Cotton, C. A. 1944: *Volcanoes as Landscape Forms*. Christchurch: Whitcombe and Tombs.

There are now several books devoted to individual volcanoes, including:
Chester, D. K., Duncan, A. M., Guest, J. E. and Kilburn, C. R. J. 1985: *Mount Etna: The anatomy of a volcano*. Stanford: Stanford University Press.
Herbert, D. and Barnossi, F. 1968: *Kilauea: case history of a volcano*.
Simkin, T. and Fiske, R. S. 1983: *Krakatau 1883. The volcanic eruption and its effects*. Washington: Smithsonian Institute Press.
Tazieff, H. 1975: *Nyiragongo, the forbidden volcano*. London: Cassell.
Thorarinsson, S. 1969: *Surtsey, the new island in the North Atlantic*. London: Cassell.

Leading journals in volcanology are *Bulletin Volcanologique* (re-titled *Bulletin of Volcanology* since 1986) and *Journal of Volcanology and Geothermal Research*. A lighter but very worthwhile digest of up-to-date information is *Volcano News*, published privately by Chuck Wood, 320 East Shore Drive, Kemah, TX 77567, USA.

Other work is published in various journals of geology, geophysics and geography. Most work concerns volcanology and petrology, with smaller amounts on geophysics and geochemistry and very little on geomorphology. Articles on volcanic geomorphology can be traced through the relevant section of *Geo-Abstracts* (A) *Landforms and the Quaternary*, Geo-Abstracts, Norwich.

208

The Bibliography of Geology published by the Geological Society of America each year contains many abstracts of papers on volcanoes.

The main glossaries of geology which include definitions of many terms related to volcanoes are:

Bates, R. C. and Jackson, J. A. 1980: *Glossary of Geology*, 2nd edn, Falls Church, Virginia: American Geological Institute.
Green, J. and Short, N. M. (eds) 1971: *Volcanic Landforms and Surface Features*. New York: Springer-Verlag.

This book has a volcanic glossary (pp. 457–513) and photographic illustrations of most volcanic features.

References

Allen, J. R. L. 1982: *Sedimentary structures. Their Character and Physical Basis*. Vol. II, Amsterdam: Elsevier.

Aramaki, S. 1961: Classification of pyroclastic flows. *International Geological Review* **3**, 518–24.

Aramaki, S. and Kushiro, I. 1983: *Arc Volcanism*. Amsterdam: Elsevier.

Aramaki, S. and Yamasaki, M. 1963: Pyroclastic flows in Japan. *Bulletin volcanologique* **26**, 89–99.

Baker, P. E., Gass, I. G., Harris, P. G. and Le Maitre, R. W. The volcanological report of the Royal Society expedition to Tristan da Cunha, 1962. *Philosophical Transactions of the Royal Society of London, Series A* No. 1075, 256, 439–578.

Bates, R. C. and Jackson, J. A. 1980: *Glossary of Geology* (2nd edn), Falls Church, Virginia: American Geological Institute.

Benson, W. N. and Turner, F. J. 1940: Mugearites in the Dunedin District. *Transactions of the Royal Society of New Zealand* **70**, 188–99.

Bernstein, V. A. 1960: On magnetometric investigations in vicinity of volcanoes. *Bulletin volcanologique* **23**, 129–33.

Blong, R. J. 1966: Discontinuous gullies on the volcanic plateau. *Journal of Hydrology* **5**, 87–99.

Blong R. J. 1982: *The Time of Darkness. Local Legends and Volcanic Reality in Papua New Guinea*. Canberra: Australian National University Press.

Blong R. J., 1984: *Volcanic Hazards*. Sydney: Academic Press.

Blot, C. 1964: Origine profonde des seismes superficiels et des eruptions volcaniques. *Bureau Centrale Seismologique International* A23, 103–21.

Booth, B. and Fitch, F. 1979: *Earthshock*. New York: Walker & Co.

Bout, P., Derruau, M. and Fel, A. 1960: The use of volcanic cones and lava flows in the Massif Central to measure the recession of slopes in Crystalline rocks. *Zeitschrift fur Geomorphologie* Supp. **1**, 140–55.

Bozon, P. 1963: Contribution to the study of volcanic landforms in the Ardeche. *Review Geographique alpine* **51**, 591–647.

Branch, C. D. 1966: Volcanic cauldrons, ring complexes and associated granites in the Georgetown Inlier, Queensland. *Bulletin of the Bureau of Mineral Resources, Geology and Geophysics, Australia.* **76**.

Breed, W. J. 1964: Morphology and lineation of cinder cones in the San Franciscan volcanic field. *Museum of Northern Arizona Bulletin* No. **40**, 65–71.

Bucher, W. M. 1933: Cryptovolcanic structures in the United States. *Proceedings of the International Geological Congress* **2**, 1055–84.

Bullard, F. M. 1962: Volcanoes of Southern Peru. *Bulletin volcanalogique* **24**, 433–53.

Bullard, F. M. 1977: *Volcanoes of the Earth*. Austin: University of Texas Press.

Bulletin Volcanologique, **45**, 1982: *Special Issue on Volcanic Gases, Aerosols and Sublimates*.

Bulletin Volcanologique, **47**, 1984: *Special Issue on Bradyseismic crisis at Phlegrean Fields, Italy*.

Carey, S. W. 1958: The isostrat, a new technique for the analysis of the structure of the Tasmanian dolerite. *Dolerite Symposium*. Hobart: University of Tasmania.

Carey, S. W. 1976: The expanding earth. *Developments in Geotectonics* **10**, 1–488. Elsevier.

Carmichael, I. S. E., Turner, F. J. and Verhoogen, J. 1974: *Igneous Petrology*. New York: McGraw-Hill.

Carne, J. E. 1903: The kerosene shale deposits. N.S.W. Geological Survey. *Memoirs of the Geological Survey of New South Wales* No. 3, 236–40.

Chester, D. K. and Duncan, A. M. 1982: The interaction of volcanic activity in Quaternary times upon the evolution of the Alcantara and Simto Rivers, Mount Etna, Sicily. *Catena* **9**, 319–42.

Chivas, A. R., Barnes, I., Evans, W. C., Lupton, J. E. and Stone, J. O. 1987: Liquid carbon dioxide of magmatic origin and its role in volcanic eruptions. *Nature* **326**, 587–9.

Chubb, L. J. 1957: The pattern of some Pacific Island chains. *Geological Magazine* **94**, 221–8.

Cloos, H. 1941: Bau und Tatigkeit von Tuffschloten: Untersuchungen an dem Schwabischen Vulkan. *Geologische Rundschau* **32**, 709–800.

Colton, H. S. 1930: Lava squeeze-ups. *The Volcano Letters* **300**, 3.

Cook, E. F. 1966: Paleovolcanology. *Earth Science Reviews* **1**, 155–74.

Coombs, H. A. 1936: The geology of Mount Rainier National Park. *University of Washington Publications in Geology* **3** (2), 131–212.

Cotton, C. A. 1944: *Volcanoes as Landscape Forms*. Christchurch: Whitcombe and Tombs.

Cotton, C. A. 1962: The volcano tectonic theory of block faulting no longer tenable. *New Zealand Science Review* **20**, 48–9.

Coulson, A. 1953: The volcanic rocks of the Daylesford district. *Proceedings of the Royal Society of Victoria* **65**, 113–24.

Davies, K. A. 1952: The building of Mount Elgon. *Memoirs of the Geological Survey of Uganda* **7**.

Dawson, J. B. 1962: The geology of Oldoinyo Lengai. *Bulletin volcanologique* **24**, 349–87.

Dawson, J. B. 1964: Carbonatitic volcanic ashes in Northern Tanganyika. *Bulletin volcanologique* **27**, 81–91.

Decker, R. W. 1986: Forecasting volcanic eruptions. *Annals and Review of Earth and Planetary Science* **14**, 267–91.

Decker, R. W., Hill, D. P. and Wright, T. L. 1966: Deformation measurements on Kilauea volcano, Hawaii. *Bulletin volcanologique* **29**, 721–30.

Downie, C. 1964: Glaciations of Mount Kilimanjaro, north-east Tanganyika. *Bulletin of the Geological Society of America* **75**, 1–16.

Downie, C. and Wilkinson, F. 1962: The explosion craters of Basotu, Tanganyika Territory. *Bulletin volcanologique* **24**, 389–420.

Dulhunty, J. A. 1967: Mesozoic alkaline volcanism and Garrawilla lavas near Mullaley, New South Wales. *Journal of the Geological Society of Australia* **14**, 133–8.

Eaton, J. P. and Murata, K. J. 1960: How volcanoes grow. *Science* **132**, 925–38.

References

Edwards, A. B. 1941: The crinanite laccolith of Circular Head, Tasmania. *Proceedings of the Royal Society of Victoria* 53, 403–15.

Eichelberger, J. C., Carrigan, C. T., Westrich, H. R. and Price, R. H. 1986: Non-explosive silicic volcanism. *Nature* 323, 598–602.

Fernandez Caldas, E. and Yaalon, D. H. (eds) 1985: *Volcanic Soils: Weathering and Landscape Relationships of Soils on Tephra and Basalt.* Catena Supplement 7.

Finch, R. H. 1933: Block Lava. *Journal of Geology* 41, 769–70.

Fisher, R. V. 1966: Rocks composed of volcanic fragments and their classification. *Earth Science Reviews* 1, 287–98.

Fisher, R. V. and Schmincke, H. U. 1984: *Pyroclastic Rocks*. New York: Springer-Verlag.

Fitch, F. 1964: The development of the Beerenberg Volcano, Jan Mayen. *Proceedings of the Geologists' Association* 75, 133–65.

Franklin, J. M., Lydon, J. W. and Sangster, D. F. 1981: Volcanic-associated massive sulphide deposits. *Economic Geology* 75th Anniversary Volume, 485–627.

Gèze, B. 1964: Sur la classification des dynamismes volcaniques. *Bulletin volcanologique* 27, 237–57.

Gibbs, H. A. and Wells, N. 1966: Volcanic ash soils in New Zealand. *Bulletin volcanologique* 29, 669–70.

Greeley, R. 1971: Geology of selected lava tubes in the Bend Area, Oregon. *State of Oregon Department of Geology and Mineral Industries Bulletin 71.*

Greeley, R. and Hyde, J. H. 1971: Lava tubes of the Cave Basalt, Mount St Helens, Washington, *NASA Technical Memorandum, NASA TM X-62 022*, 33 pp.

Green, J. and Short, N. M. 1971: *Volcanic Landforms and Surface Features.* New York: Springer-Verlag.

Griggs, R. F. 1918: Scientific results of the Katmai expedition of the National Geographic Society: 1. The recovery of vegetation at Kodiak. *Ohio Journal of Science* 19, 1–57.

Griggs, R. F. 1921: Our greatest national monument. *National Geographical Magazine* 40, 219–92.

Gupta, H. K. 1980: *Geothermal Resources: an energy alternative*. Amsterdam: Elsevier.

Hatheway, A. W. and Herring, A. K. 1970: Bandera lava tubes of New Mexico, and lunar implications. *Communications of the Lunar and Planetary Laboratory* 8, 299–327.

Hay, R. L. 1960: Rate of clay formation and mineral alteration in a 4000-year-old volcanic ash soil on St Vincent, British West Indies. *American Journal of Science* 258, 354–68.

Heiken, G. and Wohletz, K. 1984: *Volcanic Ash*. California: University of California Press.

Heiken, G. 1982: Geology of geothermal systems. In: Edwards, L. M., Chillingar, G. V., Rieke, H. H. and Fertl, W. H. (eds) *Handbook of Geothermal Energy*, pp. 177–217. Houston: Gulf.

Hirschboeck K. K. 1980: A new worldwide chronology of volcanic eruptions. *Palaeogeography, Palaeoclimatology, Palaeoecology* 29, 223–41.

Holmes, A. 1965: *Principles of Physical Geology*. London: Nelson.

Hotz, P. E. 1952: Form of diabase sheets in south-eastern Pennsylvania. *American Journal of Science* 250, 375–88.

Hunt, C. B. 1938: A suggested explanation for the curvature of columnar joints in volcanic necks. *American Journal of Science* 236, 142–9.

Imbo, G. 1928: Variazions cicliche nella successione dei periodi di reposos Etnei. *Bulletin volcanologique* Nos. 15–18.

Iwasaki, I., Ozawa, T. and Yoshida, M. 1966: Differentiation of volcanic emanation around the boiling point of water in geothermal regions. *Bulletin volcanologique* 29, 517–27.

Jaggar, T. A. 1931: Volcanic cycles and sunspots. *The Volcano Letter* No. 326.

Kaizuka, S. 1965: Some problems of tephrochronology in Japan. *VII Conference of the International Association for Quaternary Research, Boulder Abstracts*.

Karapetian, K. I. 1964: Some regularities in areal volcanism. *Bulletin volcanologique* 27, 381–3.

Kear, D. 1957: Erosional stages of volcanic cones as indicators of age. *New Zealand Journal of Science and Technology* B38, 671–82.

Kennett, J. P. 1981: Marine tephrochronology. In: Emiliani, C. (ed.) *The Oceanic Lithosphere. The Sea*. New York: Wiley-Interscience.

King, B. C. 1949: The Napak area of southern Karamoja, Uganda. *Memoirs of the Geological Survey of Uganda* 5.

Kjartansson, G. 1940: Nyr hell i'r i Hekluhrauni, *Natturufraedingurinn* 19, 175–84.

Kjartansson, G. 1966: Sur la recession glaciaire et les types volcaniques dans la region du Kjolur sur le plateau centrale de l'Islande. *Revue de Geomorphologie Dynamique* 16, 23–39.

Korsch, R. 1982: Mount Duval: geomorphology of a near-surface diapir. *Zeitschrift fur Geomorphologie* 26, 151–62.

Kruger, P. and Otte, C. 1973: *Geothermal Energy*. Stanford: Stanford University Press.

Kuno, H., Ishikawa, T., Katsui, Y., Yagi, K., Yamasaki, M. and Taneda, S. 1964: Sorting out pumice and lithic fragments as a key to eruptive and emplacement mechanism. *Japanese Journal of Geology and Geography* 35, 223–38.

Lamb, H. H. 1971: Volcanic activity and climate. *Palaeogeography, Palaeoclimatology, Palaeoecology* 10, 203–30.

Langford-Smith, T. (ed.) 1980: *Silcrete in Australia*. Armidale, Australia: Department of Geography, University of New England.

Leavitt, S. W. 1982: Annual volcanic carbon dioxide emission; an estimate from eruption chronologies. *Environmental Geology* 4, 15–21.

Lewis, J. F. 1968: Tauhara volcano, Taupo Zone. I. Geology and structure. *New Zealand Journal of Geology and Geophysics* 11, 212–24.

Lipman, P. W. 1967: Mineral and chemical variations within an ash-flow sheet from Aso Caldera, southwestern Japan. *Contributions in Mineralogy and Petrology* 16, 300–27.

Lorenz, V. 1973: On the formation of maars. *Bulletin Volcanologique* 37, 183–204.

Luce, G. V. 1969: *The End of Atlantis*. London: Thames and Hudson.

McBirney, A. R. and Williams, H. 1965: Volcanic history of Nicaragua. *University of California Publications in Geological Science* 55, 1–65.

McCall, G. J. H. 1963: Classification of calderas – Krakatoan and Glencoe types. *Nature*, 197, 136–8.

McCall, G. J. H. and Bristow, C. M. 1965: An introductory account of Suswa Volcano, Kenya. *Bulletin volcanologique* 28, 333–67.

McCraw, J. D. 1967: The surface features and soil pattern of the Hamilton Basin. *Earth Science Journal* 1, 59–74.

Macdonald, G. A. 1953: Pahoehoe, aa, and block lava. *American Journal of Science* 251, 169–91.

Macdonald, G. A. 1962: The 1959 and 1960 eruptions of Kilauea volcano,

References

Hawaii, and the construction of walls to restrict the spread of lava flows. *Bulletin volcanologique* **24**, 249–94.

Macdonald, G. A. 1967: Forms and structures of extrusive basaltic rocks. In: *Basalts* (eds H. H. Hess and A. Poldervaart), pp. 1–61, New York: Wiley.

Macdonald, G. A. 1972: *Volcanoes*. Englewood Cliffs, N.J.: Prentice-Hall.

McKee, C. O., Johnson, R. W., Lowenstein, P. L., Riley, S. J., Blong, R. J., de Saint Ours, P. and Talai, B. 1985: Volcanic hazards, surveillance, and eruption contingency planning. *Journal of Volcanology and Geothermal Resources* **23**, 195–237.

Malin, M. C. 1980: Lengths of Hawaiian lava flows. *Geology* **8**, 306–8.

Marathe, S. S., Kilkarni, S. R., Karmarkar, B. M. and Gupte, R. B. 1980: Variations in the nature of Deccan Trap volcanicity in time and space. *Memoirs of the Geological Society of India* **3**, 143–52.

Markhinin, E. K. 1962: On the possibility of estimating the amount of juvenile water participating in volcanic explosions. *Bulletin volcanologique* **24**, 187–91.

Mathews, W. H. 1947: Tuyas, flat-topped volcanoes in North British Columbia. *American Journal of Science* **245**, 560–70.

Meinzer, O. E. (ed.) 1949. *Hydrology*. New York: Dover.

Menard, H. W. 1964: *Marine geology of the Pacific*. New York: McGraw-Hill.

Middlemost, E. A. K. 1985: *Magmas and Magmatic Rocks*. London: Longman.

Mohr, P. 1983: Ethiopian flood basalt province. *Nature* **303**, 577–84.

Moore, J. C. 1967: Base surge in recent volcanic eruptions. *Bulletin volcanologique* **30**, 337–63.

Moore, J. G. 1975: Mechanism of formation of pillow lava. *American Scientist* **66**, 551–9.

Morimoto, R. and Ossaka, J. 1964: Low temperature mud-explosion of Mt Yake. *Bulletin volcanologique* **27**, 49–50.

Moriya, I. 1978: Topography of lava domes, Komazawa *Chiri*. *Bulletin of the Department of Geography, Momazawa University, Japan* **14**, 55–69. In Japanese. Summary in *Volcano News* **15**, 4–6.

Murai, I. 1961: A study of the textural characteristics of pyroclastic flow deposits in Japan. *Bulletin of the Earthquake Research Institute, Tokyo University* **39**, 133–254.

Murata, H., Dondoli, C. and Saenz, R. 1966: The 1963–65 eruption of Irazu volcano, Costa Rica. *Bulletin volcanologique* **29**, 765–93.

Naum, T. R., Buntariu, E. and Giurescu, M. 1962: Volcanic karst in the Caliman Massif, Eastern Carpathians. *Anals of the University of Bucaresti. Series Stiint National Geology and Geography* **32**, 143–79.

Neumann van Padang, M. 1963: The temperature in the crater region of some Indonesian volcanoes before the eruption. *Bulletin volcanologique* **26**, 319–36.

Newell, R. E. and Walker, G. P. L. (eds) 1981: Volcanism and climate. *Journal of Volcanology and Geothermal Resources* **11**, 1–92.

Newhall, C. G. and Self, S. 1982: The Volcanic Explosivity Index (VEI): an estimate of explosive magnitude for historical volcanism. *Journal of Geophysical Research* **87**, 1231–8.

Nichols, R. L. 1936: Flow units in basalt. *Journal of Geology* **44**, 617–30.

Nichols, R. L. 1939: Squeeze-ups. *Journal of Geology* **47**, 421–5.

Ninkovich, D. and Heezen, B. C. 1965: Santorini tephra. In: eds W. F. Whittard and R. Bradshaw, *Submarine Geology and Geophysics*. pp. 413–52, London: Butterworths.

Noguchi, K. and Kamiya, H. 1963: Prediction of volcanic eruption by measuring the chemical composition and amounts of gas. *Bulletin volcanologique* **26**, 367–78.

Nockolds, S. R., Knox, R. W. O'B. and Chinner, G. A. 1978: *Petrology for Students*. Cambridge: Cambridge University Press.

Oba, Y. 1966: Geology and petrology of Usu volcano, Hokkaido, Japan. *Journal of the Faculty of Science, Hokkaido University* Series IV, **13**, 185–236.

Ollier, C. D. 1964a: Tumuli and lava blisters of Victoria, Australia. *Nature* **202**, 1284–6.

Ollier, C. D. 1964b: Caves and related features of Mount Eccles. *Victorian Naturalist* **81**, 64–71.

Ollier, C. D. 1967a: Landforms of the Newer Volcanic Province of Victoria. In: J. N. Jennings and J. A. Mabbutt (eds) *Landform Studies from Australia and New Guinea*. Canberra: Australian National University Press.

Ollier, C. D. 1967b: Maars. Their characteristics, varieties and definition. *Bulletin volcanologique* **31**, 45–73.

Ollier, C. D. 1981: Gulemwawaya: a cave in welded tuff at Budoya, Fergusson Island, Papua New Guinea. *Helictite* **19**, 33–4.

Ollier, C. D. 1982a: The Great Escarpment of eastern Australia: tectonic and geomorphic significance. *Journal of the Geological Society of Australia* **29**, 13–23.

Ollier, C. D. 1982b: Geomorphology and tectonics of the Dorrigo Plateau, N.S.W. *Journal of the Geological Society of Australia* **29**, 431–5.

Ollier, C. D. 1984a: Geomorphology of the South Atlantic Volcanic Islands, Part I: The Tristan da Cunha Group. *Zeitschrift fur Geomorphology* **28**, 367–82.

Ollier, C. D. 1984b: Geomorphology of the South Atlantic Volcanic Islands, Part II: Gough Island. *Zeitschrift fur Geomorphology* **28**, 393–404.

Ollier, C. D. 1985: Lava flows of Mount Rouse, Western Victoria. *Proceedings of the Royal Society of Victoria* **97**, 167–74.

Ollier, C. D. and Brown, M. C. 1965: Lava caves of Victoria. *Bulletin volcanologique* **28**, 215–30.

Ollier, C. D. and Brown, M. J. F. 1971: Erosion of a young volcano in New Guinea. *Zeitschrift fur Geomorphology* **15**, 12–28.

Ollier, C. D. and Harrop, J. F. 1958: The caves of Mount Elgon. *Uganda Journal* **22**, 158–63.

Ollier, C. D. and Joyce, E. N. 1964: Volcanic physiography of the western plains of Victoria. *Proceedings of the Royal Society of Victoria* **77**, 357–76.

Ollier, C. D. and Pain, C. F. 1981: Active gneiss domes in Papua New Guinea: new tectonic landforms. *Zeitschrift fur Geomorphology* **25**, 133–45.

O'Shea, B. E. 1954: Ruapehu and the Tangiwai disaster. *New Zealand Journal of Science and Technology* **B36**, 174–89.

Palfreyman, W. E. and Cooke, R. J. S. 1976: Eruptive history of Manam Volcano, Papua New Guinea. In: Johnson, R. W. (ed.) *Volcanism in Australasia*. pp. 117–32, Amsterdam: Elsevier.

Park, S. C. F. 1961: A magnetite 'flow' in northern Chile. *Economic Geology* **56**, 431–6.

Peterson, D. W. 1986: Summary of Mt St Helens activity, 1980–1986. *Volcano News* **24**, 2.

Peterson, D. W. and Swanson, D. A. 1974: Observed formation of lava tubes. *Studies in Speleology* **2**, 209–22.

Pike, R. J. 1978: Volcanoes on the planets: some preliminary comparisons of gross topography. *Proceedings of the 9th Lunar and Planetary Science Conference*, 3239–73.

Prider, R. T. 1960: The leucite lamproites of the Fitzroy Basin, Western Australia. *Journal of the Geological Society of Australia* 6, 71–118.

Pullar, W. A. 1967: Uses of volcanic ash beds in geomorphology. *Earth Science Journal* 1, 164–77.

Raggatt, H. G., Owen, H. B. and Hills, E. S. 1945: The bauxite deposits of the Boolara-Mirboo North area, South Gippsland, Victoria. *Commonwealth of Australia Ministry of Supply and Shipping Mineral Resources Bulletin* 14.

Re, M. D. 1963: Hyaloclastites and pillow lavas of Acicastello (Mt Etna). *Bulletin volcanologique* 25, 281–4.

Reck, H. 1915: Physiographische Studie uber Vulkanische Bomben. *Zeitschrift fur Vulkanologie* Erganzungsband 1914–1915, 1, 124.

Reeves, C. V. 1978. A failed Gondwana spreading axis in southern Africa. *Nature* 273, 222–3.

Richards, A. F. 1965: Geology of the Islas Revillagigedo, 3. Effects of Erosion on Isla San Benedicto 1952–61 following the birth of Volcan Barcena. *Bulletin volcanologique* 28, 381–403.

Rinehart, J. S. 1980: *Geysers and Geothermal Energy*. New York: Springer-Verlag.

Rittman, A. 1962: Trans. E. A. Vincent *Volcanoes and their Activity*. New York: Interscience.

Romano, R. 1982: Succession of the volcanic activity in the Etnean area. In: R. Romano (ed.) *Mount Etna*, pp. 27–48. Memorie della Societa Geologica Italiana 23.

Ruxton, B. P. 1968: Rates of weathering of Quaternary volcanic ash in north-east Papua. *Transactions of the 9th International Soil Science Congress* Adelaide, 4, 367–76.

Ruxton, B. P. and McDougall, I. 1967: Denudation rates in northeast Papua from potassium-argon dating of lavas. *American Journal of Science* 265, 545–61.

Saarinen, T. F. and Sell, J. L. 1985: *Warning and Response to the Mt St Helens Eruption*. Albany: State University of New York Press.

Saggerson, E. 1963: Geology of the Simba-Kibwezi area. *Geological Survey of Kenya*. Report No. 58.

Schmidt, P. W., Currey, D. T. and Ollier, C. D. 1976: Sub-basaltic weathering, damsites, paleomagnetism and the age of lateritization. *Journal of the Geological Society of Australia* 23, 267–370.

Searle, E. J. 1964: *City of Volcanoes*. Auckland: Paul.

Selby, M. J. 1966: Soil erosion on the pumic lands of the central North Island. *New Zealand Geographer* 22, 194–6.

Self, S. and Sparks, R. S. J. (eds) 1981: *Tephra Studies*. Dordrecht: Reidel.

Shand, S. J. 1938: *Earth Lore*. New York: Dutton.

Sheets, P. D. and Grayson, D. K. (eds) 1979: *Volcanic Activity and Human Ecology*. New York: Academic Press.

Sigurdsson, H., Carey, S., Cornell, W. and Pescatore, T. 1985: The eruption of Vesuvius in AD 79. *National Geographic Research* 1, 332–87.

Simkin, T. and Fiske, R. S. 1983: *Krakatau 1883 – the Volcanic Eruption and its Effects*. Washington: Smithsonian Institute Press.

Simkin, T. L., Seibert, I., McClelland, L., Bridge, D., Newhall, C., and Latter, J. H. 1981: *Volcanoes of the World. A Regional Directory, Gazeteer, and Chronology of Volcanism during the last 10,000 years*. Stroudsburg, Pennsylvania: Smithsonian Institute, Hutchinson Ross.

Skeats, E. W. and James, A. V. G. 1937: Basaltic barriers and other surface features of the Newer Basalts of Western Victoria. *Proceedings of the Royal Society of Victoria* 49, 245–78.

Smith, R. L. and Bailey, R. A. 1968: Resurgent cauldrons. In *Geological Society of America Memoirs* 116, 613–62.

Sparks, R. S. J., Pinkerton, H. and Hulme, G. 1976: Classification and formation of lava levees on Mount Etna, Sicily. *Geology* 4, 269–71.

Spry, A. 1962: The origin of columnar jointing, particularly in basalt flows. *Journal of the Geological Society of Australia* 8, 191–216.

Spry, A. and Banks, M. R. 1962: The geology of Tasmania. *Journal of the Geological Society of Australia* 9, 107–362.

Stearns, H. T. 1926: Volcanism in the Mud Lake area, Idaho. *American Journal of Science* 211, 353–63.

Stearns, H. T. 1935: Geology and ground-water resources of the island of Oahu, Hawaii. *Hawaii Division of Hydrography Bulletin* 1, 479 pp.

Stearns, H. T. 1949: Hydrology of volcanic terranes. In: O. E. Meinzer (ed.) *Hydrology*. New York: McGraw-Hill.

Stearns, H. T. 1966: *Geology of the State of Hawaii*. Palo Alto, California: Panin Books.

Stearns, H. T. and Macdonald, G. A. 1946: Geology and ground-water resources of the island of Hawaii. *Hawaii Division of Hydrography Bulletin* 9.

Stephenson, P. J. et al. 1967: The Ambrym Island Research Project (New Hebrides). ANZAAS 39th Congress, Section C (abstract).

Stephenson, P. J., Stevens, N. C. and Tweedale, G. W. 1960: Lower Cainozoic igneous rocks, Geology of Queensland, ed. D. Hill and A. K. Denmead. *Journal of the Geological Society of Australia* 7, 355–69.

Stipp, J. J. and McDougall, I. 1969: Geochronology of the Banks Peninsula volcanoes, New Zealand. *New Zealand Journal of Geology and Geophysics* 11, 1239–60.

Sutherland, F. L. 1966: The tertiary volcanics of the Tamar Valley, Northern Tasmania – a preliminary report. *Australian Journal of Science* 29, 114–15.

Suzuki, T. 1977: Volcano types and their global population percentages. *Bulletin of the Volcanological Society of Japan* 22, 27–40.

Swanson, D. A. 1973: Pahoehoe flows from the 1969–1971 Mauna Ulu eruptions, Kilauea Volcano, Hawaii. *Bulletin of the Geological Society of America* 84, 615–26.

Taylor, G. A. M. 1958: *The 1951 Eruption of Mount Lamington, Papua*. Canberra: Australian Department of National Development.

Tazieff, H. 1962: *Volcanoes*. London: Prentice Hall International.

Tazieff, H. 1975: *Nyiragongo, the forbidden volcano*. London: Cassell.

Tazieff, H. and Sabroux, J. 1983: *Forecasting Volcanic Events*. Amsterdam: Elsevier.

Tazieff, H. and Tonani, F. 1963: Fluctuations rapides et importantes de la phase gazeuse eruptive. *Comptes Rendus hebdomadaire Séance Academie des Sciences, Paris* 257, 3985–7.

Thorarinsson, S. 1954: *The eruption of Hekla, 1947–48, II. 3. The tephra fall from Hekla on March 29th 1947*. Reykjavik: Societas Scientiarum Islandica.

Thorarinsson, S. 1956: *Hekla on Fire*. Munich: Hanns Reich.

Thorarinsson, S. 1967: *The Eruption of Hekla, 1947–1948*. Vol. 1 of *The Eruptions of Hekla in Historical Times: a Tephrochronological Study*. Reykjavik: Leiftur.

217

References

Thorarinsson, S. 1969: The Lakaglgar eruption of 1793. *Bulletin volcanologique* 33, 910–29.

Tricart, J. 1965: Geomorphology and underground water of the Santiago Basin, Chile. *Bulletin of the Faculty of Letters, Strasbourg.* TILAS, 43, 605–74.

Tricart, J., Dollfus, O. and Michel, M. 1962: Note sur quelques aspects geomorphologique de la Foret de Pierre de Huaron (Andes Centrales Peruviennes). *Revue de Geomorphologie Dynamique* 13, 125–9.

Tsuya, H. and Morimoto, R. 1963: Types of volcanic eruptions in Japan. *Bulletin volcanologique* 26, 209–22.

Tuttle, O. F. and Gittins, J. (eds) 1966: *Carbonatites.* New York: Wiley.

Ugolini, F. C. and Zasoski, R. J. 1979: Soils derived from tephra. In Sheets, P. D. and Grayson, D. K. (eds) *Volcanic activity and human ecology.* pp. 83–124, New York: Academic Press.

Upton, B. G. J. and Wadsworth, W. J. 1966: The basalts of Reunion Island, Indian Ocean. *Bulletin volcanologique* 29, 7–23.

Van Bemmelen, R. W. 1930: The volcano-tectonic origin of Lake Toba (North Sumatra). *Proceedings of the Pacific Science Congress* 2, 115–24.

Wace, N. M. and Ollier, C. D. 1984: Biogeography and geomorphology of South Atlantic islands. *National Geographic Society Research Reports: 1975: Projects*, 733–58.

Walker, F. 1958: Recent work on the form of dolerite intrusions in sedimentary terrains. *Dolerite Symposium*, pp. 88–92, Hobart: University of Tasmania.

Walker, G. P. L. 1971: Compound and simple lava flows, and flood basalts. *Bulletin volcanologique* 35, 579–90.

Walker, G. P. L. 1973a: Explosive volcanic eruptions – a new classification scheme. *Geologische Rundschau* 62, 431–46.

Walker, G. P. L. 1973b: Lengths of lava flows. *Philosophical Transactions of the Royal Society of London. A,* 274, 107–18.

Walker, G. P. L. 1980: The Taupo Pumice: product of the most powerful known (ultraplinian) eruption. *Journal of Volcanology and Geothermal Resources* 8, 69–94.

Waring, G. A., Blankenship, R. R. and Bentall, R. 1965: Thermal springs of the United States and other countries of the world – a summary. *Professional Papers of the U.S. Geological Survey* 492, 1–383.

Watanabe, T., 1940: Eruptions of molten sulphur from the Siretoko-Iosan Volcano, Hokkaido, Japan. *Japanese Journal of Geology and Geomorphology* 17, 289–310.

Watanabe, T. 1970: Volcanism and ore genesis. In: T. Tatsumi (ed.) *Volcanism and Ore Genesis.* Tokyo: University of Tokyo Press.

Waters, A. C. 1960: Determining direction of flow in basalts. *American Journal of Science* 258A, 350–66.

Watkins, N. D., Sparks, R. S. J., Sigurdsson, H., Huang, T. C., Federman, A., Carey, S. and Ninkovich, D. 1978: Volume and extent of Minoan tephra from Santorini: new evidence from deep-sea sediment cores. *Nature* 271, 122–6.

Wellman, P. 1986: Intrusions beneath large intraplate volcanoes. *Exploration Geophysics* 17, 135–9.

Wentworth, C. K. 1943: Soil avalanches on Oahu, Hawaii. *Bulletin of the Geological Society of America* 53, 53–64.

Wentworth, C. K. and Macdonald, G. A. 1953: Structures and forms of basaltic rocks in Hawaii. *Bulletin of the U.S. Geological Survey* 994, 98.

Wilcoxson, K. 1967: *Volcanoes.* London: Cassell.

Williams, H. 1936: Pliocene Volcanoes of the Navajo-Hopi Country. *Bulletin of the Geological Society of America* **47**, 111–71.

Williams, H. 1941: Calderas and their origin. *University of California Publications in Geological Science* **25**, 239–346.

Williams, H. 1952: The great eruption of Coseguino, Nicaragua, in 1835: *University of California Publications in Geological Science* **29**, 21–46.

Williams, H. 1960: Volcanic collapse basins of Lakes Atitlan and Ayarza, Guatemala. *International Geological Congress* Part **21**, 110–18.

Williams, H. and McBirney, A. R. 1964: Petrological and structural contrast of the Quaternary volcanoes of Guatemala. *Bulletin volcanologique* **27**, 61.

Williams, H. and McBirney, A. R. 1979: *Volcanology.* San Francisco: Freeman & Co.

Wilson, J. T. 1963: Evidence from islands on the spreading of ocean floors. *Nature* **197**, 536–8.

Wohletz, K. H. and Sheridan, M. F. 1983: Hydrovolcanic explosions II. Evolution of basaltic tuff rings and tuff cones. *American Journal of Science* **283**, 385–413.

Wood, C. 1971: The nature and origin of Raufarholshellir. *Transactions of the Cave Research Group of Great Britain* **13**, 245–56.

Wright, J. B. 1967: Contributions to the volcanic succession and petrology of the Auckland Islands. II. Upper parts of the Ross volcano. *Transactions of the Royal Society of New Zealand (Geology)* **5**, 71–87.

Wright, J. V., Smith, A. L. and Self, S. 1980: A working terminology of pyroclastic deposits. *Journal of Volcanology and Geothermal Resources* **8**, 315–36.

Yokoyama, I. 1974: Mode of movement and emplacement of Ito pyroclastic flow from Aira Caldera, Japan. *Science Reports of the Tokyo Kyoiku Daigaku, Sec. C.* **12**, 17–62.

Zen, M. T. 1965: The future danger of Mt Kelut. *Bulletin volcanologique* **28**, 275–82.

Index

Index